Deleuze and Guattari's 'What is Philosophy?'

BLOOMSBURY READER'S GUIDES

Titles available in this series

Aristotle's 'Politics': A Reader's Guide, Judith A. Swanson
Badiou's 'Being and Event': A Reader's Guide, Christopher Norris
Berkeley's 'Principles of Human Knowledge': A Reader's Guide, Alasdair Richmond
Deleuze's 'Difference and Repetition': A Reader's Guide, Joe Hughes
Deleuze and Guattari's 'A Thousand Plateaus': A Reader's Guide, Eugene W. Holland
Descartes' 'Meditations': A Reader's Guide, Richard Francks
Hegel's 'Phenomenology of Spirit': A Reader's Guide, Stephen Houlgate
Heidegger's 'Being and Time': A Reader's Guide, William Blattner
Hobbes's 'Leviathan': A Reader's Guide, Laurie M. Johnson Bagby
Kant's 'Critique of Aesthetic Judgement': A Reader's Guide, Fiona Hughes
Kierkegaard's 'Fear and Trembling': A Reader's Guide, Clare Carlisle
Levinas' 'Totality and Infinity': A Reader's Guide, William Large
Locke's 'Second Treatise of Government': A Reader's Guide, Paul Kelly
Marx and Engels' 'Communist Manifesto': A Reader's Guide, Peter Lamb
Nietzsche's 'Beyond Good and Evil': A Reader's Guide, Christa Davis Acampora and Keith Ansell Pearson
Nietzsche's 'Thus Spoke Zarathustra': A Reader's Guide, Clancy Martin
Rousseau's 'The Social Contract': A Reader's Guide, Christopher Wraight
Spinoza's 'Ethics': A Reader's Guide, J. Thomas Cook
Wittgenstein's 'Philosophical Investigations': A Reader's Guide, Arif Ahmed
Wittgenstein's 'Tractatus Logico-Philosophicus': A Reader's Guide, Roger M. White

Forthcoming from Bloomsbury

Kant's 'Critique of Practical Reason': A Reader's Guide, Courtney D. Fugate
Marx's 'Grundrisse': A Reader's Guide, Simon Choat

READER'S GUIDES

Deleuze and Guattari's 'What is Philosophy?'

REX BUTLER

BLOOMSBURY
LONDON • NEW DELHI • NEW YORK • SYDNEY

Bloomsbury Academic
An imprint of Bloomsbury Publishing Plc

50 Bedford Square	1385 Broadway
London	New York
WC1B 3DP	NY 10018
UK	USA

www.bloomsbury.com

BLOOMSBURY and the Diana logo are trademarks of Bloomsbury Publishing Plc

First published 2016

© Rex Butler, 2016

Rex Butler has asserted his right under the Copyright, Designs and Patents Act, 1988, to be identified as Author of this work.

All rights reserved. No part of this publication may be reproduced or transmitted in any form or by any means, electronic or mechanical, including photocopying, recording, or any information storage or retrieval system, without prior permission in writing from the publishers.

No responsibility for loss caused to any individual or organization acting on or refraining from action as a result of the material in this publication can be accepted by Bloomsbury or the author.

British Library Cataloguing-in-Publication Data
A catalogue record for this book is available from the British Library.

ISBN: HB: 978-1-84706-586-5
PB: 978-1-84706-587-2
ePDF: 978-1-44111-217-0
ePub: 978-1-44119-063-5

Library of Congress Cataloging-in-Publication Data
A catalog record for this book is available from the Library of Congress.

Typeset by Fakenham Prepress Solutions, Fakenham, Norfolk NR21 8NN

CONTENTS

Abbreviations vii

1 Context 1
2 Overview of Themes 15
3 Art 33
4 Philosophy 69
5 Science and Logic 107
6 The Brain and Geophilosophy 153
7 Reception 171

Notes 189
Index of Names 207
Index of Concepts 211

ABBREVIATIONS

The following abbreviations are used in this book:

By Gilles Deleuze

B	*Bergsonism*, Zone Books: New York, 1988
'D'	'The Method of Dramatization', in *Desert Islands and Other Texts, 1953–74*
DI	*Desert Islands and Other Texts, 1953–74*, Semiotext(e): New York, 2004
DR	*Difference and Repetition*, Columbia University Press: New York, 1994
EP	*Expressionism in Philosophy: Spinoza*, Zone Books: New York, 1990
F	*The Fold: Leibniz and the Baroque*, University of Minnesota Press: Minneapolis, 1993
FB	*Francis Bacon: The Logic of Sensation*, University of Minnesota Press: Minneapolis, 2003
'G'	'The Idea of Genesis in Kant's Philosophy', *Angelaki* 5 (3) (2000): 57–70
H	*Empiricism and Subjectivity: An Essay on Hume's Theory of Human Nature*, Columbia University Press: New York, 1991
KCP	*Kant's Critical Philosophy: The Doctrine of the Faculties*, Athlone Press: London, 1984

LS	*The Logic of Sense*, Columbia University Press: New York, 1990
MI	*Cinema I: The Movement-Image*, Athlone Press: London, 1986
NP	*Nietzsche and Philosophy*, Athlone Press: London, 1983
PS	*Proust and Signs*, Braziller: New York, 1972
TI	*Cinema 2: The Time-Image*, University of Minnesota Press: Minneapolis, 1989

By Gilles Deleuze and Félix Guattari

AO	*Anti-Oedipus: Capitalism and Schizophrenia*, Viking Press: New York, 1977
TP	*A Thousand Plateaus: Capitalism and Schizophrenia*, University of Minnesota Press: Minneapolis, 1987
WP?	*What is Philosophy?*, Verso: London, 1994

CHAPTER ONE

Context

In some ways, the conditions for philosophy have never been better. Walk into any relatively serious bookshop and there are philosophy books everywhere. There are works by philosophers, such as Hegel's *Logic*. There are selections of works by philosophers, such as *Five Dialogues by Plato*. There are academic monographs on philosophers, such as *Wittgenstein's Private Language*. There are introductory guides on philosophers, such as *How to Read Heidegger*. There is a whole variety of books introducing philosophy altogether, such as *Classics of Western Philosophy*. There are practical manuals, teaching philosophy as a technique like any other, such as *50 Philosophical Ideas You Need to Know*. There are books that treat philosophy in terms of popular cultural objects, such as *The Matrix and Philosophy: Welcome to the Desert of the Real*. There are books that apply philosophy to everyday situations or seek to show how philosophy might help us function better, such as *What's It All About?: Philosophy and the Meaning of Life*. Finally, there are all those books that fuse philosophy with religion, often of a New Age kind, and that read like a combination of Eastern mysticism, self-help and the Harvard Business School, such as *This I Believe: The Personal Philosophies of Remarkable Men and Women*.

Then there are all those activities that claim to do what philosophy does. We have marketers and brand designers in the advertising industry who seek to create 'awareness'. We have artists and writers who claim – or are claimed by others – to be challenging the norms of society. (And for them there are lots of books with titles like *Nietzsche for Artists* or *Leibniz for Authors*.) There are theologians who maintain they are doing what philosophers should be doing by proposing higher values by which to live. In blogs and on the internet, there are millions of people who hold themselves up as opinion-makers, forcing people – if this is what philosophy does – to think again. There is a general coming together of creativity and critical thinking in the so-called 'creative industries'. Indeed, philosophy is found everywhere today, in television shows, newspaper columns, radio programmes, public forums and ideas festivals, with a plethora of issues discussed from a philosophical perspective. There are public debates from a philosophical point of view on all kinds of subjects – from the ethics of daily life to the justification of war, from the existence of God to medical euthanasia – with the opposing sides challenging each other in order to produce a final consensus.

And yet, in other ways, things have never been worse for philosophy. In those serious bookshops, the shelf-space devoted to philosophy shrinks every year, or actual philosophy books are increasingly mixed in with books that pass themselves off as philosophy: guides, introductions, applications, self-help, spirituality. Indeed, those bookshops that once stocked philosophy are themselves now disappearing to online retailing. Philosophy, if it still exists at all, does so more and more only as a marketing niche, a brand, a product, a lifestyle option, a sign of status or social distinction. And this applies to the discipline of philosophy itself, which has lost its critical edge, its ability to propose alternative values or to tell us how to live. Now philosophy is not truly negative or challenging to the status quo, but rather contents itself with teaching us how to live better within the existing order, in fact, how to succeed within it. It is reduced to a kind of therapy. And it is surrounded by pretenders, all of those other disciplines that claim to be doing philosophy. Philosophy is reduced to carrying out innumerable surveys or summaries of itself. Or to endless debates of the relevant issues, which do not change anything or think anything different, and whose only aim is to keep the debate going endlessly in order to justify itself.

It is precisely in these 'new' conditions for philosophy that philosopher Gilles Deleuze and psychoanalyst and political activist Félix Guattari wrote their *What is Philosophy?*, which was published in French in 1991 and translated into English in 1994.

Undoubtedly the French philosophical environment from which they were coming was different from the English one. Because of the language difference, French philosophy was to some extent protected from the onslaught of English-language publishing and popularization. There still existed in France – thanks to the way philosophy was taught in high school – a real popular-academic basis for philosophy. And yet, even some twenty years before the situation we are describing, they saw the same ambiguous desire for philosophy. It was the wish, but, better, the demand, that philosophy make itself popular, accessible, that it enter public debate, be part of civil conversation. In 1977 Deleuze had published a scathing critique of the so-called Nouveaux Philosophes – such thinkers who would later come to public attention as André Glucksmann, Alain Finkelkraut and Bernard Henri-Lévy – who held such ambitions for philosophy, and who rejected Communism and asserted universal 'human rights', accusing them of betraying the victims in whose name they spoke.[1] And Guattari, for his part, if not quite a defender of the integrity of philosophy in the same terms, had long battled what he saw as the increasing alienation and commodification of culture. In a manifesto co-written with the Italian Autonomist philosopher Antonio Negri, for example, he declared: 'Think, live, experiment and struggle in another way: such will be the motto of a working class which can no longer perceive itself as "self-sufficient"'.[2]

In *What is Philosophy?*, Deleuze and Guattari set out their alternative conception of philosophy from that of the neo-liberal, capitalist state. As they write, they are not 'ideas men' (*WP?*, 10), who come up with a new brand or concept. They do not belong to computer science, marketing, design or advertising, in which the 'only events are exhibitions, and the only concepts are products that can be sold' (*WP?*, 10). They then go on to offer a more extended list of what philosophy is not, which goes against many of the ways in which philosophy is usually thought and justified. Philosophy for Deleuze and Guattari is not 'contemplation, reflection or communication' (*WP?*, 6). It is not a matter of 'knowing oneself' or 'wondering that there is being' (*WP?*, 7). It is not even to be assessed in terms of whether it is true or not in relation to some outside referent. Above all, it is not to be understood in terms of the generation of 'opinions' or the discussion of 'issues', the terms in which philosophy is most often validated today. As Deleuze and

Guattari assert: 'Every philosopher runs away when he or she hears someone say, "Let's discuss this"' (*WP?*, 28). From such conversations nothing new can arise because they operate only in terms of what is already known. They can merely repeat what everybody already recognizes, and the cynic who apparently stands outside the consensus secretly wants everybody's approval. As Deleuze and Guattari write late in the book, taking aim at this Anglo-American notion of philosophy as consensus by imagining a dinner party at Richard Rorty's:

> For example, some cheese is brought to the dinner table, someone extracts a pure quality from it (for example, a foul smell); but, at the same time as he abstracts the quality, he identifies himself with a generic subject experiencing a common affection (the society of those who detest cheese – competing as such with those who love it). (*WP?*, 145)

But, if Deleuze and Guattari distinguish what they do from philosophy as 'opinion', they do not simply stand outside it. Indeed, when they observe that philosophy in the sense in which they speak started in Ancient Greece, this is not because the Greek language has some inherent connection with philosophy, or because Ancient Greeks were somehow closer to Being, as Hegel and Heidegger thought, but because it was in Ancient Greece, with its incipient democracy and trade with foreign nations, that we had for the first time the free exchange of opinions (*WP?*, 87–8). There is played out in Ancient Greece the contest between philosophy and its rivals, those who dispute philosophy, and even between philosophy and its friends, those who likewise claim to be doing philosophy. And the fundamental task of philosophy, when confronted with this situation, is not merely to offer another opinion but to seek to break with opinion, by deciding which one of these opinions is 'true'. If Plato marks the beginning of philosophy, then, it is because his method is not fundamentally about identifying the essence of things but about adjudicating the claims of the various contenders for philosophy. He attempts to find that 'knowledge' behind opinion, a kind of *Urdoxa* or proto-opinion, which would explain or justify something as opinion. This is the basis of his so-called dialectical method, in which the 'universals of contemplation are supposed to gauge the respective values of rival opinions so as to raise them to the level of knowledge' (*WP?*, 79) – a method that Deleuze and Guattari do not entirely break with.

Nevertheless, if Deleuze and Guattari warn against philosophy as opinion, which carries with it the danger of repeating the assumptions of the past, they also make it clear that philosophy is not simply a search for the new and unconventional for their own sakes. If they reject ready-made solutions, they are not therefore asserting that there is no method to philosophy, no way of saying what philosophy does, or even what different philosophies have in common. There *is* a kind of logic or method to philosophy, which is what Deleuze and Guattari attempt to outline in their book. It is the problem of how philosophers 'speak' to each other and how to write a 'history' of philosophy. (Indeed, the fact that Deleuze and Guattari are involved in the question of the relationship between philosophical systems is suggested by their use of the word 'baptism' (*WP?*, 8) to refer to the transfer of a concept from one philosophical system to another, a word taken from the American linguistic philosopher Saul Kripke to indicate how a word applies to a referent in the absence of any 'uniquely identifying property'.[3]) All of this is to point to 'chaos' as the opposite problem from opinion: that without some sort of method, thought would no sooner appear than disappear. It would merely be part of the external world, an effect of the particular circumstances that brought it about, and unable to pass beyond them. As Deleuze and Guattari write: 'Nothing is more disturbing than a thought that escapes itself, than ideas that fly off, that disappear hardly formed, already eroded by forgetfulness or precipitated into others that we no longer master' (*WP?*, 201). And yet again, philosophy arises in response to chaos, and chaos is what drives it and what must periodically be let back in, as with the slit that D. H. Lawrence imagines poets and artists cutting into the umbrella we hold above our heads in order to let the light in (*WP?*, 203).

The true task of philosophy, then, is to avoid both opinion – the repetition of an unchanging same – and chaos – a difference that no sooner appears than disappears. It must virtualize, as it were, both the discursive actuality of opinion and the material actuality of chaos. Against the generality of opinion, which takes itself as real and true, it must propose a certain 'counter-effectuation' (*WP?*, 159). Against the physicality of chaos – by which we mean all historical, social and biographical determinations that would reduce thought to its context – it must produce a certain 'effectuation' (*WP?*, 159). The two processes are not the same and in fact move in opposite directions. One is the virtualization of the actual at the end of things and the other is the virtualization of the actual at the beginning. And Deleuze and Guattari have a beautiful metaphor in *What is Philosophy?* for the line connecting them. They speak of a 'web' that the 'spider' can go either up or down (*WP?*, 122). And in *What is Philosophy?*, as we will see, they seek to bring out the specificity of philosophy by comparing it with art and science (and logic), which are what connect it to chaos and opinion respectively. In one way, philosophy can only think itself through art and science: a philosophy without art is merely a science, and a philosophy without science is merely an art. But, in another way, philosophy is also the thinking of (the conditions of possibility of) art and science: something like science in the case of art, and something like art in the case of science. Philosophy in *What is Philosophy?* is to be found not simply in philosophy, but also in art and science. Indeed, in some ways, it is nothing other than the very relationship between art, philosophy and science.

And in *What is Philosophy?* Deleuze and Guattari provide a subtle 'biographical' treatment of these issues, involving what we will learn to call their philosophical 'personae'. One of the dangers of what they call 'old age' (*WP?*, 2) – and here they are referring not only to the biographical old age of those who practise it, but to the old age of philosophy itself – is that we are no longer able either to 'effectuate' chaos or 'counter-effectuate' opinion (*WP?*, 214). It is undoubtedly this old age that Deleuze and Guattari understand themselves as being in when they write their book. It is an old age, as they say, that allows them the time to reflect upon philosophy in order to ask certain questions of it (*WP?*, 3). But the real question is whether the question 'what is philosophy?' itself constitutes a proper subject for philosophy or is merely one of those endless self-reflections that are the very 'plague of philosophy' (*WP?*, 28). This is one of the essential questions to put to *What is Philosophy?*: whether it is actually doing philosophy or is simply about philosophy? Whether Deleuze and Guattari are able to propose a proper effectuation or counter-effectuation in their old age, or whether they fall back into a 'mental chaos outside the plane of composition' or upon 'readymade opinions or clichés?' (*WP?*, 214). And the question must also be put – as Deleuze and

Guattari imply – to the 'old age' of philosophy itself. Is philosophy still possible today? Or has it come to a certain 'end', as a number of previous philosophers (Heidegger, Wittgenstein, Derrida) have thought? (*WP?*, 9). But perhaps philosophy has always been in this 'old age'. Perhaps it has always faced this problem of the effectuation of chaos and the counter-effectuation of opinion. And perhaps it is the difficulty or even impossibility of doing these things that in fact leads to philosophy.

* * *

It is undoubtedly true that Deleuze and Guattari were in a biographical and philosophical 'old age' by the time they came to write *What is Philosophy?* For Deleuze, who was born in 1925 and had worked in the Philosophy Department of Paris-VIII University at Vincennes for some twenty-one years, it was something like his twentieth book, stretching all the way back to *Empiricism and Subjectivity: An Essay on Hume's Theory of Human Nature* in 1953. For Guattari, who was born in 1930, it was only his eighth book, but his main career had been as a practising analyst at an experimental clinic at La Borde in the Loire Valley, some 110 kms south of Paris. *What is Philosophy?* was the fourth book they had written together, over a twenty-year partnership that, at least during their own lifetimes, was to bring each their greatest fame. It was *Anti-Oedipus*, published in 1972, that was their first collaboration. It came about after they first met in 1969, introduced by their friend Jean-Pierre Muyard at Limousin in the French countryside, where Deleuze was convalescing after having a tubercular lung removed. Extraordinarily, for all his ill health, Deleuze had just completed two huge volumes of philosophy, one of which he had submitted to complete his Doctorate, the final hurdle for those wishing to rise to the highest level of the French academic system, and the other of which is frequently described as one of the greatest books of twentieth-century philosophy: *Expressionism in Philosophy: Spinoza* (1968) and *Difference and Repetition* (1968). In a sense, therefore, when Deleuze met Guattari he was looking for something new. He was suffering a burn-out from the rigours of French academic philosophy and its emphasis either on monographic studies of specific philosophers or encyclopaedic summaries of the history of philosophy. As Deleuze was later to say: 'In my earlier books, I had tried to describe a certain exercise of thought, but describing it was not yet exercising thought in that way. With Félix, all that became possible'.[4]

Anti-Oedipus for its part was an exuberantly anti-academic book written in an alternately poetic and polemical style. Its subject was a critique of what it called the sad, neurotic 'Oedipal triangle' (*AO*, 3) of the bourgeois or capitalist family; and to make its case it traversed an extraordinary number of disciplines, from sociology to economics, from music to anthropology. In its first wave of reception, particularly in the English-speaking world, it was praised for being a revival of Freudo-Marxism, but the book was anything but that. If anything, it was a critique of psychoanalysis for no sooner discovering desire than repressing it, reducing it to what it called 'daddy-mommy-me' (*AO*, 51). And the book similarly challenged Marx for no sooner discovering the liberatory power of capital for 'decoding all flows' (*AO*, 226) than seeking to restrict it or direct it towards its supposedly proper use. In this sense, of course, Deleuze and Guattari break with the dominant theoretical models of the time, including in thinking that May 1968 represented no simple liberation but demonstrated how we are also able to desire our own repression – desire our own repression, moreover, in the very form of what is said to liberate us.

Deleuze and Guattari then follow up *Anti-Oedipus* with *A Thousand Plateaus*, which appears in French in 1980. The link to *Anti-Oedipus* is explicitly made, with the two volumes being named as making up the series 'Capitalism and Schizophrenia'. The book was a long time coming, appearing some eight years after *Anti-Oedipus*. In part, this was because of the overwhelming popular success of *Anti-Oedipus*, which brought with it a considerable burden of expectation and responsibility for both Deleuze and Guattari. Indeed, certain political consequences of the book, such as inspiring the Italian Autonomia movement, would occupy Guattari for much of the following decade. More profoundly, the delay can be explained by the difficulty of preserving the great stylistic and conceptual breakthrough represented by *Anti-Oedipus*. In fact, Deleuze and Guattari continued to work together throughout the period. In 1975, they put out a small volume on Franz Kafka, in which, as opposed to the usual theological or existential readings that emphasize his characters' search for meaning in a godless universe, they point to the humour, earthy sexuality and creative new ways of living that are expressed in Kafka's great parables. In 1976, they published a short text, 'Rhizome', in which they set out a radical new conception of desire that is laid out horizontally and 'rhizomatically' like a weed rather than vertically and 'arborescently' like a tree (*TP*, 17). What is made clear, as in *Anti-Oedipus*, is precisely the productive aspect of desire, the fact that it is not imaginary but transcendental, at once breaking with existing reality and seeking to bring about another reality.

A Thousand Plateaus when it finally appears is a gigantic book, some 600 pages in its English translation. It is composed of a series of 'plateaus', each of which records a 'self-vibrating region of intensity whose development avoids any orientation towards a culminating point or end' (*TP*, 22). For example, the plateau '1914: One or Several Wolves?' marks the date when Freud first wrote about his famous Wolf Man patient; the plateau 'Year Zero: Faciality' records the year of the birth of Christ; and the plateau '7000 BC: Apparatus of Capture' indicates the date of the putative origin of the modern state. The book is first of all an extraordinary experiment in collage or assemblage, deliberately bringing together – in a manner beyond even *Anti-Oedipus* – the most disparate disciplines and knowledges and, according to the authors themselves, able to be read (as apparently it was written) in any order. In some ways, its formal construction must be understood as the attempt to instantiate practically the abstract arguments of *Anti-Oedipus*, to produce some formal equivalent to its arguments concerning the 'machinic' (*TP*, 22) nature of desire. Desire is not seen as individual but as social, precisely what connects the individual to the world. Indeed, in *A Thousand Plateaus* it is evident that Deleuze and Guattari are attempting to write nothing less than a 'universal history' (*TP*, 459), tracing a passage from the origins of human civilization – 10,000 BC is the date of the earliest plateau – all the way through to the present – 28 November 1947 is the date of the latest.

It was to be an even longer period before Deleuze and Guattari collaborated again. Some eleven years were to pass between *A Thousand Plateaus* and *What is Philosophy?* What accounts for the delay? As is obvious, *A Thousand Plateaus* was exhaustive, all-inclusive, definitive, encyclopaedic. Although not as successful in its reception as *Anti-Oedipus* – a number of critics considered it overblown and extended beyond its proper limits – its very gigantism undoubtedly represented the end of something. It is simply impossible to imagine Deleuze and Guattari continuing further down the same line of theoretical militancy and experimentation. It is also true that, if the 1970s were a period of freedom, counter-culture and political possibility, the 1980s were a period of retreat, recession and withdrawal. In Britain, the Conservative government of Margaret Thatcher took power in 1979. In America, the period of triumphant Reaganism began in 1980. And in France, the Socialist government of François Mitterrand lost its parliamentary majority and was forced to 'co-habit' with the right-wing Jacques Chirac from 1986 on. It was indeed called in France the decade of 'la grande lessive', in which the liberatory effects of May 1968 were if possible forgotten or even consciously rolled back. The French Leftist infatuation with Cuba and China soured. Eurocommunism as a political force, principally in Italy but also in France, came to a sudden end. The Berlin Wall fell in 1989, and the Soviet Union itself collapsed in 1991.

For Deleuze and Guattari themselves, the decade of the 1980s was also a period of reflection and retrenchment. For Guattari, the clinic at La Borde, at which he had worked since the late 1950s, continued to take much of his time, and he was forced to defend its methods of anti-psychiatry from continuing attacks. And Guattari himself had difficulties with his personal life throughout the period. As noted by François Dosse, author of a joint biography of Deleuze and Guattari, there was an unhappy marriage and a long depression, both in response to his own personal circumstances and to the general state of the world.[5] Deleuze, for his part, after his period of collaboration with Guattari, which took him out of his usual reclusive ways and involved him in a number of political causes, returned during the 1980s to his life-long habit of teaching and writing. Vincennes, which was initially established in the wake of May 1968 as a way of siphoning off dangerous revolutionary energies, had gradually returned to the norms of French academic life, and Deleuze taught a weekly course there (and later at Saint-Denis, when it moved), which became famous, eventually attracting students from all round the world. It was in this class that Deleuze generated the material for the string of brilliant monographs he was to write throughout the 1980s, on subjects as diverse as Leibniz, cinema and the English painter Francis Bacon.

Students of Deleuze and Guattari often speculate on what made Deleuze decide – for it was he who had the more active public profile and publishing schedule – to resume his collaboration with Guattari with *What is Philosophy?* What was it that made *What is Philosophy?* different from the other books Deleuze was writing at the time? Was there some special quality about the book that made Deleuze feel as though he needed Guattari, or that we can see coming out of Guattari? Certainly, it is true that the book can be – and has been – read as continuous with Deleuze's other work. Indeed, it is the case that a number of preliminary excerpts from the book – for example, the essay 'The Conditions of the Question: What is Philosophy?', which appeared in the prestigious American journal *Critical Inquiry* – first appeared under Deleuze's name alone.[6] Famously, in the experimental milieu of *A Thousand Plateaus* in 'Rhizome', Deleuze and Guattari speak in the following terms about their collaboration: 'The two of us wrote *Anti-Oedipus* together. Since each of us was several, there was already quite a crowd' (*TP*, 3). And Deleuze has offered the following account of their collaboration, in the kind of beatific language he often reserved for public explanations of his actions: '[Passing what was to be worked on back and forth,] each of us worked like an inlay or quotation in the other's text, but at a certain point we no longer knew who had written what'.[7] However, as has subsequently emerged, from Guattari's own perspective things looked a little different. As he noted in the journal he kept contemporaneously with the composition of *Anti-Oedipus*, there was a sort of exasperation he felt at the way he perceived his work to be taken over by Deleuze: 'I don't really recognize myself in the *Anti-Oedipus*. I need to stop trying to run behind the image of Gilles and the polishedness, the perfection he brought to the most unlikely book'.[8] And, if anything, it is likely that this tendency was even more the case with *What is Philosophy?*

In the end, we are forced to conclude with Dosse that Deleuze's decision to make Guattari a co-author of *What is Philosophy?* was something like an act of charity on his part, to mark an old friendship. And that perhaps it was undertaken to give the by-now frail Deleuze, whose respiration and general health had deteriorated significantly over the intervening years, a final push to allow completion of the book, in part by reminding him of the joyous days of their first collaboration some twenty years before.[9] Certainly, *What is Philosophy?* is not written with the same high-pitched revolutionary energy and does not cover or at least does not explicitly play out the same encyclopaedic swathes of knowledge as the earlier *Anti-Oedipus* and *A Thousand Plateaus*. The book is considerably shorter than either, the writing plainer and more unadorned, and instead of actually dramatizing its knowledge its references are condensed, allusive, almost cryptic. If the book is difficult, then, it is not because of its language or logic, but because so much is assumed of its reader, not only familiarity with the work of the great artists, philosophers and scientists whose names run throughout its pages, but also Deleuze and Guattari's arguments about them. If *Anti-Oedipus* and *A Thousand Plateaus* are open and introductory in tone, primers for those coming to philosophy from the outside, we would say – and this would go against the book's own claim to be 'pedagogic' (*WP?*, 12) – that *What is Philosophy?* is summary or valedictory in tone, written for insiders, those who already know their philosophy. It is as though Deleuze and Guattari are looking back, as they say they are, from the vantage of old age, at both the history of philosophy and their own place within it.

What is Philosophy?, indeed, can seem to have a valedictory aspect. Looked at from a teleological perspective, it can appear a fitting conclusion both to Deleuze's and Guattari's lives and to their careers. Guattari was to die in 1992, just one year after *What is Philosophy?* was published. Deleuze was to die some three years later in 1995, after long medical complications, and having abandoned his last attempted book, on the 'grandeur of Marx'. *What is Philosophy?* in this light can be seen to be almost prescient; to offer a summary of Deleuze's and Guattari's thought; to speak, in their own words, of 'what it is I have been doing all my life' (*WP?*, 1) And the book has undoubtedly been read this way. But, in terms of the logic of the book itself, philosophy is not to be reduced to its historical and biographical context in this fashion. Philosophy, though it arises at a particular time and communicates through ordinary language, is not to be confused with these. Its proper time is what Deleuze and Guattari call a 'meanwhile' (*WP?*, 158), and Deleuze's and Guattari's deaths do not constitute any meaningful conclusion from which we might look back, but are a pure contingency, which breaks off their project at the only proper place philosophy inhabits, which is 'in the middle' (*TP*, 25). And in *What is Philosophy?*, Deleuze and Guattari do not speak only of 'looking back' but also of things 'hurrying on' (*WP?*, 7), as though there is still so much to do. And, in fact, we assert that *What is Philosophy?* is not merely about philosophy, offering a survey or summary of it, but actually *does* philosophy, is involved in the creation of new concepts, in a way that resists summary, even by Deleuze and Guattari themselves.

CHAPTER TWO

Overview of Themes

It is strange that Deleuze and Guattari call their book *What is Philosophy?* (In being so called, it joins a long line of others with the same title, from those by Heidegger and Ortega y Gasset to those by Edmond Holmes and Elmer Sprague.) It is strange because Deleuze for his part opposed such ontological questions throughout his work, including *What is Philosophy?* itself. In *The Logic of Sense*, for example, he writes of the Ancient Greek philosopher Diogenes replying to such a question by carrying a fish about on the end of string (*LS*, 154). More seriously, in *Difference and Repetition*, he objects to the question in the following terms: 'The question is always traced from giveable, probable or possible responses' (*DR*, 156). And in *What is Philosophy?*, Deleuze and Guattari reject altogether the question and answer form, which they compare to a TV quiz show: 'As the creation of thought, a problem has nothing to do with a question, which is only a suspended proposition, the bloodless double of an affirmative proposition that is supposed to serve as its answer' (*WP?*, 139). As opposed to this, Deleuze sees philosophy as asking the questions 'how many?', 'how?', 'in which case?', which would contest the notion of a universal that is to be found across different examples, or a universal that is to be reached by adding together a number of examples. Against this classic philosophical-scientific method, Deleuze and Guattari propose a concept of philosophy that does not work empirically through the gradual analysis or assembling of examples, to which counter-examples would always be possible, but one in which all of its components are immediately co-present, crossed at 'absolute speed' by a point of 'absolute survey' (*WP?*, 21), and admitting no outside. And what is produced is not any generality or commonality across various examples, but a set of 'variations' (*WP?*, 20), which is not things as they are but as they could be, not the concept that different examples have in common but the difference that allows any particular instance of the concept to be given.

Indeed, Deleuze and Guattari's ultimate point in *What is Philosophy?* is that few, if any, disciplines work through the question 'what is?' For Deleuze and Guattari, philosophy's attempt to imagine thought proceeding like this – and they are referring predominantly to the Anglo-American tradition of analytic philosophy – is 'puerile' and 'impoverished' (*WP?*, 139), and not even true to the facts. Take, for example, science, the supposed model for this kind of philosophical logic. As Deleuze and Guattari make clear in *What is Philosophy?*, scientists and mathematicians do not proceed by syllogistic steps or the patient accumulation of evidence: 'Mathematical equations do not enjoy a tranquil certainty, which would be like the sanction of a dominant scientific opinion, but arise from an abyss that makes the mathematicians "readily skip over calculations", in anticipation of not being able to bring about or arrive at the truth without "colliding here and there"' (*WP?*, 203). In *Difference and Repetition*, Deleuze speaks of biological classification – he takes the point from the vitalism and evolutionism of Bergson – as ending not in some common quality that defines forever each class and species. Rather, each successive level of classification is revealed as containing only a series of differences, as revealed by the category below, with the apparently smallest difference (species) having to be understood as in effect holding together the greatest number of differences. What is passed on from genus to species, in other words, is the power to differ, and any particular classification is revealed only as the site of a division to come (*DR*, 31). Finally, even with such a rationalist philosopher as Leibniz – and the point is not unrelated to what we have just said – Deleuze is able to read his principle of sufficient reason not as necessarily implying a convergence of possible worlds, as is commonly thought, but as opening up a thinking of a divergence or maximum difference between them. The 'same' Biblical Adam may be both a sinner and virtuous (*LS*, 131). The 'same' equation for a conic section in mathematics may express

itself as a circle, an ellipse, a hyperbola, a parabola or a straight line (*LS*, 130).
But all of this must be understood very carefully. For all of Deleuze and Guattari's seeming rejection of the methods of logic and empiricism, they do nevertheless attempt to answer the question of what philosophy is. Against the prevailing anarchist readings of their work, in which they are seen to reject reason and propose instead a form of schizophrenia, *What is Philosophy?* is in fact written and argued logically. The various parts of the book are meaningfully enchained, laid out in sensible propositions that refer to recognizable objects. Deleuze and Guattari do not refuse the classic ontological question 'What is philosophy?', and in a way even argue for its necessity. Those readings of their work that contend they replace meaning with use, like that of Fredric Jameson in *The Political Unconscious*, are simply mistaken.[1] On the contrary, Deleuze and Guattari are interested in what allows the possibility of an answer to such a question – and even the question itself. What allows the production of 'good sense', which Deleuze defines as the 'fixed and sedentary ordering of differences' (*LS*, 132), that allows one thing to be distinguished from another? What allows 'common sense', which Deleuze defines as the 'function of identification' (*LS*, 132), that allows different things to be included within the same category? What is it that makes possible the understanding of philosophy as a form of recognition, of the recovery of what is already known? It is not this image of thought as such that Deleuze and Guattari object to in *What is Philosophy?*, but the fact that it remains unquestioned, that its conditions of possibility are not accounted for, that its genesis, or how it came about, is not explained.

Deleuze and Guattari do question these assumptions, which form the basis of opinion, in several ways in *What is Philosophy?* First of all, in a manner typical of 'politically correct' critiques of the 1990s, they make the point that those opinions put forward as natural and universal are not natural and universal but the viewpoint only of a white European minority at a particular moment in time. As they write: 'But does not the transcendent subject hide European man, whose privilege it is constantly to "Europeanize", as the Greeks "Greekized", that is to say, to go beyond the limits of other cultures that are preserved as psychosocial types' (*WP?*, 149). (And along these lines, they would probably not object to someone like Pierre Bourdieu's speaking of the way that Kant's pure universal taste is in fact impure, historical and class-specific.[2]) But Deleuze and Guattari go further than this. What they see as constituting authentic philosophy is the project of doing away with *all* preconceptions as to what thought is or should be. It would be to hold to the principle that there is *nothing* that naturally or innately belongs to thought, that all definitions of it reveal themselves merely to be the reflections of a particular place and time. To this extent, we would say that Deleuze and Guattari's deepest affinity is to something like Kant's project of transcendental 'critique', which aims to rid thought of its errors or illusions in order to leave only what is necessary for experience to be possible. It is an impulse that they see as characterizing philosophy from the very beginning. In Plato, it is always a matter of passing beyond opinion to truth through reminiscence, stimulated by the 'beauty of the perceived' and the 'test of the good' (*WP?*, 148). In Descartes, the inaugural power of the Cogito would break with any Platonic reminiscence, in challenging every 'objective presupposition' (*WP?*, 26) and replacing it with a subjective and pre-philosophical understanding. And in Kant, there is a going beyond of Descartes, insofar as 'nothing warrants a claim of the [thinking] I' (*WP?*, 31), that is, the ordinary and unprejudiced subject his method is seen to presuppose.

But Deleuze and Guattari's point, following each of the thinkers they study, is that at a certain moment this questioning of assumptions comes to an end. If each thinker is able to question the assumptions of the one before, they do so only to reintroduce the same sorts of assumptions themselves. They do not properly conceive of that 'plane of immanence' (*WP?*, 36) that would be at once the only way not to have concepts that are ungrounded, and that 'reserve' or 'reservoir' (*WP?*, 36) from which all concepts come. If in Plato the Idea is not reduced to reminiscence, truth is still presented as the 'presupposition of an already there' (*WP?*, 29). If in Descartes natural appearance is criticized as illusion, there is nevertheless not a thinking of the 'time' (*WP?*, 31) that would allow this 'I' to be determined. If in Kant there is proposed an immanent critique in which things are questioned in their own terms, philosophical concepts continue to be related to lived experience through 'a priori propositions or judgement as functions of a whole of possible experience' (*WP?*, 142). For

Deleuze and Guattari, it is only Spinoza who properly thinks this plane of immanence, pursuing thought to its limit without some presupposition bringing it to a halt, and thus in some ways is the 'Christ' (*WP?*, 60) of philosophers. (Perhaps the only equivalent to Spinoza in thinking a thought that is not subject to any higher judgement is Nietzsche, which is why he might be called the 'anti-Christ' of philosophers.) But, strictly speaking, this 'plane of immanence', this imageless 'image of thought' (*WP?*, 37), is impossible to realize. Thought, as Kant was in fact the first to make clear, is inseparable from illusion, mistake, error, which is why the plane of immanence cannot finally be maintained. Or, as Deleuze and Guattari put it, it is at once what must be thought and cannot be thought, persisting only as a certain 'nonthought within thought' or 'nonphilosophy within philosophy' (*WP?*, 218).

As we say, in their attempt to grasp the conditions of thought, Deleuze and Guattari can be seen as post-Kantian. However, they also differ from Kant in that they seek to find the conditions of *real* and not merely *possible* experience. That is to say, what Deleuze ultimately objects to in Kant is that the transcendental Ideas that are said to make experience possible – God, the world and the soul – are too broad or too general. They do not arise out of a thinking of actual experience but are imposed upon it, and thus provide the conditions not of how experience actually is but only of how it should be. And at the same time Deleuze also criticizes Kant for the way that these transcendental conditions are merely a reflection of the empirical, an empirical that is constructed in the image of the possible. What is said to condition remains in the image of what is conditioned, and thus the transcendental is unable to propose anything fundamentally different from what is but only an extension of it. This is the complex, double-edged aspect of Deleuze's description of his philosophy as a 'transcendental empiricism' (*DR*, 143), as opposed to Kant's 'transcendental idealism', for it implies a criticism of the transcendental for being both unrelated to the empirical and insufficiently different from the empirical.[3] In a way, that is, Deleuze's transcendental empiricism is at once more transcendental than the transcendental, a thinking of what makes something like Kant's transcendental Ideas possible, and nothing other than the empirical, insofar as Deleuze wants to think the real conditions of real experience. It is what we might call, slightly amending the title of one of the commentaries on

What is Philosophy?, a 'critique of pure critique':[4] an attempt to apply the method of Kant's transcendental critique to those transcendent, that is, unquestioned or assumed, facts that underpin Kant's first two Critiques (the 'fact' of experience in the *Critique of Pure Reason*, the 'fact' of morality in the *Critique of Practical Reason*). But it is a critique that would be undertaken with no prior aim or image of truth in mind, and perhaps in that sense would no longer be a critique, insofar as critique always implies the refusal or rejection of something in the name of something 'better' or 'superior', often determined in advance. Deleuze's transcendental empiricism rejects nothing in advance in attempting to account for everything. But everything would now be possible only for an entirely other reason, a condition that is absolutely other to what it conditions. As Deleuze writes in the context of Nietzsche's Eternal Return: 'It is the thought of the Eternal Return that selects. It makes willing something whole... . It makes willing a creation. It brings about the equation willing = creation' (*NP*, 69). And in *What is Philosophy?*, Deleuze and Guattari call this hyper-transcendental condition that is also nothing else but what is 'Mime', that which 'confines itself to perpetual allusion without breaking the ice': 'A mime neither reproduces the state of affairs nor imitates the lived; it does not give an image but constructs a concept' (*WP?*, 159-60).

It is Husserl and his project of phenemonology that several critics see Deleuze as closest to at this point. In a similar way to Deleuze, Husserl through his famous transcendental reduction tried to suspend our ordinary, empirical relationship to the world and instead force us to think what allows this experience. Husserl attempted not to impose these conditions onto experience, but sought as much as possible to have these conditions arise out of experience. It was Husserl who was the first to constitute a kind of transcendental empiricism – and Deleuze briefly makes the connection in *Difference and Repetition* (*DR*, 137) – in that, in a way beyond Kant, he sought to think the transcendental conditions of experience through experience itself. Again, it would be the attempt not to exclude anything in advance or to declare how things should be, but to the extent possible to record how things actually are, to have the conditions of thought not be something different from what is actually thought. (Although with Husserl, too, Deleuze and Guattari argue that, while his transcendental reduction sought to 'renew our concepts by giving us perceptions and affections that would awake us to the world' (*WP?*, 149–50), he ultimately invoked a 'transcendent – not transcendental – subject, to which this experience would be immanent' (*WP?*, 46). In other words, it would be a subject that was not phenomenologically produced, but simply assumed or taken for granted. And it is at this point in *What is Philosophy?* that Deleuze and Guattari turn to Sartre, whose Husserlian-derived notion of an 'impersonal transcendental field' (*WP?*, 47) – as opposed to the Husserlian concept of a transcendental Other – in relation to which I am formed and which operates as a kind of guarantor of my representations, opens up both an outside to consciousness and consciousness to its outside.)

The crucial breakthrough that Husserl made, particularly in his later works, which Deleuze and Guattari can be seen to be wanting to preserve, is the thinking of the transcendental conditions of experience in terms of *genesis*. What Deleuze feels is missing in Kant, but that can be found, or at least is suggested, in Husserl – although it was in fact first proposed by an early critic of Kant, Salomon Maïmon, and later taken up in the nature-philosophy of such German Idealists as Fichte and even Hegel – is an emphasis on how the transcendental categories are not preconstituted or do not exist once and for all but are *produced*, put together as part of an ongoing encounter with the world. In the later Husserl, 'perceptions and affections' are not merely epiphenomenal, affecting an already constituted subject, but are themselves the very materials out of which a subject will come to be constituted. In Husserl's later phenomenology, that is, not only is the transcendental subject subject to the critique of empiricism, insofar as it cannot import anything that is not to be found in experience, but empiricism itself is transcendental, is never simply itself but already contains the conditions for its own reception and constitution. We always get the thing together with what has allowed us to perceive it. As Deleuze writes in *Difference and Repetition*, at once distinguishing his project from Husserl's early, 'static' phenomenology with its famous transcendental reduction (the attempt to determine the sensible as 'that which remains once representation is removed') and declaring his affinity with Husserl's later, 'genetic' phenomenology, in which the empirical is the transcendental ('when he apprehends directly in the sensible that which can only be sensed, the very being of the sensible'):

It is strange that aesthetics (as the science of the sensible) could be founded on what *can* be represented in the sensible. True, the inverse procedure is not much better, consisting of the attempt to withdraw the pure sensible from representation and to determine it as that which remains once representation is removed (a contradictory flux, for example, or a rhapsody of sensations). Empiricism truly becomes transcendental, and aesthetics an apodictic discipline, only when we apprehend directly in the sensible that which can only be sensed, the very being *of* the sensible (*DR*, 56–7).

In fact, the same question of 'aesthetics' as the sensible producing its own possibility of reception is to be found in Deleuze's early book on Kant, in which he criticizes Kant for his failure properly to derive his transcendental categories and instead merely to assume them. It is in Kant's last great work, the *Critique of Judgement* – incidentally, one of Deleuze and Guattari's signal works of 'old age' in *What is Philosophy*? – that we find Kant retrospectively deriving the authentic grounds of his first two Critiques. In the Third Critique, in the experience of the sublime, each of Kant's three faculties, Understanding, Reason and Imagination, is exceeded and pushed towards its limit. Each in its own way fails to think the sublime and falls back upon itself. But paradoxically it is at this point, where each faculty is exceeded by and confronted with a formlessness that it cannot identify, that each reaches a kind of accord in which it is able to recognize itself in the other. And at this moment it is revealed that the original condition for each of the faculties is indeed this relationship. If in the judgement of beauty, there is a 'free and indeterminate accord' (*KCP*, 49) between faculties, which still implies a kind of authority and self-determination, in the experience of the sublime there is a 'dissension' (*KCP*, 51) that is not an accord and not a freedom, but a forced necessity precisely because no single faculty exists before its relationship with the others. Put otherwise, if the Third Critique takes place under the faculty of Imagination, as the First Critique took place under Understanding and the Second under Reason, Imagination for its part is only a name for this relationship between the faculties. As Deleuze writes: 'In this accord [between Reason, Imagination and ultimately Understanding], the soul [Imagination] is felt as the indeterminate suprasensible unity of all the faculties;

we are ourselves brought back to a focus, as a "focal point" in the suprasensible' (*KCP*, 51). Imagination, we might say, occurs twice in the Third Critique: once as genus and once as species. It is that genus which includes itself as one of its species. It is that 'suprasensible' point – suprasensible because it is only where each faculty reaches its own internal limit – at which Understanding, Reason and Imagination meet.

* * *

In many ways, *What is Philosophy?* works like Kant's Third Critique. Indeed, we might say that *What is Philosophy* is Deleuze's Third Critique, after his First Critique of *Difference and Repetition* and Second Critique of *Anti-Oedipus*. *What is Philosophy?*, like the Third Critique, is about three faculties – called art, philosophy and science – and, as in Deleuze's reading of the Third Critique, Deleuze and Guattari's aim is to show how each engenders the other, comes about in its relationship with the other two. Deleuze and Guattari raise at several points in *What is Philosophy?* the question of art, philosophy and science touching or crossing over into one other. They speak of the philosophical concept becoming 'the concept of function or sensation' and the scientific function becoming 'the function of sensation or the concept' (*WP?*, 199). Moreover, they speak of the fact that 'none of these elements can appear without the other being still to come, still indeterminate or unknown' (*WP?*, 199). In other words, *What is Philosophy?* is the playing out of Deleuze's reading of Kant's Third Critique in terms of genesis: what is at stake there is how art, philosophy and science are given not in themselves but only in their relationship with each other when confronted with a sublime 'indeterminate' or 'unknown' – Deleuze and Guattari's word for it at the end of the book is simply a 'No' (*WP?*, 218). (And, furthermore, it is a relationship that, as with Imagination in the Third Critique, takes place under the head of philosophy. In *What is Philosophy?*, philosophy is not only one of the terms engaged with those others, but also thinks the relationship between these terms. The connection between philosophy and 'aesthetics' in the wider Kantian sense is indicated by Deleuze and Guattari suggesting that a 'function is beautiful' or a 'concept is beautiful' (*WP?*, 132), and speaking of the way that philosophy requires a certain 'taste' (*WP?*, 7) for the well-made concept.) Indeed, more than the relationship between art, philosophy and science – this has been an emerging theme in Deleuze scholarship for some time – we might say that what *What is Philosophy?* ultimately traces is the passage from physical chaos or materiality through sense or virtuality and on to logical propositions and representational consciousness. In this regard, it is not entirely inappropriate to compare *What is Philosophy?* to something like Hegel's *Phenomenology of Spirit*, although we might perhaps better title it *The Phenomenology of the Brain*. In part, *What is Philosophy?* is the story of how philosophy comes to realize itself or be realized (but also in a crucial sense – and this is how Deleuze and Guattari would differ from Hegel – philosophy would be lost in being realized or realized in being lost).

To put this more directly, what we see in *What is Philosophy?* is a certain passage from art, through philosophy and on to science and logic. In this passage – and this should remind us of what we said in the previous chapter – art 'contracts' (*WP?*, 211) or holds together for a moment its materials, thus beginning the process of breaking with the chaos in which something disappears as soon as it appears. Philosophy then takes the sensations and intensities that art leaves us with and further abstracts and unifies them so that they form self-contained and 'self-positing' (*WP?*, 11) concepts. These now virtual Ideas or concepts are then progressively 'actualized' (*WP?*, 23) in science, so that they make up first individuated things and bodies and then wider classes of objects and subjects. These objects and subjects are then further abstracted or 'generalized' (*WP?*, 135), in order that they can be represented and shared with others. A kind of arc is traced in the book, therefore, from the actual to the virtual and then back to the actual. Philosophy as a breaking with its initial conditions is ultimately embodied first in the bodies of science and then in the propositions of logic. But this is to say that, if philosophy in the end becomes as opinion or logical proposition, it is also a way of contesting or counter-actualizing the currently existing state of affairs, of holding it up against that virtuality out of which it came. This is why, again, Deleuze and Guattari speak of a 'spider's web' in their book – a spider's web that the whole book can be understood to be – and of the way the movement between the actual and the virtual is always two-way, even if not reciprocal or equivalent. There are always at once the actual and the virtual; one is not possible without the other. Even though Deleuze and Guattari are not simply opposed to the actual, they also make it clear that the actual is not possible outside the virtual, by which they mean the 'becoming' (WP?, 112) of things, the process by which they become what they are. Even when things are at their most actual, when all is actual, there is still the virtual; all this is possible only because of the virtual.

This conception of art, philosophy and science as aligned and mutually engendering one another, however, goes against many readings of *What is Philosophy?*, and even against several suggestions in *What is Philosophy?* itself. It can appear, indeed, as though art, philosophy and science are three different attempts to 'cast a plane over chaos' (WP?, 197, 202). That is, it can appear as though art, philosophy and science each independently grapples with the problem of chaos as though for the first time, with each responding to it in its own way. Thus, as Deleuze and Guattari can say of Greek philosophy in *What is Philosophy?*: 'Philosophy, science and art are no longer organized as levels of a single projection and are not even differenciated according to a common matrix, but are immediately posited or reconstituted in a respective independence' (WP?, 91). Or perhaps more generally: 'Art should not be thought to be like a synthesis of science and philosophy, of the finite and infinite routes. The three routes are specific, each as direct as the other, and they are distinguished by the nature of the plane and by what occupies it' (WP?, 198). And this presumed independence between art, science and philosophy has been followed by such commentators as Ronald Bogue, who writes: 'Art, too [like philosophy and science] commences in chaos'.[5] And by Elizabeth Grosz, who writes: 'Each plane, Deleuze and Guattari suggest, cuts chaos in a different way, through a different angle, which is why each is unique, irreplaceable and incommensurable with each other'.[6] In all of this there is the idea that art, philosophy and science are essentially parallel activities, each enacting an entire process on its own; and that the ultimate effect of philosophy's engagement with other fields – for it cannot be denied that Deleuze writes extensively on such topics as film and visual art – is to test the limits of a philosophy that remains fundamentally unchanged. It is a modesty of philosophy – for philosophy does not attempt to speak for those others; they each retain their own authority – and yet it is philosophy that remains Deleuze's central subject, which stands outside those other fields and speaks of its relationship to them as though from somewhere else. *What is Philosophy?* would in the end be a book *about* philosophy, in a classic act of philosophical self-reflection and self-possession.

The reading of *What is Philosophy?* that emerges from the emphasis on the post-Kantian question of genesis, on how the various fields of thought emerge rather than being assumed, is different. The most important distinction, of course, is that art, philosophy and science are not independent but interconnected, the separate stages on a trajectory leading from material chaos through to propositional consciousness. And this would be to say that each does not deal anew with chaos, but each represents a successive stage of engagement: art comes first, then philosophy and finally science and logic. Although each does in a way continue to engage with chaos – and chaos, as we will see, is what drives the movement from one to the other – each is progressively more 'distant' from it, mediated as it were by what comes before it. And there is much evidence for this ordering of art, philosophy and science in *What is Philosophy?*, from Deleuze and Guattari speaking of the 'advance' or 'succession' (*WP?*, 203) of the various disciples, to the laying out of the different layers of what they call the 'brain subject' in the order art, philosophy and science (*WP?*, 211–16). But the second consequence of this post-Kantian perspective is that when Deleuze and Guattari speak of art, philosophy and science they are not, or not simply, speaking about what we ordinarily mean by these things but about the three different stages in this genesis. Art refers to that first moment of genesis that takes us from chaos to liberated 'compounds of sensation' on a 'plane of composition' (*WP?*, 185). Philosophy takes these elements from a 'plane of immanence' (*WP?*, 35) and puts them together to form concepts or Ideas. Science takes these virtual Ideas and actualizes them on a 'plane of reference' (*WP?*, 119). And logic takes these actualized singularities and generalizes them to constitute 'opinions' or 'propositions' (*WP?*, 142).

It is at this point that we might make a comment both about the terms Deleuze and Guattari use in *What is Philosophy?* and about the overall organization of the book. A number of recent critics, such as Joe Hughes in *Deleuze and the Genesis of Representation*[7] and Levi Bryant in *Difference and Givenness: Deleuze's Transcendental Empiricism and the Ontology of Immanence*,[8] have argued that the same essential schema involving the passage from a first, dynamic genesis going through a moment of virtuality and then on to a final, static genesis runs through all of Deleuze's books (and through Deleuze's collaborations with Guattari, which makes the case for the essential continuity between the two oeuvres, or even more strongly that Deleuze is effectively the author of the works they wrote together). The real subject of Deleuze's *The Logic of Sense*, for example, beneath its discussion of Lewis Carroll, Antonin Artaud and the Greek Stoics, is the movement from a first, dynamic genesis of physical effects through a virtual plane of sense and on to a final, static genesis of good and then common sense. The real subject of *Anti-Oedipus*, against its seeming critique of an Oedipalized psychoanalysis and assertion of a schizophrenic desire, is the progression, historical as well as ontological, from dispersed molecular affects to aggregated molar objects. And Deleuze's *Difference and Repetition*, for all its detailed philosophical treatment of the themes of difference and repetition, is concerned first with the production of time, then with the Ideas that result from this and finally with the expression of these Ideas as spatial objects with qualities in the world. In other words, what these commentators insist upon is that, at least across a certain period of Deleuze's career, from the late 1960s until the early 1970s, and across a wide variety of subject matter (some directly philosophical and some not), there is a remarkable consistency of approach to be found. Deleuze remains throughout concerned to trace how, through a series of identifiable stages, we go first from a passive or dynamic synthesis, through a transcendental field of sense or intensity and then on to an active or a static synthesis in order to proceed from an undifferentiated chaos or materiality to a differenciated field of representation.

It is a continuity that Hughes for one sees as running all the way through to *What is Philosophy?* But perhaps one of the reasons this consistency has not been noted, suggests Hughes, is that the same terms or the same structural positions within the overall genesis have been given different names in Deleuze's different treatments. Hughes describes Deleuze's shifting terminology from book to book as 'incoherent but systematic'.[9] And Claire Colebrook explains: 'A philosophy or form of writing that aims to affirm the mobility of life must also be mobile, creating all sorts of connections and following new pathways. For this reason, there is an almost circular quality to Deleuze's work: once you understand one term then you can understand them all, but you also need to understand all the terms even to begin to understand one'.[10] Thus in *The Logic of Sense*, the chaos of *What is Philosophy?* is called the schizophrenic depths, and the plane of immanence is called the transcendental field of sense. In *Anti-Oedipus*, the plane of immanence of *What is Philosophy?* is called the field of intensity, and the passage from philosophy through to science and logic corresponds to the successive historical periods of the territorial age, the age of the despot and modern capitalism. In *Difference and Repetition*, the plane of immanence and philosophical concepts of *What is Philosophy?* are called multiplicity and Ideas, and the passage through science and logic is repeated in the sequence individuation, dramatization and differenciation. The mathematical calculus that is used in *What is Philosophy?* to speak of static genesis is used in *Difference and Repetition* to speak of Ideas, and in *The Fold: Leibniz and the Baroque* (1988) to speak of passive genesis. And, indeed, perhaps the other reason why the consistency of this theme of genesis throughout Deleuze's and Deleuze and Guattari's work has not been immediately noted is that in different books Deleuze emphasizes different aspects of its overall trajectory, and even calls it different names. In *The Logic of Sense*, genesis goes through a primary order, a secondary organization and a tertiary order and the emphasis is on static genesis. In *Anti-Oedipus*, the process is divided up into desiring production and social production, with each half having a radically different language (psychoanalytic and historical respectively). In *Difference and Repetition*, dynamic genesis culminates in the future and static genesis is the passing of this future into the present, with this overall narrative being interrupted by intervening chapters.

This genesis is also the fundamental subject of *What is Philosophy?* The first point we would want to make is the book's consistency with the rest of Deleuze's and Deleuze and Guattari's work. Although the terms *What is Philosophy?* uses are not the same as in others of their writings, its overall subject matter is. And this is to say that, although the particular terms used in *What is Philosophy?* are different, the role they play within Deleuze and Guattari's argument is comparable to that in others of their books. Thus, even though Deleuze and Guattari do not use the language of *Difference and Repetition* of Ideal elements between which differential relationships are formed by an aleatory point passing between them, when they speak in *What is Philosophy?* of a concept made up of components crossed by a state of survey in infinite movement (*WP?*, 20), the various terms match up with another because they occupy similar structural positions. And this is to say that each term in *What is Philosophy?* takes its meaning contextually, in its relationship with all the others. The book itself forms a kind of concept, of which its various terms would be the components. And this has the important consequence that, when Deleuze and Guattari speak of art, philosophy, science and logic in *What is Philosophy?*, each of these is first to be understood by the place it fills within a wider narrative of genesis, which is the book's real subject. Art corresponds to dynamic genesis, philosophy to the transcendental realm of sense and science and logic to static genesis. That is, again, before art, philosophy, science and logic relate to anything that corresponds to the world – and it is important to realize that this is part of Deleuze and Guattari's attempt to break with philosophy as a form of 'recognition' (*WP?*, 139) – they are terms within an overall structure (and this is another reason why art, philosophy and science are not independent, simply three separate 'castings over chaos'). However, again, perhaps the reason why this structure has not until recently been recognized is that, like so many other of Deleuze's and Deleuze and Guattari's books, *What is Philosophy?* is not narrated in the order of this genesis. It is philosophy that is dealt with first, then science and logic and finally art. Hughes in his elaboration of the notion of genesis in the work of Deleuze draws a distinction between the 'story' – the actual order that leads from unconscious sensations to conscious representations – and the 'plot' – the way this story is told.[11] Deleuze and Guattari narrate the story of *What is Philosophy?* in the order philosophy, science and art, we might say, because – insofar as we can understand each of Deleuze's books as emphasizing a different aspect of genesis – they want to bring out in it the role of philosophy. In this respect, it is *Difference and Repetition* (the chapters 'The Image of Thought' and 'Ideas and the Synthesis of Difference') and *The Logic of Sense* (the chapters on 'Aion', 'The Communication of Events' and 'Univocity') that are the true precursors to *What is Philosophy?* It is these three books that could be said to constitute the properly 'philosophical' trilogy in Deleuze's oeuvre.

In what sense, then, is philosophy the true subject of *What is Philosophy?* Or, to put it another way, where is the real philosophy in *What is Philosophy?* As we say, the philosophy we find in *What is Philosophy?* is not philosophy as it is usually defined. Deleuze and Guattari understand philosophy not as reflection, contemplation or communication, but rather as a thinking of genesis. That 'virtuality' they describe philosophy as being is a conception of the world in terms of its 'becoming': the fact that what is is only because of what comes before and after it. As they write: 'The actual is not what we are but rather what we become, what we are in the process of becoming' (*WP?*, 112). And this thinking of becoming within the actual is, to recall what we said earlier, also the thinking of the conditions of the sensible in the only terms in which they can be thought, from within the sensible itself. But this is to say that, if philosophical thinking arises as a result of the genesis of the sensible, this thinking is itself this genesis. In a performative way, this thinking *is* the genesis or becoming it speaks of: it not only speaks of a certain virtuality within the sensible, it represents this very virtuality. But all of this is to suggest that philosophy as this thinking does not simply stand outside of the genesis but is also subject to it. Philosophy is not to be grasped in itself, but only in the relationship between art, philosophy and science. It is for this reason, again, that Deleuze and Guattari say that philosophy is not a matter of reflection or, for that matter, self-reflection. It is also why they say there is no 'concept of all concepts' (*WP?*, 35). So where, then, do we see in *What is Philosophy?* that place from where philosophy is re-marked? Or, to put this another way, where is it that we see philosophy both as what thinks genesis and itself subject to genesis? It is the *brain*, like philosophy, that is the 'junction' (*WP?*, 208) of art, philosophy and science. It is the brain that, like the philosophical concept in relation to its components, constitutes a 'state of survey without distance' (*WP?*, 210). And it is the brain, and not philosophy as such, that thinks this unity. Philosophy is only one of the three 'planes' (*WP?*, 208) that make up the brain. But we would emphasize that not even the brain is capable of any final reflection or self-reflection. The brain is split between the 'subjective' brain, which reflects, and the 'objective' brain, which is reflected upon (*WP?*, 210), without its being possible to draw a clear line between them. As Deleuze and Guattari insist, it is not a matter of any 'brain behind the brain', but only of the brain surveying itself without any 'supplementary dimension' (*WP?*, 210). And, indeed, in one of the most complicated equivalences of all, we would say that this self-reflection at the end of genesis finally produces something like the chaos we have at the beginning. Self-reflection attempts to master chaos, but in the end only leads to it, which is why the process of genesis is never complete.

Accordingly, in explicating *What is Philosophy?* for this *Reader's Guide*, we re-order its chapters in order to bring out this question of genesis. We begin with art (the chapter 'Percept, Affect and Concept'), move on to philosophy (the chapters 'What is a Concept?', 'The Plane of Immanence' and 'Conceptual Personae') and end with science and logic (the chapters 'Functives and Concepts' and 'Prospects and Concepts'). We then close with the chapter on the brain ('From Chaos to the Brain') and the chapter on philosophy in relation to history and geography ('Geophilosophy'). Our point in connecting these two chapters is that the genesis of thought in the brain – philosophy as the creation of thought in the depths of the 'synaptic fissures' (*WP?*, 206) – is the same as the most evident historical and geographical origins of philosophy in Ancient Greece. In both, there is the absolute enigma of philosophy as an unlocatable 'event' (*WP?*, 112), which is to be distinguished from every place and present, that occurs nowhere else but in the actual, in the brain. To conclude here, then, the answer to the question the book asks is to be found not in any particular part of the book, but in the entire book itself. But, beyond this, there is *nowhere* from where the question is able to be answered. Philosophy is only its own becoming or, better, it is the being of its own becoming. And it is for this reason that we might understand the book offering a certain 'pedagogy' (*WP?*, 12) of the concept. Deleuze says elsewhere that pedagogy is a matter not of 'doing like' but of 'doing with' (*DR*, 23), and this would be to say that philosophy does not exist without an other. That is, if in one way it is a matter of following a particular philosophical system, in another way this system would not exist before this following. The secret of *What is Philosophy?* is that the book and its subject, the book and its genesis, the book and its commentary come about at the same time in a mutual and inseparable becoming. And this would be to say that neither appears before the other, neither is definitively able to speak of the other. It is for this reason that the book would be forever open to the future, a future Deleuze and Guattari define as a 'new world that is never-ending, that is always in the process of coming about' (*WP?*, 112).

CHAPTER THREE

Art

What is art for Deleuze and Guattari? It has certainly been noted that throughout Deleuze's and Deleuze and Guattari's work – and not just in *What is Philosophy?* – art is a privileged object of inquiry. Deleuze for his part wrote a number of studies on specific artists and art forms. And Deleuze and Guattari, in *A Thousand Plateaus* as well as *Kafka: Toward a Minor Literature* (1975), also engaged extensively with art. Art is often seen by Deleuze and Guattari's commentators to function as a kind of 'other' to philosophy, in line with their general project of contesting thought with its 'outside'. Thus Deleuze and Guattari take up art in order to confront philosophy with its limits, conceived of either as some overturning of reason or some unconscious desire. As Simon O'Sullivan writes in *Art Encounters Deleuze and Guattari*: '[With art] our typical ways of being in the world are challenged, our systems of knowledge are disrupted. We are forced to thought'.[1] Or as Isabelle Ginoux puts it in 'On the History of Philosophy Considered as One of the Fine Arts', in a perhaps slightly more sophisticated version: 'The work of Gilles Deleuze presents itself as a triptych where aesthetics and the history of philosophy enfold, in the manner of outer leaves, a central panel dedicated to the elaboration of a philosophy of difference and repetition'.[2] But all of this must be understood very carefully. Art is not simply an external limit to philosophy, which in classic philosophical manner has the effect that it is philosophy that ultimately thinks the truth of art. But neither, as we have said before of some of the readings of *What is Philosophy?*, is it a matter of art merely constituting another 'throw over chaos' with philosophy, operating in parallel with it, as though the two were unrelated.

Perhaps the first point to recognize is that, for all their various treatments of art, Deleuze and Guattari are not actually interested in art in the usual sense. They are not concerned with the question of the proper hierarchy or relations between the different arts. They do not judge art aesthetically or attempt to constitute a canon of any kind. They do not, with rare exceptions, speak about art with reference to the generally recognized media, movements or social histories. And, in many of their studies of single artists, they do not use the results to generalize about comparable art forms or periods or even about other work by the same artist. As they write in *A Thousand Plateaus*: 'In no way do we believe in a fine-arts system: [instead] we believe in very diverse problems whose solutions are found in heterogeneous arts' (*TP*, 300). But this does not mean that they are simply uninterested in art. Art, as we will see, retains a crucial, indeed foundational, role in their thought. Rather, the question Deleuze and Guattari ask throughout their separate studies of art is: what makes art possible? Or, to put it in the common form in which they ask such questions: what is it that the possibility of art tells us? And, in a first answer to this question, we would say that for Deleuze and Guattari art is a way of *perceiving the world*. What is required for art and what art embodies is a certain perception of the world. What we have in art, the structural possibility that art represents, is a first engagement with the world and an initial organization of perception.

In art, that is, we engage with the world outside any pre-existing forms, categories or conceptual schemata. In art, there is nothing politically or morally right or wrong. There are no pre-established norms or rules that have to be followed. This is why Deleuze and Guattari are able to say, in an almost avant-garde sense, that the only duty of art is always to add more 'varieties' (*WP?*, 175) or 'possibilities' (*WP?*, 177) to the store of what is. In art, we see, to use the image Deleuze and Guattari borrow from D. H. Lawrence, as though through a 'slit in an umbrella' (*WP?*, 203): art not only views what is without expectations but cuts through already existing expectations. And what art then does is 'preserve' (*WP?*, 163) or 'monumentalize' (*WP?*, 164) these sensations. It wants to preserve them forever, even when the original object that inspired them no longer exists or the original artist who experienced them is no longer alive. The work of art becomes *in itself*, as long as the material in which it is embodied survives, the sensation or perception that was originally in something or somebody. And what art is – and what art shows – is the process by which this occurs, how it is that we are able to move from our first fleeting impressions of the world to a sensation that can last for millennia. Thus in a first stage of art a passing apprehension of the world is caught insofar as for a brief moment two separate instants are held together and seen to be of the 'same' thing. It is what Deleuze and Guattari call the *percept*. Examples of this percept in *What is Philosophy?* include the moor in the novels of Thomas Hardy, the ocean in Herman Melville's *Moby Dick* and the mirror and the city of London in Virginia Woolf's *Mrs Dalloway*. In each, there is a first separation of sensation from its surroundings, a kind of contrast and continuity against the incessant appearance and disappearance of the rest of the world. This is then followed by a second moment, in which this percept is related to an observer. It is this that Deleuze and Guattari call the *affect*. Examples of this affect given in *What is Philosophy?* include the relationship of Captain Ahab to Moby Dick or of Mrs Dalloway to London. In some ways, however, what is at stake in the affect, insofar as the one who perceives is at this stage nothing outside of what they perceive, is the relationship between two percepts. Art – and this is perhaps to offer a second answer to the question we began by posing – is not only the perception but also the *creation* of the world and of the one who perceives it. It is undoubtedly for this reason that Deleuze and Guattari emphasize the 'inhuman' aspect of art, which is precisely not post- or anti-human but pre- or before the human in an almost 'impersonal' (*WP?*, 47) sense.[3]

In other words, what is crucial to recognize is that none of the terms in Deleuze and Guattari's account of art (sensation, the world, the perceiver) exists in itself independently. Sensation does not exist outside the material in which it is embodied. The world does not exist before art but arises as a result of its perception by it. And it is not a matter in art of a fully conscious spectator who has this perception, for they are part of the world and come about only through their perception of it. As we say, art does not start with pre-existing categories, but is how these categories are produced. What we have in art is not an already represented world or a conscious spectator, but a series of geneses by which perceptions move away from an original chaos and are formed into independent, autonomous sensations that are able to be recorded, remembered and recognized. Art in fact is merely the first stage in a long process that leads from an evanescent material flux to fully actualized objects whose representations are able to be shared by conscious subjects. What it represents – but what it shows us, in that coming together of the empirical and transcendental that marks Deleuze and Guattari's work – is the first in a series of stages in the formation of human experience. Art is and is possible only because of a certain genesis that moves through percept, affect and on to the final freeing or liberation of sensation. In Deleuze and Guattari's various analyses of art we see that art is not simply a product of this genesis but also itself speaks of and allows us to speak of this genesis of representation.

Indeed, as we have already tried to make clear, art for Deleuze and Guattari is first of all a structural place within an overall trajectory of genesis and not a distinct realm of human activity. It is notable, for example, that after treating what appears to be art in the chapter 'Percept, Affect and Concept' in *What is Philosophy?*, we see the same successive moments of genesis in the chapter 'From Chaos to the Brain', which is a survey of the various capacities of the brain and its relationship to the world. Deleuze and Guattari begin there by arguing for a certain 'vitalist' (*WP?*, 213) conception of the universe, characterized by a 'contemplation' (*WP?*, 213) by the brain, in which two separate moments or elements are brought together and the one who perceives is nothing outside of what they perceive: '[The brain is] filled with itself by filling itself with what it contemplates' (*WP?*, 212). And we see this 'contraction' in such disparate natural phenomena as plants that bind the different elements out of which they are composed and rats that take on a habit that testifies to something going on behind their immediate actions (*WP?*, 212–13). There is then a following moment, in which these 'contractions' themselves are put together to produce a certain reaction or 'resonance' between them: 'Sensation is formed by contracting that which composes it, and by composing itself with other sensations that contract it in turn' (*WP?*, 212). Finally, there is a concluding moment in the formation of sensation, in which sensation is abstracted or 'withdrawn' (*WP?*, 211) in breaking with any physical or cultural causality and becoming independent (or almost) of any material determination: 'Sensation, then, is on a plane that is different from mechanisms, dynamisms and finalities' (WP?, 212). Here emerges the 'survey' (WP?, 211) or point of view onto the world and the 'plane of composition' (WP?, 211) or ensemble of all possible aesthetic 'varieties' (WP?, 213). And at this point art approaches philosophy, almost to the extent of being inseparable from it or joining up with it in the brain (WP?, 216).

We see the same three stages of genesis and final relationship to philosophy throughout Deleuze's and Deleuze and Guattari's various analyses of art. It is first of all, as we say, to think art not so much or not simply as a particular practice or product as a kind of perception of the world – a perception that is first of all in things themselves. But it is also to think, as this perception moves out of things and even out of the one who perceives, and becomes something more like what we usually think of as art, how art approaches philosophy. And this is to think – and we turn in more detail to this in the next chapter – art not as the other to philosophy or as unrelated to philosophy but as the *precondition* for philosophy. Although the chapter on art comes last in the narration of *What is Philosophy?*, as though it can only be thought through philosophy and science, this is deceptive. On the contrary, it is art that comes first in the story that *What is Philosophy?* wants to tell, and philosophy and science that are possible only on the basis of what it leaves behind. And we attempt to show all of this – both the three-part structure of genesis that marks all of Deleuze's and Deleuze and Guattari's readings of art and the way that it is art that provides the essential conditions for philosophy – through an analysis of four of Deleuze's and Deleuze and Guattari's writings on art, each taking up a different art form, in relation to *What is Philosophy?*: music in the chapter '1837: Of the Refrain' of *A Thousand Plateaus*, painting in Deleuze's *Francis Bacon: The Logic of Sensation* (1981), literature in Deleuze's *Proust and Signs* (1964) and cinema in Deleuze's *The Movement-Image* (1983) and *The Time-Image* (1985).

* * *

Deleuze and Guattari in the chapter on art in *What is Philosophy?* speak of the *Scenopoetes dentirostris*, known to Australians as the bowerbird, which every morning in order to mark off its territory 'cuts leaves, makes them fall to the ground and turns them over so that the paler, internal side contrasts with the earth' (*WP?*, 184). It seems strange that in this chapter on art Deleuze and Guattari should speak of nature, but their argument is that art is first of all a matter of the animal, or let us say nature. Deleuze and Guattari are thus opposed to many other theories of art (for example, Kant's) in seeing art not as marking a break with nature, but as nature, or more precisely the break that constitutes nature. In fact, this example of the bowerbird was first seen in the chapter '1837: On the Refrain' of *A Thousand Plateaus*, which deals principally with music. Deleuze and Guattari's argument there is that the territorial markings of the bowerbird are, fundamentally, not different from a similar 'territorialization' (*TP*, 312) that takes place in music – and, of course, the bowerbird is a famous musician. In 'On the Refrain' they look at a number of scientific accounts of animals marking off their territory through song or other ceremonial behaviour. Usually, this is seen as merely evolutionarily functional: a simple dividing up of space between the various species, each driven by an 'instinct of aggression' (*TP*, 315–16) with no other meaning. Here any musical expression would take place only after an initial marking off of territory. But Deleuze and Guattari disagree with this reductive conception. Drawing on the work of the neo-Darwinian biologist Jacob von Uexküll, they emphasize that evolution is to be understood not only as the following out of a predetermined code but also as the epigenetic interaction between the code and its environment. Thus it is that they can say that it is not an initial marking off of territory that allows a subsequent freedom of expression, but an expressive surplus that allows the initial marking off of territory, which in turn leads to a further increase in expression. As they write: 'The territory is not primary in relation to the qualitative mark; it is the mark that makes the territory' (*TP*, 315; also *WP?*, 183).

In fact, in *What is Philosophy?* Deleuze and Guattari understand the bowerbird's behaviour to be already a *second* moment in the creation of art. Before that, there is what they call 'vibration' (*WP?*, 168), which is when two passing sensations are momentarily held together by the perceiver so that the first remains when the second comes about. It is a moment often associated with flowers, not just with flower paintings (*WP?*, 175), or the 'contraction' (*WP?*, 212) by a plant of the elements that make it up, but with the way 'the field of lilies might be said to celebrate the glory of the skies' (*WP?*, 184). However, it is only with something like the marking out of territory by the bowerbird that there is a break with the material context sufficient to allow other 'causalities and finalities' (*WP?*, 184). And this second moment is connected to what Deleuze and Guattari call the 'embrace' or 'clinch' (*WP?*, 168), in which two of the sensations formed by that original contraction are themselves put together. This second moment is spoken of as the marking off of territory, but also described in terms of the 'house' (*WP?*, 186) and the 'earth' (*WP?*, 191). And the same is to be seen in *A Thousand Plateaus*. There, before the bowerbird and its marking off of territory, is what Deleuze and Guattari call the 'milieu', which is also characterized as 'vibratory', insofar as it is a 'bloc of space-time constituted by the periodic repetitions of the components' (*TP*, 313). And the bowerbird's marking off of territory is understood to be the taking into account of the relationship between two such milieus, in what Deleuze and Guattari call, using a musical analogy, 'counterpoint' (*TP*, 318). The bowerbird, when it marks off its territory, does so not in itself but only in relation to another, in the same way that the spider builds its web in order to catch the fly and the orchid colours itself to attract the wasp (*TP*, 314). As opposed to the unchanging habit or refrain of that first moment, in which the end comes back to the beginning, here with the house or territory things must be grasped in their difference from others. Things do not remain the same, but rather there is a 'continuous variation' (*TP*, 340) of an underlying motif.

Finally, however, if this breaking with milieu allows the production of territory, it also points towards a certain deterritorialization. If elements are allowed to take on different meanings and functions in order to build a house (for example, the leaves out of which the bowerbird constructs its nest), what is implied is that they are always open to a further decontextualization of this sort. As Deleuze and Guattari write: 'In many cases, a territorialized, assembled function acquires enough independence to constitute a new assemblage, one that is more or less deterritorialized, en route to deterritorialization' (*TP*, 324). The examples of this that Deleuze and Guattari give in *What is Philosophy?* – although again they originally come from *A Thousand Plateaus* – are chaffinches that suddenly assemble in their millions, and lobsters that gather in enormous numbers to set off on vast underwater migrations (*WP?*, 186). And in *A Thousand Plateaus* there is a detailed account of the Australian grass finch, which takes a stick from its nest and uses it as an autonomous or free-floating element in order to pass between hitherto separated territories as part of a courtship ritual (*TP*, 324). This is precisely that 'withdrawal' or 'unclasping' that Deleuze and Guattari speak of as constituting the third and final moment of sensation, in which sensations are not only different from others but also different from themselves. Beyond the difference between territories, which remains only part of them, we have the difference that allows territory, which opens territory up to the outside. This is the ambiguity of what Deleuze and Guattari call in *A Thousand Plateaus* the 'Natal': 'The territory has an intense centre at its profoundest depth; but, as we have seen, this intense centre can be located outside of the territory, at the point of convergence of very different and distant territories' (*TP*, 325–6). And it is for this reason that the Natal is retrospectively revealed as already present in that first moment of sensation. It is the 'rhythm' present from the beginning that drives sensation from one moment of its genesis to the next. Territory is inseparable from its deterritorialization, just as deterritorialization for its part always leads to reterritorialization.

And all of this can be thought in terms of music as an actual art form. We have, of course, already been talking about music. Deleuze and Guattari's vision of nature, as we have already seen, is that it is traversed by and even made up of rhythms. The bowerbird 'sings perched on his singing stick, a vine or branch located just above the display ground he has prepared' (*TP*, 331). The male *Troglodytidae* of the wren family 'takes possession of his territory and produces a "music box refrain" as a warning to possible intruders' (*TP*, 323). The mating dance of the stickleback fish is a zigzag, in which the 'zig is tied to an aggressive drive towards the partner, and the zag to a sexual drive towards the nest' (*TP*, 317). And the same goes for humans, whose music for Deleuze and Guattari arises out of similarly 'natural' ends. At first, there is what they call the 'song' or 'air' (*WP?*, 189). It is the first synthesis of the discontinuous flow of space and time, both artistically and developmentally. Songs and airs are those nursery rhymes and children's songs (for example, 'Frère Jacques'), in which we return to the beginning after the end, so that we can repeat them over and over again, without anything changing. It is a way of ensuring that a first moment does not disappear when a second appears, holding the two moments together in a simple 'vibration' (*WP?*, 190). It is the first elementary framing of chaos, almost by its repetition, like 'chaos jumping over itself' (*TP*, 312). In terms of the history of music proper, it corresponds to the period Deleuze and Guattari call simply the 'classical', in which we have the 'one-two of the differentiation of form divided' (*TP*, 338). But musical art is the making-expressive of such airs, the taking of them away from their original context. First, it does this by putting two airs together in a process we have already called 'counterpoint', in that what is at stake is the mutual relationship or 'becoming' between two such milieus. This, of course, corresponds to the period of the Baroque in music, associated with such composers as Mozart and even Beethoven, in which we have the 'one-two of the distinction between parts as they answer each other' (*TP*, 338). And this is extended in Romanticism, associated with such composers as Wagner and Mahler, in which there is a more general principle of 'continuous development' (*TP*, 340), in which the underlying motifs of the Baroque undergo a potentially endless series of variations. As Deleuze and Guattari put it: '[With Romanticism] the universal has become a relation, a variation' (*TP*, 340).

However, at the end of the Romantic period, with its themes and variations and its evocation of landscape or territory, there is a certain distension and opening-up of music. With such composers as Chopin and Liszt, there is a breaking of the rules of composition and no longer any underlying theme of which the music is a variation. Now, in the improvization of the compositional study (*WP?*, 190), there is an attempt to discover the ultimate expressive potential of the musical material, outside any boundaries. This is the beginning of what Deleuze and Guattari call the 'modern' (*TP*, 342). In modern music, there are no longer any identifiable motifs that the composer tries to hold together, but the complete dispersion of the organizational elements of the music – in a process Deleuze and Guattari call 'molecularization' (*TP*, 342) – in which each part differs from itself. Compositionally, this dispersion takes two contrasting forms: either long, unchanging chords to produce a 'uniform area' of sound, as in Wagner, or the continuous variation of 'broken and unrelated tones' (*WP?*, 191), as in Debussy. What is liberated in modern music is pure sensation, but also the compositional possibilities that would express it (*WP?*, 193). There is the creation of musical 'intensity' (*TP*, 343) and the discovery of that refrain or rhythm that underlies all music (*TP*, 347–8). As opposed to the memory and looking back to the past of Romanticism, in modern music there is the putting forward of a people of the future: there is no subject or audience at present, but the music itself seeks to bring about this audience through its own means. With modern music, that is, it is no longer a matter of the earth, but of the 'cosmos' or 'universe' (*WP?*, 191; *TP*, 342).

Now, all of this can appear to be the writing of a history of music, but Deleuze and Guattari insist that this is not their aim, or at least not their primary aim.[4] Rather, they argue that, if they are offering an account of formal innovation, moving from uncomposed airs through counterpoint and symphonic variation and on to the liberation of musical materiality, they are also proposing a certain logic of sensation (*TP*, 347). In a way, each distinct musical movement (Classical, Baroque/Romantic, modern) represents a successive moment in the genesis of perception. Early music is a 'vibration' (*TP*, 348), Baroque and Romantic music an 'embrace' (*TP*, 339) and modern music an 'opening up' (*TP*, 342) of sensations. And, again, the fact that this is not a simple history of music is indicated by the fact that the same 'progression' is to be seen also in nature, from the first milieus or markings of space, through the framing or territorializing of landscape and on to the final migration or deterritorialization towards the cosmos. Music is part of nature, or music is nature in the sense that out of the rhythms of music emerge both nature and the one who listens to it. Music is not simply a matter of some human or even animal that listens, because both they and what they listen to come about only in this rhythm. Music is the emergence both of nature (percept) and the one who listens (affect). And yet, again, if what we trace here is a certain progression or genesis, in another way – and this is perhaps also why what Deleuze and Guattari are proposing here is not a history of music – there is no such progression. As they say: 'Everything we attribute to an age was already present in the preceding age' (*TP*, 346). That is, as we saw before of the sublime, each successive stage of genesis is only the *failure* of the one before: the third marks the failure of the second, the second marks the failure of the first and the first for its part is merely the failure to grasp all the original chaos.

* * *

We can see something like this same sequence in painting. Deleuze and Guattari make the point in *What is Philosophy?* that painting is a kind of 'monument' (*WP?*, 164). In breaking with any original model and the one who made it, the painting has to stand up on its own. It is what preserves a sensation, Deleuze and Guattari insist, that will last as long as the materials in which it is embodied last. The examples of this that they give are of a young man in a painting whose smile will remain forever and a young woman in a sculpture who will maintain her pose for 5,000 years (*WP?*, 153). But what must be borne in mind is that this sensation captured in art will not remain strictly the same, but is a 'becoming' that is permanently open to the future. However, as Deleuze and Guattari are careful to remind us, this 'becoming', itself, would not exist without a certain framing, a certain materialization, a certain embodiment. Although sensation is always seeking to pass beyond its physical representation, it never actually can. There is a first moment in art that Deleuze and Guattari call, after Maurice Merleau-Ponty, the 'flesh', in which 'the world and the body are exchanged as correlates' (*WP?*, 178). It is perhaps a rephrasing of that 'contraction' that lies at the first moment of perception. But Deleuze and Guattari also insist – and here they follow the work of Erwin Strauss and Henri Maldiney, who while remaining phenomenologists broke with Merleau-Ponty's notion of the 'flesh' and the unified subject it implies – that this flesh by itself is too frail, too impermanent, to make itself into a monument. The flesh is still too close to that chaos out of which it emerges, insofar as it is not certain that, in it, that first moment remains by the time the second arrives. As Deleuze and Guattari write in *What in Philosophy?*: 'Flesh is only the developer which disappears in what it develops' (*WP?*, 183). As in *A Thousand Plateaus*, then, the first stage of genesis is not yet sufficient for art. It is only with the 'frame' – what Deleuze and Guattari speak of as the 'bone' within the flesh (*WP?*, 179) – that art properly exists, so that the first vibration is able to be remembered or reproduced along with the second. It is only at this juncture, as with the shift from the air to the motif in music, that art effectively breaks with nature.

Art, as Deleuze and Guattari emphasize throughout *What is Philosophy?*, is always a matter of the 'frame' or 'framing' (*WP?*,

179). It is the frame that produces art. If the first moment of contraction creates a sensation by holding together two different moments, it is the frame that produces a 'becoming' in holding two such sensations together – and for this reason art is always a 'bloc' or 'compound' (*WP?*, 164) of sensations. It is the frame that, as Deleuze and Guattari say, allows us to put the pieces of two 'differently oriented planes' together to form what they call a 'house' (*WP?*, 179). Art for them is always a matter of putting these 'planes' together, and each great artist has a different and identifiable way of doing so. Giacometti's 'receding horizontal planes differ from right to left and seem to come together on the thing (the flesh of the small apple), but like a pincer' (*WP?*, 180). Soutine's houses are 'knocked up against one another and prevent one another from falling back into chaos' (*WP?*, 204). Monet's houses 'rise up like a slit through which chaos becomes the vision of a rose' (*WP?*, 204). And this juxtaposition of different planes that do not immediately belong together produces an affect corresponding to that second moment in the genesis of perception called 'resonance'. It is a resonance that in *What is Philosophy?* and other of Deleuze's and Deleuze and Guattari's works is associated with 'memory' (*WP?*, 176). But at the outer limits of this framing, these planes join together to form a universe or single great plane (*WP?*, 180). It is a total joining up of planes, but also an opening up of the frame or house to what is outside it. The chaos that the walls of the house were built to protect us against now re-enters as a kind of cosmic force or intensity. It is an intensity that Deleuze and Guattari often associate with fields of unmodulated colour (*WP?*, 180). And yet, if the deterritorialization of this third moment of genesis arrives at the end, it is also retrospectively revealed as what lies at the beginning. The framing or territorialization of the second moment is possible only because of the deterritorialization of the third, or the third arrives only to make clear a failure or impossibility already at stake in the second. The chaos of the beginning (as figured by the broken tones of the flesh) re-emerges as an equivalent to the abstract intensity of the 'plane of composition' (as figured by the plane of monochrome colour) at the end (*WP?*, 189).

In fact, the considerations in *What is Philosophy?* of painting in terms of flesh and framing, section and house, colour and the opening out onto the cosmos are heavily indebted to Deleuze's discussion of the great English painter Francis Bacon, in *Francis Bacon: The Logic of Sensation*. Bacon paints using a vocabulary of scumbles, smears and semi-abstract marks, repeatedly wiping out and reapplying the paint and incorporating chance and accident, in order to capture his subjects unawares, before they compose themselves, as though in the process of coming about. If he is a figurative painter, he is figurative in the sense not of some representational fidelity to an original model, but of what Deleuze calls, after Jean-François Lyotard, the figural (*FB*, 5). It is to refer to a primal body – what Deleuze describes as 'the body without organs' (*FB*, 40) – crossed by unconscious impulses before its self-formation or self-consciousness. As Deleuze puts it at the beginning of the book: 'If the painter keeps to the figure, it will be to oppose the "figural" to the figurative. The figurative (representation) implies the relationship of an image to an object that it is supposed to illustrate' (*FB*, 6). It is to suggest – to take up the title of the book – the sensation that comes before sense. It is sensation not as subjective perception and affection, but as pre-subjective percept and affect. Bacon's paintings are not representational, narrative or symbolic, but seek a direct and unmediated relationship with the spectator's nervous system (*FB*, 32). As in the films of Alfred Hitchcock, it is the scream that he paints and not what is being screamed at: the percept becomes the affect (*FB*, 34). The subject of Bacon's paintings is the subject of art. But what is also to be seen in Bacon's paintings is the creation of the subject, or the movement towards the subject, through art. In Bacon's paintings there is the coming about of the subject (both the subject in the painting and the subject who looks at the painting) through the successive stages of 'vibration' (*FB*, 60), 'resonance' (*FB*, 61) and 'forced movement' (*FB*, 61). In other words, as so often in Deleuze's and Deleuze and Guattari's treatments of art, Bacon's paintings are understood as a disguised 'allegory' of the genesis of perception. To turn to the other half of the title of the book, what is being argued for here is a certain *logic* of sensation, revealing the genesis both of Bacon's art and of the subject of art.

Bacon's work starts with a series of seemingly accidental marks, scrapings, second thoughts and interruptions – what Deleuze calls Bacon's 'graph' or 'diagram' (*FB*, 82). But Deleuze emphasizes that this is not a matter of preliminary sketches on a previously blank surface, as in the common conception of artistic technique, but on the contrary a break with something – a chaos or even opinion – that is there before he begins. As Deleuze explains, Bacon does not assume the figure, but has to extract or isolate it, either hold it together against the dissipation of nature or cut it free from the assumptions of narrative. And this can be seen in those bars, rings or contours of colour that separate the figures from their background. Or, to put this more precisely, Bacon's figures come about as a result of this distinction. The background, as it were, encompasses or wraps itself around the figure in what Deleuze speaks of as a kind of systole or contraction. As he writes: 'The material structure curls around the contour in order to imprison the Figure ... The Figure becomes a Figure only through this movement' (*FB*, 14–5). What is brought about is a tension or trembling, a spasm or perhaps more accurately a 'waiting for a spasm' (*FB*, 15). The figure does not merely sit still within its ring, as though caught once and for all, but is traversed by a series of forces or sensations, as though there were some inner force held within, or as though the emerging organs of the body were that force held. In a way, the body in Bacon is only its contraction of the outside, and yet something else emerges from this, as a further difference or independence of the body draws itself off from this initial framing. Again, as Deleuze puts it: 'But the body is not simply waiting for something to finish itself; it exerts an effort upon itself in order to become a Figure' (*FB*, 15).

The body in Bacon is unable to sustain this tension, this heldness, this hysteria, for long. If the first moment of Bacon's painting consists in a contraction or wrapping around of the background to produce a stillness or immobility, it is followed soon after by a second moment, in which the body explodes or reaches out towards the background. If in that first moment the background wraps itself around the body in a systolic contraction, in a second moment the body wraps itself around the background in a diastolic expansion. After an internal trembling or gathering together, in which the body and its environment are held in a fragile tension, there is a deformation or release of tension, in which the body passes out of itself, either through one of its organs or through its projection onto an exterior object. An example of this, of course, is the mouth through its scream; but Bacon's figures can also pass outside themselves through the tip of an umbrella, a hypodermic needle, or, in *Figure at a Washbasin* (1976), through the blackness of a drain (*FB*, 15–16). Here – to go back to the analysis of the earlier *The Logic of Sense* – if this second moment can be seen as a mere reversal of the first, it is also different, in that it is not a connection but a conjunction (*LS*, 262) between parts. The body is not a simple effect of the objects around it, as though it incorporates them, but is the origin or cause of these objects, as though they were images or reflections of the body. In this regard, the mirror is an important object in Bacon, operating as a reflection of the body, even if it does not actually reflect it (*FB*, 17). And this second moment in the 'order of sensations' (*FB*, 37) puts in place the systolic-diastolic system that constitutes the basis of Bacon's art. The frame between inside and outside does not just exclude or cut off but also joins, opens up, deterritorializes. However, if this frame or contour allows us to put together body and background, it also opens the painting up to what cannot be framed, what passes outside the frame. Deleuze's example of this is those broad fields of colour that we see in the backgrounds of Bacon's painting, which, if they represent the putting together of planes on the second level, seem also to go beyond the edge of the painting in a kind of abstraction (*FB*, 111–13). We can see this particularly in Bacon's late work, where he aspires to paint no longer bodies but the forces they stand for: a jet of water, a wave, the wind of a tempest (*FB*, 28). And Deleuze's ultimate example of this – reminding us of another great English artist, Lewis Carroll – is the smile that remains when the face behind it disappears (*FB*, 23).

We have described here the three different 'orders' of sensation in Bacon's work, as though it is a question throughout of the relationship between the background and a single figure. But, while this can be seen through a single figure, it is a progression that can best be seen as it applies to different types of Bacon's paintings: those that feature a single figure (usually single-panelled), those that feature two figures (usually diptychs) and those that feature three figures (usually triptychs). It is the single-panelled works that Deleuze associates with 'vibration' or the first appearance of the world. It is the diptychs that he associates with 'resonance' or the reproduction of that first synthesis. And it is the triptychs that he associates with 'forced movement' or the attempt to synthesize the first two syntheses. In the single-figure works, the figure is held fixed by the background. In the two-figure works, we have a relationship – sometimes across the panels – not just of the figure to the background, but of one figure to another. And in the three-figured works, there is a relationship between two figures, but also a third 'witness' or 'attendant' figure (*FB*, 59), as though what is at stake is at once the 'resonance' or 'embrace' of the second moment plus a certain withdrawal from or even failure of this resonance. Deleuze several times throughout the *Logic of Sensation* repeats this taxonomy, recalling that distinction we have previously seen in *What is Philosophy?* But he goes on to make the point that, if the single figure corresponds to 'vibration', two figures to 'resonance' and three figures to 'forced movement', all three moments are also simultaneously present in each canvas. As Deleuze says, the 'second period does not so much contradict the first as is added to it' and 'it is not only the third period that invents the synthesis of the two' (*FB*, 27). In other words, if a kind of 'force' (*FB*, 49) or 'time' (*FB*, 53) emerges at the end of Bacon's art, this trajectory is also 'retrogradable' (*FB*, 69), a finality in retrospect present from the beginning.

* * *

Deleuze had in fact earlier elaborated the 'succession' involved in sensation in a study on the novelist Marcel Proust. *Proust and Signs* breaks with previous treatments of Proust's multi-volume masterpiece *In Search of Lost Time*, written between 1909 and 1922, by not seeing Proust's famous principle of 'involuntary memory' as the key to the novel. As is well known, *In Search of Lost Time* tells the story of the narrator Marcel and how he came to write the narrative that we read. The book is an extraordinarily detailed and apparently autobiographical account of Proust's life, covering his years in Parisian high society in the early 1900s, his various loves and their inevitable disappointment and his eventual seclusion from the world, which would lead to the writing of his novel. *In Search of Lost Time* – as with those other works of art Deleuze writes about – is therefore the story of a certain apprenticeship or pedagogy, of how Proust came to write his masterwork. What Deleuze attempts to show is that how Proust learnt to perceive the world parallels how he learnt to write his novel (just as the novel also shows its reader how to perceive the world). It is impossible to say, in other words, whether it is Proust who creates the novel or the novel that creates Proust. Proust becomes in effect a reader or creation of his own work. And the work does not simply re-create a pre-existing world but is part of it (*PS*, 98). It shows how the world comes about, just as it shows how it is that the subject in the world comes about. In this sense, the book is not an autobiography of its author because the author does not exist before his book. And it is not the story of how the book came to be written, as though it were a reflection upon the process from somewhere else, but an authentic genesis, in which the story of the conditions necessary for art (perception) are what art is and what would allow any such self-reflection (*PS*, 137).

The true movement of *In Search of Lost Time*, then, is a progression through the various orders of signs, which is also a movement through the different stages of dynamic genesis. And the journey of life – the idea in the book of a necessarily 'lost' time and the fact that 'intelligence' always arrives too late – means that we have to go through each one of these stages before moving onto the next. Each arises out of the failure of the one before, although the end also 'redeems' what preceded it. It is, above all, a question of genesis, of the work of art at once arising out of and allowing certain perceptions. As Deleuze writes: 'No one has insisted more than Proust on the following point: that the truth is produced, that it is produced by orders of machines which function within us, that it is extracted from our impressions' (*PS*, 129). The first order of signs is what Deleuze calls the 'worldly' signs (*PS*, 5). They are to begin with the signs of the social environment Marcel inhabits: the realm of social customs and etiquette, of knowing what to do or say in a particular situation. It is a snobbery that closes off or partitions milieus, that decides who does and who does not belong and what should be said in response to what: 'Nothing funny is said at the Verdurins, and Mme. Verdurin does not laugh; but Cottard makes a sign that he is saying something funny, and Mme. Verdurin makes a sign that she is laughing' (*PS*, 6). (In this regard, Proust is close to Bacon: art is first of all a break with opinion, opinion in the sense *What is Philosophy?* also alludes to, opinion as 'milieu'.) The next order of worldly signs are those of love. Again, it is a question of Marcel the narrator learning to read the signs of love, what they stand in for, what is really being said by them. Marcel in his jealousy over his lover Albertine tries to see the signs of her future infidelity and betrayal to come. He seeks to predict what will occur next, to make guesses on the basis of the other women he has previously known. As with the laws of society we have just discussed, there is an attempt by intelligence to grasp events, to make a prediction as to what follows what in the present. But this attempt inevitably fails: just as custom or fashion always changes, so Marcel can only ever see the signs of infidelity too late, in retrospect and not as they actually occur. The attempt to put together two instances of the same thing fails, reveals only a subjective or an objective association. The voluntary or conscious use of the faculties to draw out a general rule always falls short, needs to be explained by another, deeper order of signs.

The second distinct order of signs is what Deleuze calls the 'sensuous' (*PS*, 11) signs. These signs are the subject of the famous involuntary memory of *In Search of Lost Time*, and are opposed to the voluntary and conscious efforts of decoding and memory that organized the social signs and signs of love. Here the connection between the sign and what it stands in for is more abstract, impersonal, breaks with both subjective and objective associations. The well-known example of this in *In Search of Lost Time* is the relationship between the madeleine Marcel takes with his tea and the Combray of his youth: 'With the flavour of the madeleine, Combray has risen up in all its splendour; but we have by no means discovered the cause of such an apparition' (*PS*, 55–6). In other words, with involuntary memory there is neither the instinctive or habituated response of the social signs nor the attempt to find a common quality to what at first appears different of the signs of love. Rather, the sign and its referent meet across their difference from each other (*PS*, 54). And, again, almost as an attempt to think the failure of the first order of signs to hold two things together in the present, there is in this second order of signs a thinking of the past, but a past that never actually took place (the sign and the object it evokes through memory never co-existed, but inhabit radically different temporalities). The sign, therefore, increasingly breaks with both any objective origin and any subjective consciousness. Beyond any external resemblance, what is suggested is an 'essence' (*PS*, 60) that the two phenomena have in common, which is almost Platonic in its suspension of time and passing beyond of space (and this is, indeed, the way that Proust is often read). And yet, as Deleuze insists, this explanation still does not go to the end, does not get to the deepest truth of the sign. Although involuntary memory breaks with the object and subject, it does not explain how we are able to produce or replicate signs. It does not offer a true genesis or explanation of signs, of how they come about or what causes them.[5]

It is only with the last order of signs in *In Search of Lost Time* that we get to art proper and that the previous order of signs becomes subject to art. It is the final moment of the apprenticeship to signs that retrospectively justifies and makes sense of what comes before. The chief evocation of this in Proust's novel is the composer Vinteuil's sonata that the narrator listens to, in which violin and piano endlessly twine around each other, as though reproducing some 'original struggle' (*PS*, 47) between them. Of course, this can appear like that relationship across the difference between two incommensurable elements of involuntary memory, but this third order differs from this in that what is achieved is a final unity between the two parts. The effect does not remain a mere 'resonance' (*PS*, 133) between the two, but each part actually becomes the other in what Deleuze speaks of as the 'metamorphosis' brought about by the style of art: 'Style is essentially metaphor. But metaphor is essentially metamorphosis, and indicates how the two objects exchange their determinations, exchange even the names which designate them, in the new medium which confers the common quality upon them' (*PS*, 47). More precisely, it would be a matter not merely of unifying the two parts, but rather that out of their struggle a 'superior viewpont' arises, what Deleuze calls the 'absolute and ultimate Difference' (*PS*, 41), which would be not the difference between things or the difference between differences but something that is different from itself. Again, however, it is crucial to realize that this third moment does not simply exist outside the first or second, but is a thinking of their failure (*PS*, 132). If in one way this viewpoint can be understood as a kind of immaterial withdrawal beyond the perspective of any subject, in another way it can never be made entirely immaterial, is nothing outside what it sees.

In 1972, Deleuze added an extra chapter to *Proust and Signs*, 'Antilogos, or the Literary Machine'. It was written just after *The Logic of Sense* and just before *Anti-Oedipus*, and it affords an excellent opportunity to see the crossover between Deleuze's literary criticism and his philosophy. It is in 'Antilogos' that

Deleuze states for the first time the sequence of signs in terms that are recognizable to us from *What is Philosophy?* He begins by describing the social signs and signs of love as 'partial objects', by which he means to refer both to 'fragments without totality, vessels without communication and partitioned scenes' and to a general law that, while not 'uniting into a whole', 'covers distance, separations, partitionings' (*PS*, 133). It is an order (and, remember, it is close to the original chaos of the world) that Deleuze associates with 'death' (*PS*, 132), by which he means that it inhabits only the present or the realm of 'time wasted'. Deleuze then speaks of a second order of signs that bring about a 'resonance', which is an 'indescribable link of an alliance' (*PS*, 134) and the attempt to put partial objects together in a way that goes beyond the resemblance of a general law. Deleuze speaks of this second order in terms of a certain Eros, a 'joy so powerful that it suffices to make us indifferent to death' (*PS*, 55), and of a past in itself that makes possible the passing of the present (*PS*, 56–7). Finally, Deleuze speaks of a third order, which is that of the signs of art, in terms of a 'forced movement' in which the difference between the two moments of resonance is 'extended measurelessly' and they 'touch simultaneously' (*PS*, 141), and which he associates with Thanatos or the death drive. And it is only with this last order that we might say time is regained, regained in the sense that it is always yet to come (*PS*, 141). With the 'force' (*PS*, 161) and 'essence' (*PS*, 136) of this third order of signs, we have something like the 'intensity' and 'plane of composition' of the last stage of art in *What is Philosophy?*, which are what will lead us to philosophy. Indeed, Deleuze even ends the original edition of *Proust and Signs* with the chapter 'The Image of Thought', which addresses the connection between art and philosophy, the 'superior viewpoint' of art and something like the 'aleatory point' (*PS*, 152) of *What is Philosophy?*

In fact, art in *Proust and Signs* is said to begin only with the third stage of the sign, with the development of style, which puts two different objects together in a 'revealing medium' (*PS*, 47) that brings out what is common to them. This would be as opposed to the second stage of involuntary memory, in which the sensuous linking of two moments implies a 'relationship with something different' (*PS*, 58). And this, of course, would be different from what Deleuze and Guattari say in *What is Philosophy?*, in which art is said to begin with the 'frame' of the second stage, and it is different too from what they say in *A Thousand Plateaus*, in which art is understood to begin with something like the lyrebird and its marking off of territory. But the crucial thing is that the same order and relationship between the three levels of signs remains in *Proust and Signs*, and ultimately we would argue that all three correspond to what Deleuze and Guattari mean by art in *What is Philosophy?* And in *Proust and Signs* Deleuze makes the point that, if art in the form of style arrives only at the end after a long search, it is also art that has been there from the beginning, driving the narrative of Proust's book: 'All the stages must issue into art, we must reach the revelation of art: then we review the stages, we integrate them into the work of art itself, we recognise essence in its successive realizations, we give to each degree of realization the place and the meaning it occupies within the work' (*PS*, 64). But, again, if the first and second orders await the third as their completion, this third is possible only after it has passed through the first and second – this is precisely the genesis and creation at stake in Proust's novel. More specifically – and we must remember that Deleuze originally writes *Proust and Signs* just after his book on Kant – each subsequent order arises out of the failure of the one before. This is, of course, the theme of 'disappointment' (*PS*, 25) and the idea that intelligence always arrives too late; but in 'The Image of Thought' Deleuze explicitly relates it to the logic of Kant's sublime: 'The sensuous sign does us violence: it mobilizes the memory, it sets the soul in motion; but the soul in its turn excites thought, transmits to it the constraint of the sensibility, forces it to conceive essence, as the only thing that must be conceived' (*PS*, 166). It is the idea that thought always takes place under a kind of constraint, is not exercised voluntarily, but always in relation to something that goes beyond it. And it is also to say that, if Proust's novel is not only a work of art but also a certain thinking or reflection upon art – 'it is a work of art which produces upon itself its own effects' (*PS*, 136) – this is not at all a question of self-reflection or autobiography, but precisely produces a split within it, a split we might indeed call a viewpoint.

* * *

After collaborating with Guattari on *A Thousand Plateaus*, Deleuze wrote two volumes on cinema, *The Movement-Image* and

The Time-Image, which were decisively to influence film theory. They marked a break with the dominant modes of looking at and analyzing film at the time, cine-semiotics and psychoanalysis, both of which understood film as a kind of 'language' and the task of the analyst as the revealing of some hidden or repressed content or meaning. In a way, Deleuze in his books begins with a moment earlier than this, with what make this language possible. Rather than analyzing the meaning of the cinematic image, he looks at the image itself and how it is formed. What we see in cinema, as in all of Deleuze's studies of art, is a history of perception, a logic of sensation. And the crucial thing that cinema makes clear is that this perception takes place before or without the human. What we absolutely have in cinema – this is the very meaning of the camera – is another kind of perception. As Deleuze writes: 'Cinema goes beyond human perception towards another perception, in the sense that it reaches to the genetic element of all possible perception, that is, to the point which changes, which makes perception change, the differentiation of perception itself' (*MI*, 83). And to help Deleuze to think this, he turns to Henri Bergson, who – despite his resistance to actual cinema – outlines the essential conditions of this 'cinematic' thinking of perception. Bergson's essential insight is that cinema is not just a matter of movement subsequently being added to an originally still image or snapshot, but that from the beginning it is a matter of the image being in movement or even that the image comes about only because of movement: a movement-image. This is part of Bergson's larger point – adopted by Deleuze from the beginning of his work – that perception does not arise from somewhere outside the world (for example, human consciousness), but must be explained genetically as arising within the world. And in the same way the cinematographic image is not of the world, but forms the world:

> My eyes, my brain, are images, parts of my body. How could my brain contain images since it is one image among others. External images act on me, transmit movement to me, and I return movement: how could images be in my consciousness since I am myself image, that is, movement? (*MI*, 58)

Deleuze's *The Movement-Image* and *The Time-Image* can be seen to offer a certain history of cinema, moving from the early silent films of Griffith, Chaplin and Eisenstein through Hollywood and Italian Neo-Realism and on to the modern cinema of Godard, Herzog and Wenders. But, again, as in all Deleuze's studies of art – both across whole art forms, as with music in *A Thousand Plateaus*, or a single artist's oeuvre, as with Bacon in *Logic of Sensation* – Deleuze proposes not merely a history of art but an 'allegory' of the successive stages of perception.[6] Indeed, the history that Deleuze relates across the two volumes uncannily resembles that found in *What is Philosophy?* The first type of image Deleuze identifies in *The Movement-Image* is the 'perception-image' (*MI*, 64). It is the image that all of the other kinds of image in cinema start with. In it, we see as though for the first time, in a kind of fundamental seizing or apprehension of the world, a holding together for an instant of disparate perceptions. Deleuze speaks of it as though the result of a certain 'cooling down' (*MI*, 68) of the original chaos, which allows an initial framing of the world. (And, of course, the perception-image and the cinematic image in general allow us to travel a reverse genesis, from the 'solid' state of human perception back through a liquid state and on to an original 'gaseous' state (*MI*, 84).) The classic cinematic expression of this perception-image is the Soviet film-maker Dziga Vertov's *Man with a Movie Camera* (1927), in which we are immersed in an intricately dizzying, pulsating world that we have never seen before, in which there is no superior viewpoint outside the material, and in which things seems to disappear amongst the furious cutting almost as soon as they appear. Images are simply strung together without any narrative or unifying consciousness – or, if there is a consciousness, it is merely one 'image' among others. That is, the one perceiving (the cameraman in *Man with a Movie Camera*) is only what they perceive. Their consciousness is only the thing that they see: 'It is the vibration, the elementary solicitation of which movement is made up at each instant, the clinamen of Epicurean materialism' (*MI*, 83).

The next type of image Deleuze identifies is the close-up or 'affection-image' (*MI*, 65). The close-up with its object extracted from its surroundings and its creation of a 'partial object' can appear to be no higher a principle than the first perception-image, as though all it enacts is a similar framing. But Deleuze rejects this, placing the affection-image on a higher level than the perception-image and emphasizing that it has nothing to do with 'partial objects' (*MI*, 95). In fact, the affection-image might be understood as a further slowing down or, better, cooling down of the relationship between images, placing a greater distance between them. The face in a close-up, Deleuze explains, is made up of two inseparable halves: the face as reflected and the face as reflexive or reflecting. In the first, the face immediately responds to what it senses or feels. It is an 'intensive' form, something that 'passes from one quality to another, to emerge on to a new quality' (*MI*, 89). In the second, the face is not immediately responsive to what surrounds it, but introduces a certain gap or pause, as though it is thinking or reflecting. In this sense, it is a face that expresses a certain quality, a holding or composing of itself as a whole. As Deleuze writes: 'It is [on the one hand] a coincidence of subject and object and [on the other hand] the way in which the subject perceives itself, or rather experiences itself or feels itself "from the inside"' (*MI*, 65). In other words, with the reflective face it is as though the face is reacting not so much to some object but reacting to itself reacting to the object. If the first perception-image creates or draws out a difference between things, this second affection-image relates these differences to each other. And it is this increased 'abstraction' that allows Deleuze to speak of the affection-image – whose emblematic instances are the colour red and a close-up of a knife – in terms of a certain 'potential' or 'possibility' (*MI*, 98): not so much red as the potential of red, not so much fear as the possibility of fear. And all of this is also why Deleuze associates the close-up with a spiritual 'choice': it would be not so much an actual choice, putting us back in the determinations of the world, but a choice to choose, after which every actual choice always implies an otherwise (*MI*, 110).

The third kind of image Deleuze considers is the 'action-image' (*MI*, 65). In historical terms, it corresponds to what we might call Hollywood cinema, all the way from Griffith in the 1910s through to the Westerns and film noirs of the 1950s and early 1960s. It is the cinema of the social, of narrative continuity, of the relations between characters and between characters and their environment. And this relationship can be understood to proceed in either one of two ways. The first is what Deleuze calls the 'large figure' of the action-image, in which the situation acts upon the character, who responds, thus changing the situation. As Deleuze describes it: 'The whole incurves itself around the group, the character or the home, constituting an encompasser' (*MI*, 131). An example of this given by Deleuze is the gunfight of *Who Shot Liberty Valance?* (1962), in which great and distant forces converge on a single concentrated incident. The second way is what Deleuze calls the 'small action', in which, on the contrary, it is the action of the character that changes the situation, which in turn changes the character. Here it is not great and far-flung forces that converge upon an act, but a 'slight difference in the action, or between two actions, that leads to a very great distance between two situations' (*MI*, 162). An example of this is Chaplin's *The Great Dictator* (1940), in which the 'same' gesture made by the humble Jewish barber becomes terrible and monstrous when repeated by the dictator Adenoid Hinckel (*MI*, 171–2). And the action-image itself – and this should remind us of what Deleuze says in his book on Bacon, written some two years before – is the attempted synthesis of this 'contraction and expansion' (*MI*, 151). That is, if we can make a distinction between the large- and small-forms of the action-image, with particular directors largely associated with either one or the other, the two also cannot be separated, and each director must be seen to be working in both. Ultimately, the action-image gathers up all elements, both large and small, putting things that are most different together and keeping apart things that appear closest. As Deleuze writes: 'It is not the line which unites into a whole, but the one which connects or links up the heterogeneous elements, while keeping them heterogeneous' (*MI*, 194).

However, as Deleuze points out towards the end of *The Movement-Image*, the action-image breaks down and opens up a crisis in European cinema at some time around WWII (and the question remains whether this happens for socio-historical reasons, for example, the destruction caused by the War, or for internal reasons, the passing of a certain threshold in the genesis of perception (*MI*, 211–12)). We see this crisis manifested in such different forms as Hitchcock's reflection on the classic crime or thriller formulae and the Neo-Realist films made immediately following the War by Roberto Rossellini and Vittorio De Sica. In Hitchcock's films, actions are increasingly replaced by mental relations, the complex series of alliances formed around the original crime. In the films of Italian Neo-Realism, spatial co-ordinates are often missing or unclear – the films were frequently shot amongst the rubble of recently liberated cities – and their characters operate without any sense of an underlying social order. As Deleuze writes, drawing a contrast with the synthesis or territoriality brought about by the action-image: 'The image [in the crisis of the action-image] no longer refers to a situation which is globalising or synthetic, but rather to one which is dispersive ... The line or the fibre of the universe which prolonged events into one another, or brought about the connection of positions of space, has broken' (*MI*, 207). This 'crisis' leads to films in which the connection between narrative events is weak, and the film appears to have lost confidence in its own ability to tell a story. And this should remind us of that 'withdrawal' by which Deleuze and Guattari characterize that third moment of genesis in art, and perhaps even more generally of that 'hollowing out' (*WP?*, 195) they say characterizes contemporary art.

Finally, however, there is not just the crisis of the old form, but the coming about of a new form, which Deleuze calls the time-image. This is the distinctly 'modern' cinema of such directors as Godard, Resnais and Tarkovsky. It is characterized by the confusion between the actual and the virtual (in principle, there is no way of deciding in these films the status of what we see: reality or dream, action in the present or flashback) and the liberation of sounds and images from any really existing source (these films are often characterized by non-relational soundtracks and images that appear to have no easily identifiable source). And in these films there is suggested a different form of time: no longer a linear time in which the present comes out of the past and leads into the future, but a time in which the present and past co-exist, which is what Deleuze calls Aion or the transcendental condition of time (*TI*, 81–2). Deleuze frequently describes this cinema as a cinema of 'thought' or the 'brain', and it is understood as the continuation – and completion – of the Hitchcockian cinema of mental relations. Indeed, we might even say that this cinema of the time-image *is* philosophy, which is not at all to say that it is a kind of 'philosophical' thinking or deals with 'philosophical' issues. Rather, we would say that it occupies the place of philosophy insofar as it stands in for the next stage in the genesis of perception after 'art'. Deleuze in *The Time-Image* is speaking of that genesis that leads from the image to thought and the percept to the concept, and the time-image has all of those qualities that will come to be associated with philosophy. It arises out of the failure of 'recognition' (*TI*, 4), it is the thinking of the pure form of time (*TI*, 81–2), it begins with a metaphysical surface or plane of immanence (*TI*, 68–9), it involves the inseparability of the actual and the virtual (*TI*, 273), and it is even a form of pedagogy (*TI*, 248).

* * *

What finally is to be seen in these four examples of the study of art that we have looked at in Deleuze's and Deleuze and Guattari's oeuvres? We notice that in each of them there is a similarity, if not a strict identity, to the treatment of art in *What is Philosophy?* (And *What is Philosophy?*, for its part, offers summaries of many of these previous studies.) We start with 'chaos', with those immediate fleeting appearances in which nothing is able to be thought or presented, insofar as it is subject to the 'infinite speed with which any form taking shape in it vanishes' (*WP?*, 158). Then there is 'vibration', which because it is 'durable, because it rises and falls' (*WP?*, 168), forms a first bloc of sensation in which the sensible is recorded and preserved in the present. There is then the 'embrace' or 'clinch', in which two of these blocs of sensation 'resonate in each other' (*WP?*, 168), so that there is produced a certain recollection or remembrance, as duration is stretched out in the past. Finally, there is a 'withdrawal', in which these two blocs of sensation 'draw apart, release themselves, but so as to be brought back together' (*WP?*, 160), thus opening up a kind of future. In *A Thousand Plateaus*, we move from 'chaos' (*TP*, 311), through the 'vibration' of Classicism, which 'differenciates the unity of the beginning' (*TP*, 338), the 'counterpoint' of the Baroque and the 'embrace' of Romanticism, in which there is a 'consolidation of co-existence and succession' (*TP*, 330), and on to the 'unclasping' of modern music, which 'molecularizes' sound matter so that it becomes capable of 'harnessing nonsonorous forces such as Duration and Intensity' (*TP*, 343). In *Francis Bacon*, there is an initial 'given' or 'cliché' (*FB*, 71), a 'vibration', which produces a 'pure presence' (*FB*, 45) of the body, then a 'resonance', in which two sensations are coupled together in counterpoint like 'wrestlers' (*FB*, 57), and finally a 'forced movement', in which rhythms take on an 'extraordinary amplitude' and produce in us a sense of the 'powers of the future' (*FB*, 51). In *Proust and Signs*, we begin with 'time wasted', in which events simply pass us by without being recorded. Then there are the 'repetitions' of love, which 'transmute the particular into the general' (*PS*, 72). There is then the 'resonance' of involuntary memory, in which the 'past co-exists with the present' (*PS*, 87). Finally, there is a 'forced movement of greater amplitude', in which 'time is regained' (*PS*, 24). In *The Movement-Image* and *The Time-Image*, we begin with a 'plane of immanence' – not to be confused with the 'plane of immanence' of *What is Philosophy?* – which is the 'infinite set of all images' (*MI*, 58). Then there is the perception-image, in which there is a 'correlation of two images that are different' (*MI*, 82). The following affection-image would be a 'genetic or differential sign' (*MI*, 110) that would unite a 'time of after and a time of before' (*MI*, 122). Finally, there is the action-image and its crisis, in which 'perception is cut off from its motor extension, action from the thread which joined it to a situation and affection from adherence or belonging to characters' (*MI*, 215), in a simultaneous completion and passing beyond of the movement-image, as it transforms into the time-image and its new 'experience of thought' (*TI*, 215).

But beyond these similarities across Deleuze's and Deleuze and Guattari's various treatments of art, we find the same three-part division of the first moment of genesis throughout a whole series of books that appear to have nothing to do with art. In *Difference and Repetition*, we have the 'excitations' (*DR*, 96) of discontinuous matter, which are subject to a process of 'contraction', in which two distinct moments are held together by a 'contemplative soul' to constitute 'time as a present' (*DR*, 79). This is followed by a 'resonance', which is not simply the holding together of two passing moments but involves 'another time in which the first synthesis can occur' (*DR*, 79). Finally, we have a 'forced movement' (*DR*, 117), in which the present is no longer able to be represented but is different from itself, thus opening up a certain 'whole of time' (*DR*, 110). In the immediately succeeding *The Logic of Sense*, we begin with the depths in which bodies and things are indiscriminately mixed with no clear limits between them. There is then a present that 'measures out the action of bodies and causes' in a kind of 'mixture or blending' (*LS*, 186). This is followed by a past and future that 'divide the present of every instant and subdivide it ad infinitum into past and future' (*LS*, 188). Finally, between the two presents of 'Chronos' or linear time, there is a 'thread pertaining to Aion, a kind of eternity or endless futurity' (*LS*, 191). In Deleuze and Guattari's *Anti-Oedipus*, we begin with pulverized and unidentifiable objects and flows (*AO*, 324). Then in a first 'connective synthesis of production', there is a 'connection of these particular objects and flows' (*AO*, 69). This is followed by a 'disjunctive synthesis of recording' that 'affirms the disjointed terms' (*AO*, 76), thus introducing a form of lack or absence. Finally, in a third 'conjunctive synthesis of consumption-consummation', in a 'crossing of a threshold' there is produced a 'pure intensity' in an abandoning of all 'form and quality' (*AO*, 84).

The question is what is revealed by this series of parallels, which go beyond *What is Philosophy?* and those other treatments of art to such apparently unrelated subjects as the difference that makes possible identity (*Difference and Repetition*), the emergence language from the depths of bodies (*The Logic of Sense*) and the origins of desiring-production (*Anti-Oedipus*)? It is the fact that all of these stand in for the moment of *dynamic genesis* in the overall production of representation. This is ultimately Deleuze's and Deleuze and Guattari's real subject: to reveal how experience is formed outside pre-existing categories, and instead how these categories arise out of experience. That is to say, their project is fundamentally *post-Kantian*. In the Transcendental Deduction of the *Critique of Pure Reason*, Kant attempted to demonstrate how we pass from a manifold of disorganized appearance through to the unified form of an object that is able to be thought by means of a series of cognitive syntheses. It is these syntheses that take what is originally given to intuition and, through the application of a series of conceptual categories, transform it into a series of representations that are the basis for true knowledge about the world. (In the overall architecture of the *Critique*, it is a conceptual determination that is added to spatio-temporal intuitions in the syntheses, while in the reciprocal operation of schematism it is spatio-temporal reality that is given to abstract conceptual determinations.) Each of these three stages of synthesis involves a different faculty and operates through a different means. The first synthesis is that of apprehension in intuition, which involves the synopsis of the manifold a priori through sense. Here an original diversity both of time and space and of what appears in time and space is gathered together and represented as a single moment. This is followed by a second synthesis of reproduction in imagination, which involves the synthesis of the manifold, but this time through imagination. This responds to the necessity that, insofar as that first apprehension would pass away when the second arrives, this second must also bring back the first, in order that we might have a 'complete representation'[7] of experience. Finally, there is a third synthesis of recognition in the concept, which involves the unification of the two prior syntheses through apperception. This comes out of the idea that the second synthesis and its reproduction of the first would not be sufficient unless we could recognize them as the same or as belonging to the same subject. This is done by positing a certain object = x, which is a general object-form that allows a subject to recognize various of its representations as the same. It is this third synthesis that precisely unifies those previous two syntheses according to categories that are the rules for the determination of objects-in-general that are subject to cognition. And what is produced by way of these three syntheses – and it is important to realize that this third synthesis is no longer passive and unconscious unlike those first two – is both the linear and transcendental forms of *time* themselves, in which the sensations given to intuition are unified and the self is able to affect the self, that is, think or become self-conscious. At the end of Kantian Transcendental Deduction, we have the form of the object in general under which representations are unified and a subject able to attribute these representations to itself. And all of this takes place in Kant through the regular unwinding of faculties under the final supervisory faculty of apperception, which underwrites the succession of syntheses from the beginning, and guarantees the successful coming together of the conceptual form of the object and the subject able to think it.

Deleuze and Deleuze and Guattari, as we can see, essentially replay this Kantian sequence in their outlining of dynamic genesis. It is perhaps in the chapter 'Repetition in Itself' of *Difference and Repetition*, as several commentators have recognized, that Deleuze most clearly sets out his conception of dynamic or passive genesis, at once repeating but also importantly differing from the Kantian prototype.[8] In terms that are already familiar to us from the various accounts of art we have looked at, we begin with chaos, in which 'one instance does not appear unless the other has disappeared' (*DR*, 70). This is like the Kantian manifold, with which the process of synthesis begins. Then there is the first moment of the synthesis of Imagination, in which, 'like a sensitive plate, it retains one case [or moment] when the other appears' (*DR*, 70). This corresponds to the Kantian faculty of sense, which gathers together an original diversity to produce an immediate apprehension, thus producing, at least according to the reading of Martin Heidegger in his *Kant and the Problem of Metaphysics*, a present.[9] The second moment of passive genesis is Memory, in which a 'former present finds itself represented in the present one' (*DR*, 80). This corresponds to the Kantian faculty of Imagination, which at the same time as it senses new experience also reproduces old experience, so that it does not simply pass away but persists, thus producing a past. Finally, the third moment of passive synthesis is Thought, in which a 'passive self experiences its own thought – its own intelligence, that by virtue of which it can say I – being exercised in it' (*DR*, 86). This corresponds to the Kantian faculty of apperception, which responds to the fact that the reproduction of the past by Imagination would be insufficient unless there were some way of recognizing that these previous moments were the same, just as other moments to come also could be, thus opening up a future. And throughout Deleuze's and Deleuze and Guattari's writings on art – even with regard to not obviously temporal media – it is always this question of time that is at stake, and not merely time in its empirical dimension (the distinct temporalities of past, present and future), but time as such or transcendental time (the Heideggerean 'time before time' or the 'simultaneity' of past, present and future that allows their temporal separation). As Deleuze and Guattari write of Proust in *What is Philosophy?*: 'The plane of composition emerges gradually from compounds of sensation that [Proust] draws up in the course of lost time, until appearing in itself with time regained, the force, or rather the forces, of pure time that have now become perceptible' (*WP?*, 189).

However, if Deleuze and Guattari repeat aspects of Kant's analysis in aligning art with dynamic genesis, they nevertheless differ from Kant in significant ways. First of all, if like Kant there is a sequence of distinct faculties or operations that takes us from a discontinuous diversity that cannot be preserved through to composed blocs of sensation on an aesthetic plane of composition, unlike Kant no faculty exists outside any other and there is no transcendental faculty guaranteeing the success of these syntheses from the beginning.[10] As Deleuze makes clear in *Difference and Repetition*, the third faculty of Thought is to be seen only through the other two, indeed, the *failure* of the other two, and it does not entirely succeed itself in unifying them as in Kant (*DR*, 88–91).[11] With the 'withdrawal' (*WP?*, 168) at the end of art there is no final unity or recognition, but only, as Deleuze and Guattari put it in *What is Philosophy?*, a 'higher deterritorialization' (*WP?*, 197). At the conclusion of the 'history' of art, there is only what Deleuze and Guattari call the 'coloured void' (*WP?*, 181) with its 'force' (*WP?*, 181) and 'making of the illegible form of time legible' (*WP?*, 182). Indeed, as much as anything, the third stage of dynamic synthesis and the conclusion of the 'history' of art are marked by a doing away with what was previously put together, with an 'abstraction' and perhaps even 'sublimation' that is characterized by a 'scattering' (*WP?*, 196), 'deframing' (*WP?*, 187) and 'opening up onto an infinite cosmos' (*WP?*, 197). It is this 'dissipation' of elements that philosophy inherits and begins with. (In fact, it is this trajectory that can be seen to lie behind Deleuze and Guattari's distinction between an 'earlier' form of art, associated with figuration and perspective, in which 'sensation is realised in the material' (*WP?*, 193), as in those syntheses we looked at, and a 'later' form of art, associated with abstraction and the overcoming of perspective, in which the 'material passes into sensation', as it 'ascends into an aesthetic plane of composition' (*WP?*, 193), which can appear almost dematerialized in its 'almost virtuality' (*WP?*, 183) and coming close to the 'maximum of the concept' (*WP?*, 181) of philosophy.) Equally, if there is no determinate object-form at the end of dynamic genesis in Deleuze and Guattari, there is also no subject. In Kant, the entire progress of synthesis takes place under the apperception of the active subject of the third synthesis, but in Deleuze and Guattari there is no such retrospective underwriting by a conscious subject, only what they call an 'aesthetic figure', which they describe as the 'conditions under which the arts produce affects' (*WP?*, 66), and which does not stand outside the processes of genesis but arises only through them, perhaps even disappearing at the end of genesis along with the object when the 'planes' or 'frames' (*WP?*, 187) of sensation can no longer be held together. It is again for all these reasons that dynamic genesis in Deleuze and Guattari does not cover the whole span from original manifold through to the general form of the object and the subject able to think its representations of it as its own, but is merely the first stage in a much longer process.

In all of this, Deleuze and Guattari undoubtedly follow phenomenologist Edmund Husserl (and to a lesser degree Heidegger) in their rethinking of the Transcendental Deduction from *The Critique of Pure Reason*. Although Deleuze and Guattari are consistently critical of phenomenology in *What is Philosophy?*, in fact their refashioning of Kant in their conception of art follows from a famous insight of Husserl in his *Ideas I* (1913). In *Ideas I*, Husserl demonstrated that in the first edition of the *Critique* (1781) even though the active and conscious faculty of apperception forms the transcendental ground of subjectivity it nevertheless relies on the passive and unconscious syntheses carried out by sense and imagination. However, as Husserl points out, by the time of the second edition of the *Critique* (1787), apperception is manifestly present from the beginning, with those other faculties being denied the ability to synthesize at all outside apperception. As Husserl writes in *Ideas I* of this second Kant turning away from the insights of the first:

> It becomes evident to us that Kant's mental regard was resting on [phenomenology], although he was still unable to appropriate it or recognize it as a field of work, a strict eidetic science proper. Thus for example, the transcendental deduction in the first edition of the *Critique of Pure Reason* was actually operating inside the realm of phenomenology, but Kant misinterpreted that realm as psychological and therefore he himself abandoned it.[12]

And we can see Husserl's own subsequent phenomenological method coming out of this early insight. In his first, 'static' phenomenology, there is an attempt through phenomenological 'reduction' to see objects in themselves, suspending what he called our 'natural attitude', by which he meant our assumptions, expectations and everyday behaviours regarding them. After cutting the object free in this way, we would hopefully find the true and regular principles underlying the order of things. What is ultimately sought to be discovered is how things appear to a consciousness that is the origin and source of the world. But in Husserl's second, 'genetic' phenomenology, coming out of his critique of Kant, he does not attempt to see things 'in themselves', which is to say how they appear to a preconstituted consciousness, but rather how this appearance itself appears or is constituted. That is to say, appearance is no longer described but *analyzed*. It is understood no longer as some atomistic stopping point that can be got at by cutting it off from what surrounds it in any logical or phenomenological reduction, but as *produced* in time and in relation to a body that is no longer a source but itself only to be grasped as part of a wider field or network. As Husserl writes in his later *Formal and Transcendental Logic* (1929):

> In that case, (inquiry into) the 'static' constitution of objects, which relates to an already 'developed' subjectivity, has its counterpart in (an inquiry into) apriori genetic constitution (a subsequent inquiry), based on (the results of) the former, which necessarily precedes it.[13]

Deleuze and Guattari at several points in *What is Philosophy?* praise Husserl and compare his project of thinking experience before or outside the transcendental categories to the insights offered by art: 'Phenomenology must become the phenomenology of art because the immanence of the lived to a transcendental subject must be expressed in transcendental functions that not only determine experience in general but traverse the here and now' (*WP?*, 178). And yet, as this passage also indicates, if Deleuze and Guattari praise Husserl for effectively aligning phenomenology to the genetic conception of experience that at once is at stake in the production of art and the encounter with art allows us to grasp, they are also critical of Husserl – as in a similar way they are critical of Kant – for not following through on his own insight. For just as Kant privileged distinct faculties despite his commitment to a 'critical', that is, an immanent account of experience, so Husserl maintained the category of the subject, despite his commitment to a genetic phenomenology in which nothing would pre-exist experience but arise only in relation to it.[14] As Deleuze and Guattari write, arguing that Husserl's assumption of a pre-existing subject to which experience is immanent falls short of that properly genetic requirement his work otherwise suggests: 'By making immanence an immanence to a subject, phenomenology could not prevent the subject from forming no more than opinions that already extracted clichés from new perceptions and promised affections' (*WP?*, 150). Against this, Deleuze and Guattari in their outlining of this first moment of genesis through art seek to complete the revolution that Kant and Husserl began: there is not only no pre-existing subject to which the experience of art is immanent, but at the end of dynamic genesis the subject has still not been found and has even perhaps been done away with. Instead, as *What is Philosophy?* suggests, we have at the conclusion of art the discovery of a certain abstract 'plane of composition', which is that out of which artistic materials and techniques are drawn (although it does not exist outside them), and a certain 'withdrawal [of the subject and sensations] that is the correlate of a survey' (WP?, 211), both of which are precursors to the next stage of genesis of philosophy with its virtual 'plane of immanence' (WP?, 35), from which the components of philosophical concepts are drawn, and 'conceptual persona' (WP?, 62), with its 'infinite movement' (WP?, 59) that puts these components together to form concepts. Paradoxically, we might suggest that it is this 'sublimation' or at least 'aestheticization' of experience as it ascends into the 'plane of composition' and 'withdrawal' of the subject as seen in art that is the genetic precondition of the 'self-positing' (WP?, 11) and 'self-referentiality' (WP?, 22) of philosophy.

CHAPTER FOUR

Philosophy

Philosophy comes after art in the genesis of representation, despite the order in which *What is Philosophy?* is written. Art, as we have seen, lies in the realm of dynamic genesis, which takes us from an original 'chaos' and moves us through three successive syntheses to end up at a final 'plane of composition'. At the end of the third synthesis, we have free and liberated elements that are related only by the difference between them, the production of a 'force' or 'intensity' and a form of time that is open to the 'future', with the whole overseen by a withdrawn 'aesthetic figure' that at once puts these elements together and opens them onto the universe. And, as we have seen, these same qualities are to be found in all of Deleuze's and Deleuze and Guattari's accounts of this last stage of art. In *A Thousand Plateaus*, what holds all of the various aesthetic components together are 'transversals' (*TP*, 296). In *Logic of Sensation*, in a forced movement, the limits of sensation are broken and 'rhythm itself' (*LS*, 61) becomes sensation. In *Proust and Signs*, there is a greater amplitude that pushes the past still further back and constitutes in time an 'horizon' (*PS*, 141). And in *The Time-Image*, the character becomes a kind of 'viewer', who 'shifts, runs and becomes animated' in vain, insofar as the 'situation he is in outstrips his capacities' (*TI*, 3). In many ways, that is, this plane of composition of art can be seen as the necessary precondition for the plane of immanence of philosophy, in which the various components that make up the philosophical concept are held, waiting to be combined. The disjunctive compounds out of which art is made, which are related by difference, can be seen to be like the components out of which philosophical concepts are constructed, which are 'distinct', 'heterogeneous' and yet 'inseparable' (*WP?*, 19). The 'force' and openness to the 'future' of art can be seen to be like the 'intensity' of philosophy and the 'event' (*WP?*, 23) it helps to bring about. And the 'withdrawn' aesthetic figure and its 'deframing' (*WP?*, 187) can be seen to be like the 'conceptual persona' and its 'survey' (*WP?*, 20) and the 'deterritorialization' (*WP?*, 67) of philosophy. Art and philosophy can be understood to be sequential steps on the same phenomenological itinerary that eventually leads to fully individuated objects and self-conscious subjects. Philosophy in this regard would be something of a mid-way point between the dynamic genesis of art and the static genesis of science and logic, a moment of virtuality or incorporeality between two actualities or materialities.

This is not recognized in most accounts of Deleuze and Guattari's concept of philosophy as it is expressed in *What is Philosophy?* As we have noted before, the most common reading of the book is that art, philosophy and science are three essentially unrelated forms of thinking, each casting its own independent 'plane over chaos' and drawing up something different from it. Or, it is as though philosophy engages in the discussion of art – this is particularly prevalent in readings of Deleuze's cinema books – as though it is some distinct and preconstituted area of inquiry that can choose to do this, as though it might reflect on itself through some other object. And, indeed, there is some textual evidence for this attitude in *What is Philosophy?* There are moments where Deleuze and Guattari appear to speak of art, philosophy and science as unrelated, having nothing to do with one another: 'We call Chaoids [art, science and philosophy] the realities produced on the plane that cut through the chaos in different ways' (*WP?*, 208). Or there are moments when they appear to speak of any relationship between them as essentially contingent and occurring in no particular order: 'A first type of interference [on the plane] appears when a philosopher attempts to create the component of a sensation or a function or when a scientist tries to create functions of sensations and even functions of concepts' (*WP?*, 216–17). But there are other moments in the book when Deleuze and Guattari do appear to countenance connections between the three fields that are not extrinsic and accidental but intrinsic and necessary. And they occur not in any order, which suggests a contingent intersection, but always in the same order, which points towards a genetic succession: 'The first two aspects or layers of the brain-subject, sensation as much as the concept, are very fragile ... and science constitutes an activity of knowing and refers to a faculty of knowledge as the third layer of a brain-subject' (*WP?*, 213–14).

Art and philosophy in *What is Philosophy?* are not unrelated or momentarily confused but distinct and successive. There are, however, good reasons why this should not immediately appear to be so and why the book is not often read in this way. Although not explicitly spoken of in *What is Philosophy?*, the third passive synthesis ends with a certain *failure* of synthesis. It does not provide that recognition guided by apperception that leads to a concept of the object unified in consciousness as in Kant. It does not come up with an 'associative synthesis' that combines like with like and distinguishes the unalike as in Husserl. Rather, in the failure of the synthesis of recognition, objects disperse and the perceiving self dissolves. It is for this reason that for Deleuze and Guattari there is the subsequent stage of philosophy: because at the end of art the genesis of representation is not yet complete. It is for this reason, too, that Deleuze writes that philosophy begins with an encounter with the 'sentiendum' or what can only be sensed (*DR*, 140). Or, as he puts it in a much-cited passage, reminding us of that paradoxical distension or disjunctive synthesis of the third stage of genesis: 'The problem does not at all express an objective uncertainty, but, on the contrary, it expresses the objective equivalent of a mind situated in front of an horizon of what happens or appears: is it Richard or William?' (*LS*, 67).[1] Philosophy does not solve this dilemma – this will have to wait until a later stage of the genesis, one associated with science and logic – but outlines its conditions and why it is necessary. This would be along the lines of Deleuze's argument, ultimately derived from Bergson, that philosophy does not so much answer problems as state them (*B*, 15). And this is to say that philosophy does not choose between Richard and William but thinks why we cannot choose between them, and how we might continue to think without resolving their identity. In a way, philosophy constructs its concepts in order to maximize both their application and their singularity; or, as Deleuze puts it, it seeks as far as possible to determine its concepts without restricting in advance their particular qualities or to what objects or individuals they would apply. Art for Deleuze and Guattari – and this perhaps corresponds to our conventional sense of modern art – is radically non-selective, open to new experiences, is always bringing about new 'varieties' (*WP?*, 175), unconstrained by morality, technique or the desire to communicate. Art, in Deleuze and Guattari's sense, is an advanced or experimental realm par excellence. And philosophy inherits this openness and also has to account for experience not bound by any recognizable form or reproduction of what has already been perceived or felt.

However, if philosophy attempts to deal with the problem of recognition left unanswered by the third stage of genesis, this must entail another form of organization from it. And in *What is Philosophy?*, Deleuze and Guattari set out a long series of differences between art and philosophy. While acknowledging the potential crossover between the two activities and the fact that one can pass into the other, they insist that they must be distinguished so that their different ways of thinking are acknowledged. The plane of composition of art, in which all artistic materials and techniques are to be found, is not the plane of immanence of philosophy, out of which philosophical components are cut, no matter that there are occasions in Deleuze's work in which they are understood to touch, and even that on other occasions the plane of immanence is associated with chaos itself. The work of art, while always 'becoming other' (*WP?*, 173) and testifying to a kind of dematerialization, never quite attains the 'embodied event' (*WP?*, 176) of philosophy that is never able to be realized. The aesthetic figure of art that can become the subject of philosophy while also explaining how philosophy affects us is not the conceptual persona of philosophy, which is never to be identified with any real author or fictional character, and moves beyond any affect (*WP?*, 65–6). To summarize, no matter how much art breaks with its original referent so that it 'stands up on its own' (*WP?*, 164), no matter how abstract it becomes with its monochromes and walls of unchanging sound, it still remains material and embodied, a matter of sensation and therefore still tied to our bodies and this world. By contrast, philosophy begins with an absolutely virtual, immaterial state, which breaks with all context and determination, whether bodily, social or historical. As opposed to the relative freedom and indetermination of art in laying itself out, which is still bound to a final plane of composition through certain rules, styles and techniques, philosophy is *absolutely* free in putting together its concepts in an aleatory or game-like way that is ultimately less bound by constraints and conventions than even the most avant-garde work of art. It is for this reason – and, again, this explains why the proper relationship between art and philosophy is often not recognized – that if in one way philosophy comes out of a genesis in which it is preceded by another, in another way it appears outside any genesis and owes nothing to any preceding principle. Indeed, more than this, one of the defining qualities of philosophy for Deleuze and Guattari is that it gives itself its own origin or genesis. More than simply having no origin or owing nothing to anything else, it actually seeks to explain itself or bring itself about through a process of what Deleuze calls 'double genesis' or 'quasi-causality' (*LS*, 123). This is exactly Deleuze's difference from Heidegger in an early 1956 lecture series 'What is Grounding?' Already, there, influenced by the post-Kantians Salomon Maïmon and J. G. Fichte, as opposed to the Heideggerian problematic, in which we search for an ultimate origin of philosophy – some pre-ontological Being or essence – Deleuze seeks to think the ambiguity of the notion of grounding in philosophy, which necessarily refers both to some putative natural origin and to the resulting philosophical system: 'Must grounding be thought as a principle of things in themselves or as a simple knowledge of things for us?'.[2] It is an ambiguity addressed some twelve years later in *Difference and Repetition*, where Deleuze refers to a certain split in the gesture of philosophical grounding, which at once points towards an 'unrepresented origin' and is only thinkable within the philosophical system it founds: 'In short, sufficient reason or the ground is strangely bent: on the one hand, it leans towards what it grounds, towards the forms of representation; on the other hand, it turns and plunges into a groundlessness beyond the ground which resists all forms and cannot be represented' (*DR*, 274–5). And it is this ambiguity that Deleuze and Guattari attempt to capture in *What is Philosophy?* by referring to philosophy as at the same time 'created' (*WP?*, 5) and 'auto-poetic' (*WP?*, 11), signed by another (*WP?*, 5) and 'independent' (*WP?*, 11). Indeed, for all of the emphasis of the book on philosophy as the 'creation' (*WP?*, 5) of concepts, what is often overlooked is that this is, at least in part, a matter of the *self-creation* of concepts, the fact that they are brought about not only by the philosopher who signs them but by the philosophical system itself.

Hence the absolute ambiguity of philosophy for Deleuze and Guattari. On the one hand – and here is where they are like Heidegger – philosophy is the search for origins, the attempt to go back to the beginning of thought. Each of the major philosophical systems Deleuze and Guattari analyze in *What is Philosophy?* – Plato, Descartes, Kant, Husserl – seeks to break with things, attempts to reveal the genetic principles behind any appearance or representation. In Plato, there is a split from the appearance of things, by reason of a truth that is 'posed as presupposition, as already there' (*WP?*, 29). In Descartes, philosophy disconnects from 'every explicit objective presupposition' (*WP?*, 26), perhaps of the kind Plato relied upon, in a direct subjective stating of the truth outside any objective guarantee or protection. And in Kant there is a going beyond of Descartes, in asking what allows this subjective stating of the truth, this Cogito that 'necessarily repeats its own thinking activity to itself as an Other' (*WP?*, 32). Each successive philosophical system here goes further and further back, attempting to reveal the unspoken assumptions taken for granted by the system before. With each we get closer to some presumed 'beginning' of thought, before which there is nothing and which relies on nothing else. And this for Deleuze and Guattari is the history of philosophy as a thinking of 'immanence' (*WP?*, 44), the attempt to produce a 'thought without image' (*WP?*, 54–5). It would be the effort to do away with all transcendentals, all philosophical categories that are understood to be original or to arise outside of genesis. Indeed, Deleuze and Guattari themselves seek to belong to this history in their surpassing in turn of Kant, in whom they see a certain unquestioned subjectivity, an immanence that is still *immanent to* something: 'Kant objects to any transcendent use of the synthesis, but he ascribes immanence to the subject of the synthesis of the system as new, subjective unity' (*WP?*, 46). And yet the paradox is that this attempt to show how no thought is original, outside genesis, is itself undertaken by a thought that claims to be outside genesis. In fact, in an especially contradictory way – a contradiction that we attempt to elaborate there – we might say that not only does the thought that seeks to think the genesis of representation attempt to escape this genesis, but that it is *only* a thought that is outside genesis, that is, philosophy, that is able to think this genesis of representation.

* * *

What Deleuze and Guattari call the 'plane of immanence' is the 'image of thought' (*WP?*, 37) that philosophy gives itself. Each individual system of philosophy constitutes a different plane of immanence, but each system nevertheless has its own plane of immanence. Deleuze and Guattari describe the plane of immanence as the series of free-floating or undetermined components that each system of philosophy selects from in order to make up its concepts. It might be understood as something like the pre-existing stock or repertoire of philosophical possibilities or philosophemes that are put together in various ways in order to produce the particular philosophical systems we have seen over history. As Deleuze and Guattari write, in necessarily abstract language (for, remember, if for them this plane of immanence constitutes the image of thought, what they see lying at the origin of philosophy and what they themselves are trying to produce is a certain 'thought without image'):

> It is the plane's variable *curves* that retain the infinite movements that turn back on themselves in incessant exchange, but which also continually free other movements which are retained. The concepts can then mark out the intensive ordinates of these infinite movements, as movements which are themselves finite and which form, at infinite speed, variable *contours* inscribed on the plane. (*WP?*, 42)

To this extent, the plane of immanence might be understood to be something like the plane of composition in art, in which all artistic techniques and possibilities are displayed in their most free and independent state as that from which artists choose. And yet, as we have seen, there is a vast leap from the liberated artistic methods of the plane of composition, which are still material, embodied and sensual, to the undetermined components of the plane of immanence of philosophy, which are virtual, incorporeal and conceptual. The plane of immanence is, in fact, exactly how philosophy breaks with the plane of composition of art, so that it apparently comes out of no genesis and owes nothing to anything prior to it, not even to the plane of immanence itself.

The plane of immanence can, indeed, appear, as Deleuze and Guattari describe it at various points in *What is Philosophy?*, as a pre-existing 'reserve' or 'reservoir' (*WP?*, 36) that precedes philosophy, and from which philosophers draw in order to create their concepts. It is something like a common pool or store that is shared across philosophies, which is what would allow us to write a history of philosophy as the tracing of how various components move through particular philosophical systems and how the meaning of these components changes according to how they are combined with others from different philosophical systems. It is in this sense that Deleuze and Guattari are able to speak of the plane of immanence as 'interleaved' (*WP?*, 50), made up of different cuts or sections through an underlying substance that is perhaps itself nothing but these leaves. It is with this in mind that we might speak of the plane of immanence as a kind of underlying ground that allows different philosophies to speak to each other, contest each other and ultimately replace each other in the ongoing history of philosophy. And, more than this, the plane of immanence even precedes and allows any particular philosophical ground, for any such 'ground' is only itself another philosophical component, something drawn by a philosophical system from the range of possibilities made available by the plane of immanence. It is, indeed, for this reason that Deleuze and Guattari can propose that the ground or beginning always occurs twice in any philosophical system: both as a component within the concept and as what underlies and makes possible the concept. As they write: 'Even the first concept, the one with which philosophy begins, has several components, because is it not obvious that philosophy must have a beginning, and if it does determine one, it must combine it with a point of view or ground [*une raison*]' (*WP?*, 15). It is for this reason, again, that the plane of immanence can be understood as 'preconceptual' or even 'prephilosophical' (*WP?*, 40). It is not simply to be identified with any of the concepts actually within the philosophical system, but corresponds to something like the 'intuitive' or 'nonconceptual understanding' (*WP?*, 40) that allows them to be selected and put together. In Plato, it is the 'virtual image of an already-thought' (*WP?*, 40) that doubles every concept. In Descartes, it is a matter of a 'subjective understanding' implicitly presupposed by the Cogito. And even in Heidegger, who did as much as anybody to think the ground that allows the ground, it is a certain 'preontological understanding' (*WP?*, 40) that predisposes us towards the thinking of Being.

But – and this is the question of that 'double genesis' or 'quasi-causality' we spoke of before – if the plane of immanence precedes philosophical concepts, it also does not. If it is associated with the 'preconceptual' or 'prephilosophical', it is a preconceptual or prephilosophical that exists only *after* the concept of philosophy. The plane of immanence is not simply the totality of what is, an attempt to capture all of the world – as Deleuze and Guattari insist, it is not to be understood as any universalizing 'concept of all concepts' (*WP?*, 35) – but is always from the beginning a certain selection of the world as seen from a particular point of view. The plane of immanence does not exist all-inclusively, which would turn it into 'chaos', but only as figured each time by a philosophical system that employs it as a 'sieve' (*WP?*, 46) or 'filter' (*WP?*, 206). This is why, as Deleuze and Guattari say, if the plane of immanence is a wall, it would be a dry wall made up of stones without cement supporting each other (*WP?*, 23). Or, if it is a desert, it would be a desert that has 'no other regions than the tribes moving around on it' (*WP?*, 36–7). And this is the paradox of the plane of immanence: it is at once what precedes philosophy and only an effect of philosophy. It is at the same time a transcendental condition of philosophy and what precedes and makes possible any transcendental condition. And it is this – to go against virtually all readings of Deleuze and Guattari – that means that the plane of immanence is not to be achieved once and for all, but is a continual struggle. Indeed, we might even say that immanence *is* this perpetually renewed undertaking to achieve immanence. As soon as immanence or the plane of immanence is definitively stated as the condition of philosophy, it becomes transcendental. Or, as Deleuze and Guattari put it, 'immanent to' something (*WP?*, 45). By contrast, true immanence must be thought as the unceasing movement between the immanent and the transcendental, the fact that the immanent is always turning into the transcendental, but only because of another immanent, that is, transcendental, condition.[3] It is certainly for this reason that Deleuze and Guattari write: 'The plane of immanence is, at the same time, that which must be thought and that which cannot be thought' (*WP?*, 59). And, perhaps more importantly for our purposes, they go on to suggest that it is a matter 'not so much of thinking the plane of immanence as to show that it is there, unthought in every plane' (*WP?*, 59).

It is undoubtedly Spinoza, for Deleuze and Guattari, who is the greatest thinker of immanence. It is from Spinoza that they take their concept of the plane of immanence, and it is following Spinoza that the thinking of the plane of immanence becomes the defining test for philosophy. And it is from Spinoza, too, that Deleuze gets his concept of 'double genesis' or 'quasi-causality', which enters his work under various names following the 1968 minor half of his *these d'État, Expressionism in Philosophy: Spinoza*. (In *Difference and Repetition*, it is one of the forms of 'repetition' (*DR*, 93); in *The Logic of Sense*, it is 'counter-actualization' (*LS*, 171); in *Anti-Oedipus*, it is the 'celibate machine' and its 'auto-affection' (*AO*, 17).) The famous problem of Spinoza, inherited by Deleuze, is what is the relationship of substance to attributes to modes? In Spinoza's monist ontology, it is the divine substance that contains all of God's qualities. It is the attributes that are what we can know of God (thought and extension). And it is the modes through which God is known (they are God's creatures). And the dilemma thereby raised, originally faced by medieval theology, is whether it is the divine substance that comes first, allowing itself to be seen through its worldly attributes, or whether it is these attributes that come first, leading to an unrelated plurality of things and only the retrospective illusion of a God. In the first, there is an absolute distance between God and his effects or emanations, so that the word 'Being' or any other predicate can be used about Him only analogously, with the result that there is a real equivocality about our discourse, insofar as it must be employed in radically different ways according to whether we are referring to God or his creaturely expressions. In the second, there is no distinction at all between God and his attributes, so that there is an absolute univocality of Being which applies to all things in the world, and even those outside it, in exactly the same way. Understanding Spinoza in the first sense leads to the accusation that what he posits is a transcendent and ultimately unknowable Being, in either a neo-Platonic or negative theology, about whom nothing can be said and who is unable to exercise any moral or ethical force. Understanding Spinoza in the second sense leads to the accusation that he is a pantheist or even an atheist, for whom there can be no God and similarly no morality and ethics. And debates have continued since Spinoza's death, interpreting him in both ways – as both idealist and materialist, conservative and radical, religious and anti-religious – attracting such diverse and yet powerful interpreters as Lessing in the eighteenth century, Hegel in the nineteenth century, and in the twentieth century Russell at the beginning, Althusser in the middle and Hardt and Negri at the end.

But it is exactly in order to overcome this interpretive dilemma that Deleuze develops or invents the concept of 'expression' in Spinoza. 'Expression' is the way in which Spinoza is seen to understand the relationship between substance, attributes and modes in his work. As Deleuze writes in *Expressionism in Philosophy*: 'Each attribute expresses the essence of the substance, its being or reality ... But then attributes express themselves in their subordinate modes, each such mode expressing a modification of the attribute' (*EP*, 13–4). However, what exactly does Deleuze mean by this? The crucial thing to grasp about 'expression' – this is the innovation Deleuze makes to its traditional usage – is that it is always a two-way process. At the same time as substance is expressed through its modes, this substance comes about only through its modes. At the same time as the modes express substance, these modes also bring this substance about. As Deleuze writes, employing a vocabulary originally developed by medieval commentators on the sixth-century Roman philosopher Boethius: 'Things remain inherent in God, who complicates them, and God remains implicated in things, which explicate him' (*EP*, 175). And it is in this way that Deleuze seeks to overcome that long-running interpretive dilemma involving Spinoza, for now it is no longer simply a matter of something higher up expressing itself through something lower in a mode of inherence or complication, or of something lower giving expression to something higher in a mode of implication or explication, but always of both. To put it in Spinoza's terms, God does not so much bring Himself about as bring about the nature that brings Him about: 'God is the cause of all things in the same sense as he is of himself' (*EP*, 164). And it is this kind of recursiveness that for Spinoza is the definition of an 'adequate' idea: 'An idea never has as its cause an object that it represents; rather does it represent an object because it expresses its own cause' (*EP*, 139–40).[4] And, indeed, it is just this kind of recursiveness that we see in the relationship between the plane of immanence and the philosophical concept. If in one way it is the plane of immanence that leads to the concept, in another way it is the concept that produces the plane of immanence. It is the concept that produces the plane of immanence that produces the concept. Or, to translate this into the relationship between Nature and Thought, which are two of the attributes of substance for Spinoza and the way in which the plane of immanence and the concept are characterized in *What is Philosophy?*, we would say that there is a necessary reversibility, a 'lightning flash' or 'infinite movement' (*WP?*, 38), between them, in which we could no sooner say that Thought follows Nature than we would discover that Nature comes about only through its expression by Thought.

But this connection between Spinoza and the plane of immanence also allows us to think what an immanent thought or a thought without image would be. For what is at stake in the 'expressive' relationship between Nature and Thought is the idea that at once philosophy is entirely open to the world and that the world is entirely a creation of philosophy. Indeed, more than this, we might say that it is not because of any supposed openness to Nature that Thought might adequately express the world – both Kant and the phenomenologists attempted this, only to end up providing the rules for a merely possible experience or seeing the world as immanent to a transcendent subjectivity – but by radically determining it as an effect of Thought. For it is just at this point that what is discovered is that this Thought itself is a radical expression of Nature, that Nature that is already exactly what Thought would have it be. This has the result that in the end it is impossible to decide whether it is Nature that arises out of Thought or Thought that arises out of Nature. But, again, in all of this immanence would not be anything that is finally achieved, but just the constant passing back and forth between Nature and Thought, the expressed and expression. And, indeed, for Deleuze it is in the end not Spinoza but Nietzsche who goes furthest in this reversibility or reciprocality between substance and modes (*DR*, 304). For the profound lesson of Nietzsche's Eternal Return is both that the willed is destined and that destiny is willed. The thinker must at once follow the world entirely as it is and this world arise only as a result of the thinker's will. In the Eternal Return, for the first time, the world is seen entirely outside any higher or superior realm – Nietzsche's work in this regard constitutes an implicit critique of Kant – and yet the world must also be understood for an entirely other reason than its own (and this is the meaning of Deleuze and Guattari's rereading of the Kantian formula 'intensity = 0' (*AO*, 326–7; *TP*,

153): the world in its very immanence or flatness, = 0, testifies to a kind of intensity or implication[5]). And, indeed, it is this incessant passing back and forth between the expressed and its expression that accounts for how the Eternal Return is possible in a world – Deleuze raises this in his discussion of the doctrine in *Difference and Repetition* – of thermodynamics, of physical laws that predict that everything will eventually run out or run down (*DR*, 228). For in the same way as Spinoza, expression leads to what is expressed; intensity or let us say the plane of immanence in Nietzsche does not run out, not because it is some store or reserve that comes before, and that philosophy gives only partial expression to – for in that case it will certainly run out – but because this intensity or plane of immanence arises as an *effect of* its expression. And this leads to the eternal task of philosophy, always failed and always resumed: to express what gives rise to it, to take account of that Nature that allows philosophy to take account of Nature.

* * *

We pass from the third of the passive syntheses of art to philosophy through a process of double causality. The plane of immanence of philosophy is both the origin of philosophy, the fact that it comes out of a genesis it cannot grasp, and can be seen only through philosophy, is what allows philosophy to grasp its own origins and thus to think this genesis. Philosophy at once draws its various components from this plane of immanence as though from a 'reserve' that exists beforehand, and these components only exist and take on their meaning within the philosophical concept and its particular arrangement of components. It is for all these reasons that the philosophical concept is at the same time determined externally, 'exoconsistent' (*WP?*, 20), and determined internally, 'endoconsistent' (*WP?*, 19); 'relative' and "absolute' (*WP?*, 21); created by another and 'auto-poetic' or 'self-positing' (*WP?*, 11). But what exactly is a philosophical concept for Deleuze and Guattari, and how does it put together the various components that make it up? Deleuze and Guattari provide several examples of philosophical concepts in *What is Philosophy?* – Plato's Ideas (*WP?*, 29–32), Descartes' Cogito (*WP?*, 24–7) and Kant's reworking of the Cogito (*WP?*, 55–7) – but we might begin here with a series of examples Deleuze provides in *Difference and Repetition*: the Ancient Greek philosopher Epicurus' Idea of the atom (*DR*, 184), the French biologist Étienne Geoffroy Saint-Hilaire's Idea of the organism (*DR*, 184–5) and Marx's Idea of society (*DR*, 186). What makes up each of these Ideas is a set of initially free-floating elements that are then reciprocally determined so that we arrive at a series of entirely differentiated singularities, each of which corresponds to a particular aspect of the Idea. These Ideas are virtual in that they break with all external context and can be explained only in terms of themselves, which is also to say that they take within themselves their own context and make it one of the components of the Idea. (Indeed, it is possible that not all these Ideas – and perhaps no Idea – will ever meet these criteria, insofar as something of the material and external always remains. Beyond Geoffroy's concept of the organism, for example, which is restricted by such anatomical elements as bones that are still not differentially determined, there is now DNA, which more completely expresses a 'reciprocal and complete determination' (*DR*, 185), and possibly not even that.) Elsewhere, in *The Logic of Sense*, Deleuze suggests the linguistic structures brought about by such portmanteau words as 'snark' and 'fruminous' (*LS*, 60) in Lewis Carroll's *Alice in Wonderland*, and such scientific discoveries named after their founders as the Kelvin, Seebeck or Zeeman effect in physics (*LS*, 82), as examples of, or at least analogies for, the concept. And Daniel W. Smith, in an essay entitled 'On the Nature of Concepts', even analyzes Deleuze's own notion of the 'fold', as developed in his book *The Fold*, as an instance of a concept. As Smith writes there:

> The concept of a fold is a singularity, because folds vary, every fold is different, all folding proceeds by differentiation. No two things are folded in the same way, no two rocks, no two pieces of paper, and there is no general rule saying the same thing will always fold in the same way. In this sense, there are folds everywhere, but the fold is not a universal. Rather, it is a 'differentiator', a 'differential'. The concept of the fold is always a singularity, and it can only gain terrain by varying within itself, by bifurcating, by metamorphosing. All folds differ from each other, and differ from themselves.[6]

What is it that we can observe of such concepts? Smith says of Deleuze's concept of the fold that, unlike our usual understanding of a category or classification, there is not something in common to all its examples or some predetermined set of qualities that each example must have in common in order to fit within the category. Rather, each example is in some way distinct from all the others, so that by the end there is nothing in common to all of them. Or we might say that each new example added to the others shows us that what we previously took to be what they all have in common is not necessarily true. We might say that each new example attempts to say what all the others have in common, to be the example that states the rule; and yet it is always possible that another will come along after it to reveal that it is only another example like those others, taking on its meaning only in relation to them. What we have is a series of examples, each of which attempts to say what they all have in common, to state exhaustively the rule of the concept; but each is limited, merely different from the others, as seen from the next in line. Thus it is that each example attempts to state the ground or plane of immanence that all the others have in common – this is Deleuze and Guattari's point that the components of a concept come out of the plane of immanence – and that as the concept goes on it gets more distinct, in Deleuze and Guattari's word, more differentiated, and more comprehensive. That is, the concept as it goes along includes more examples, covers more differences, and becomes more refined, more specific, gets closer to the ultimate 'difference' that allows it to present its differences. And the concept is finally differentiated – although in a sense this never actually happens – only when we have a series of examples or components with nothing in common. It would be when each instance is absolutely singular, having nothing in common with any of the others, and the concept covers everything, includes within it something of all the world. We see something of this, for example, in Spinoza and his concept of substance: 'Substance has an absolutely infinite power of existence only by exercising in an infinity of things, in an infinity of ways or modes, the capacity to be affected corresponding to that power' (*EP*, 95). And this progressive differentiation of the concept through its examples is not unlike that mathematical operation of 'adjunction' that Deleuze speaks of, which is not any gradual approach to reality but more the resolution of an internal 'problem' that has the effect of determining reality: 'Starting from a basic "field" (R), successive adjunctions to this field (R', R'', R''') allow a progressively more precise delimitation of the roots of an equation' (*DR*, 180).[7] But again in all of this there is the paradox that there is a certain limit to the concept in that as it becomes more perfect it approaches chaos (*WP?*, 15). There can be no total concept that includes all the others or accounts for the whole of the world, not because of some actual limit to its power or some insuperable excess to the world, but because there must always be some place outside it from where it is generated or expressed (*WP?*, 34).

We can discern in all of this the reasons for Deleuze's long-running objection to Kant. Of course, in Kant – it is this that Deleuze and Guattari mean by that 'reversibility' (*WP?*, 38) between Nature and Thought necessary for philosophy – the categories and intuition come together by means of the synthesis of appreception guaranteed by the faculty of Understanding. And Kant, despite some readings of him – and even some readings of Deleuze on him – does not simply impose his categories on experience. Indeed, as with Deleuze's example of the choice between Richard or William, he precisely attempts to think experience without reducing it to the merely recognizable. The Kantian categories of Understanding are meant to be capacious and responsive to the fact of experience. As Kant writes in the *Critique of Pure Reason*: 'We can, however, with regard to these concepts, as with regard to all knowledge, seek to discover in experience, if not the principles of their possibility, at least the occasioning causes of their production'.[8] And as Deleuze reminds us in *Difference and Repetition*: 'Kant had the liveliest presentiment of such [complexes of space and time], irreducible both to the universality of the concept and to the particularity of the now here' (*DR*, 285). But Deleuze's point is that ultimately there is a subtle circularity or even a kind of infinite regress in Kant's method: if experience is modelled on the categories, these categories for their part are understood as already analogous to experience. As he writes: 'It is clear that Kant traces the so-called transcendental structures from the empirical acts of a psychological consciousness' (*DR*, 135). Indeed, Deleuze's much-discussed 'transcendental empiricism' (*DR*, 56–7) is nothing but a response to this. When he criticizes Kant for making the mistake of empiricism in 'leaving external what is separated' and the post-Kantians for making the mistake of dogmatism in 'filling that which separates' (*DR*, 170), he will oppose to this not less but *more* empiricism and dogmatism: an empiricism that is exactly the same as experience, and a dogmatism that bears no relationship to experience. And we see this with those Ideas that Deleuze discusses, in which the rule is nothing but that series of examples all different from each other. They are only their own difference from themselves, a continuous 'variation' (*WP?*, 20) that already contains within it all future occurrences (as opposed to the endless 'varieties' (*WP?*, 175) of art, which have to be made each time for the first time). And this is as the example is immediately the rule, states entirely in itself everything that will happen to it, which will then require all those others to explicate or differentiate. In a radical way – and this is something Deleuze will say in *The Logic of Sense* – the word *is* the thing. The concept makes us see each time something new in what is, continually differenciates experience, producing finer and finer distinctions, but also including more and more, as it differentiates itself. In fact, to use Deleuze's language from *The Logic of Sense*, the 'esoteric' word or word = x is equivalent to 'exoteric' reality or thing = x (*LS*, 78): both out of place, singular, ungeneralizable, whether it applies to notions like 'sexuality' or the 'Baroque', medical conditions like Alzheimer's disease or Asperger's syndrome or portmanteau words like 'snark' or 'fruminous' that actually make us see their object as though for the first time.[9]

In all of this we would say that what passes between these examples, at once joining them and showing how they are different, is the concept. Indeed, we would say that, to use the language of *What is Philosophy?*, these examples are the *components* between which the concept passes. More exactly, Deleuze and Guattari describe the concept – or at least the concept in its capacity as the 'aleatory point' (*WP?*, 152) that passes between its components – as a survey 'without distance' (*WP?*, 20). But what does this mean? Where is this survey to be located? In fact, this idea of the concept as a survey 'without distance' or outside a 'supplementary dimension' (*WP?*, 210) reminds us that the concept is nothing else than the components that make it up. Again, if we go back to the example of the fold, we will see that each component was once a concept, attempting to say what all the others had in common, just as each concept can be seen as merely another component when seen from the point of view of another concept. And it is this we can see in one of the actual examples of the concept that Deleuze and Guattari analyze in *What is Philosophy?*, Descartes' Cogito:

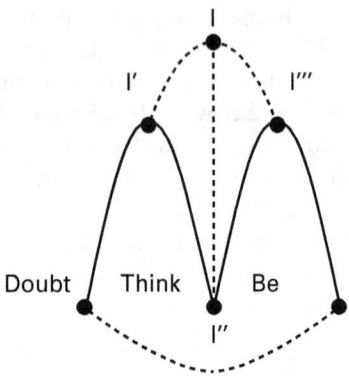

The Cogito is made up of three components: I' (doubt), I'' (thought) and I''' (being). But it is not, Deleuze and Guattari insist, a matter of simply adding these components together as though the final concept were their sum total and as though the value or meaning of these components could be understood in themselves. Rather, each additional component changes the meaning of the ones before, becoming that through which they are read. In a sense, each 'doubles' (*WP?*, 15) the others, becomes that 'transcendental' ground that explains them differently (hence again the connection of each new component with the plane of immanence). And if the concept finally produced – the Cogito or I – is to be identified or completed only with the final component, it is also only the movement between components, the state of mutual difference between them that is thereby created. It is at once the commonality that allows us to see the difference between components and only itself another, different component. That is, the concept is nothing outside its components but only the relationship between them. As Deleuze and Guattari write: 'Concepts are centres of vibrations, each in itself and every one in relation to all of the others' (*WP?*, 23). And this is to suggest that it is always possible to add another component that will again change the meaning of those others, provide another ground that will allow us to see a new difference between them. (It is in this sense that we would say that sameness is always underwritten by difference.) In the case of the Cogito, the fragmentary and momentary totality that might be expressed 'I am a thinking being' can be opened up, for example, by the addition of the component 'infinity' or, as we will see in a moment, by the addition of the component 'time': 'We can pass to other phases of being only by bridges and crossroads that lead to other concepts. Thus, "among my ideas I have the idea of infinity" is the bridge leading from the concept of self to the concept of God' (*WP?*, 26).

It is this that forms the basis of Deleuze and Guattari's model of philosophical development and of how different philosophical systems relate to one another. It is not a matter – and Deleuze and Guattari's conception of philosophy as 'variation' is not to be understood like this – of some continuous progress towards a goal, as though what we had were a series of incremental changes leading to some final truth. And it is not a matter of disputing or debating some shared reality or the meaning of common terms. This for Deleuze and Guattari is only to reduce philosophy to 'opinion' (*WP?*, 80) or, even worse, 'bad taste' (*WP?*, 80) – and, as they more generally recommend: 'Every philosopher runs when he or she hears someone say "Let's discuss this"' (*WP?*, 28). The history of philosophy, therefore, is not so much a matter of before and after as of above and below. It is not so much historical as 'geological' (*WP?*, 80), not so much developmental as 'stratigraphic' (*WP?*, 58). Philosophies and philosophers do not so much speak to each other as differentiate each other. They do not contest the terms of, or add a term to, another system without also attempting to re-interpret it completely. This is undoubtedly why, as Deleuze and Guattari say, 'there could not be two great philosophers on the same plane' (*WP?*, 51). Or – to go back to that double-sided aspect of the philosophical concept we began by discussing – each philosophical system at once completes the previous system (reality or another philosophical system, it is all the same thing), following it exactly, and inverts it entirely, providing a whole other reason for it. It is in this sense that we can say that philosophy is absolutely free, with everything always open to be re-read in any way – this is why Deleuze does not believe in the 'end of metaphysics' – and absolutely determined, with only one component at any time able to fit the existing gap in the previous system.[10] It is for this reason, too, that Deleuze and Guattari suggest that it is very hard to decide whether a particular philosopher is 'critical' or a 'disciple' (*WP?*, 57–8) of the philosophical system they take up, and why for them ever since Plato it has been difficult to distinguish 'friend' from 'rival' (*WP?*, 4) in philosophy. And we see all of this in Deleuze and Guattari's example of one philosophical system engaging with another: Kant's re-reading of Descartes. For what exactly is it that Kant does with Descartes' Cogito? He does not merely contest or disagree with him or set out some alternative system. Instead, he adds another component to Descartes' Cogito – time – and thus asks a kind of transcendental question of it: in what *time* does Descartes' determination of 'I am' as 'I think' take place? In other words, for Descartes' 'analytic' connection between 'I am' and 'I think' Kant substitutes a 'synthetic' relationship: what was once seen as the same is now seen as different and able to be bridged only by the intervening medium of time. Both 'I am' and 'I think' now only stand in for a certain form of time. As Deleuze and Guattari write:

> Kant therefore 'criticizes' Descartes for having said 'I am a thinking substance' because nothing warrants such a claim of the 'I'. Kant demands the introduction of a new component into the Cogito, the one Descartes repressed – time. For it is only in time that my undetermined existence is determinable. (*WP?*, 31)

Indeed, we see this in Deleuze and Guattari's own relationship to Kant. Kant, as we have just seen, introduces time into Descartes' Cogito. He moves closer to a proper 'genetic' account of philosophy in showing that the connection between 'I am' and 'I think' is not to be assumed, but takes place only in time. But this is still for Kant only an 'interior' time or a time that takes place within a 'subject' (*WP?*, 46). If in one way the 'I' is shown coming about, in another way it is preconstituted, a transcendental horizon within which an otherwise immanent process takes place. It is still an undetermined I or Cogito that passes between the various components of the concept, untouched by the process it oversees. Deleuze and Guattari transform all of this in their diagrammatic recreation of Kant in *What is Philosophy?*, which they say is inspired by portraits of other great philosophers by the French sculptor Jean Tinguely, in which various bits of scrap metal and machinery are combined to produce strange Rube-Goldberg-like assemblages that endlessly revolve around themselves or destroy themselves while also creating themselves:

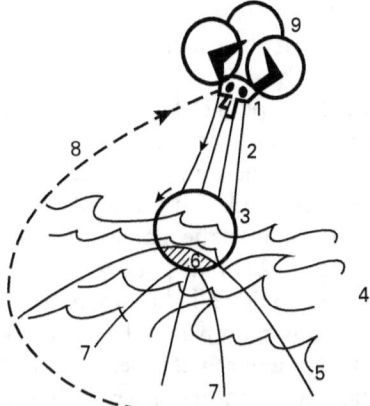

The point here, if we attempt to describe verbally what Deleuze and Guattari have drawn, is that, as opposed to Kant, for whom the subject is outside genesis, that with which the Transcendental Deduction begins, every aspect of Kant's system is connected to every other and cannot be understood outside them. That is, the deduction of the various categories of possible experience is shown to be circular, no sooner ended than having to be begun again or secretly dependent on that which it would determine. The apperception of the unity of experience, through a transcendent subject (1) that is able to mark all of its representations with the same 'I think' and a transcendent object that would remain the same through all its representations, allows the deduction of certain categories (2). These categories, mediated by the schemata (3), are able to be applied to objects given in intuition so that these objects can be granted conceptual form. Time (4) and space (5) are how these objects are offered to thought so that they can provide empirical knowledge. The passive self (6), affected by these intuited objects presented in time and space, then begins the process of forming synthetic a priori judgements (7) that allow different predicates to be attached to objects that do not necessarily contain them to extend knowledge through empirical examples in conformity with possible experience (8). And, in order to allow this attribution of a concept to possible objects when we do not know what these objects actually are, there are transcendental Ideas (the soul, the world, God) (9) that go beyond the possibility of experience, and govern the conduct of Reason, legitimizing the conformity of predicates to objects that the original transcendental apperception began with.

What, then, is the concept in Deleuze and Guattari's redescription of Kant here? It is no one part of the system, as Kant perhaps thought – for him, it was the transcendental subject – but only the relationship between them. Or if it is one of the parts of the system like the subject, this is only the name for the relation between them, that 'space' (*WP?*, 25) that puts each of them in a situation of maximum difference with all the others and all alike in their difference. (It is for this reason that Deleuze takes up Maïmon's critique of the duality between the determining concept and the determined intuition in Kant and its replacement by a principle of 'reciprocal determination' (*DR*, 173).[11]) And thus instead of the Kantian time in which the Cogito is determined – that interior or subjective time in which 'I think' becomes 'I am' – we have the time of the determination of the concept itself, which moves from undetermined or free-floating components that are unrelated through a process of reciprocal determination in which they are related to each other and on to their complete determination, in which the concept is made up of a series of unique and irreplaceable singularities that are each absolutely different from one another.[12] In other words, Deleuze and Guattari rewrite Kant's deduction of the transcendental subject as an effect of the determination of the concept. Kant's project becomes 'allegorical' of philosophy itself, as are finally all philosophical systems. All more or less approach the 'immanence' of the model Deleuze and Guattari set out, although all also fall short, do not go on to fulfil the proper 'genetic' requirements of philosophy, in the end proposing their concept as immanent to some transcendent. And the time in which the concept is determined is not Kant's 'subjective' time, but what Deleuze and Guattari call the 'Aion' (*LS*, 73–5) or the 'Aternal' (*WP?*, 111), which is the time that 'precedes' all subjective time. For precisely what Deleuze and Guattari do not want to do in their recovery of Kant is assume that time is one of the pure intuitions in which objects are presented, and therefore one of the a priori conditions for experience. Rather, what they hope to demonstrate is that it is this 'prior' putting-together of the concept that produces the possibility of Kantian time (which is, indeed, necessary: it is something like this Kantian time and space that we have seen art attempt to produce in the previous chapter and that will finally come to be realized in the chapter on science and logic). Aion is that time 'before' time in which concepts are constructed, running from undetermined elements to singular determinations in what Deleuze calls the 'sufficient reason' (*DR*, 171) of the Idea. However, if this Aion is not a linear time, in which one moment comes after another but in which the future both already has arrived and never will arrive, then this is also to say that it is not simply a matter of a *progressive* determination of the concept, as so many accounts of Deleuze and Guattari seem to assume. This Aion is also the time of the undoing of concepts or their non-arrival, the fact that they are never fully determined. Or, to put this another way – and we will be referring to this in our next chapter – even in the fully determined concept in which each component is fixed in its meaning and finds its definitive place in a system, we must also be able to see it as different, unfixed, undetermined, permanently open to another concept's taking it over and combining it in a different way. Philosophy continues to 'become' (*WP?*, 112–13) by way of a process of the linking and unlinking of components. Even the greatest and most long-lasting of philosophical systems is always able to be recreated through the adding or subtracting of components, as Deleuze indeed does in his various commentaries on other philosophers. The paradox of philosophy is that the moment of the concept's final determination, when the system is complete and no further changes are possible, is also the moment of its maximum indetermination, when the concept is at its widest and most inclusive, when its components are at their most different from each other and most able to be taken up by another.

* * *

We spoke with regard to Deleuze and Guattari's reconstruction of Kant, of the way that the final concept stands in for a kind of 'space' that moves between its various components. It is a space that, if it can be named the concept, also cannot be named, but merely takes the place of the 'ground' that all the components have in common while opening up the space for another concept to take its place, which would be what all the components, including the present concept, then had in common. And Deleuze and Guattari's name for this 'space', that moves between the components and that the concept only stands in for, is 'persona' (*WP?*, 62). Indeed, throughout Deleuze and Guattari's characterization of the concept, there is raised the question of who or what puts the components together that make up the concept. Of course, in one way these components exist only after they have been cut out from the plane of immanence, and yet in another way someone or something actually has to cut them out. Once within a philosophical concept, all the components are necessary and justify each other so that all must be chosen at once; but the question can also be asked on what basis are they are combined, insofar as they can actually only be put together one after the other. It is again in order to answer these questions that Deleuze and Guattari will speak in *What is Philosophy?* of the conceptual 'persona'. They write of this persona that it occupies a 'hazy existence half-way between concept and pre-conceptual plane' (*WP?*, 61), and that it 'plays a part in the construction of the [philosopher's] concept' (*WP?*, 63). But what exactly does this mean? How is the persona able to satisfy the dual demands of the concept we have just seen? In its most obvious sense, the persona must be understood as the figure or identity within a philosophical system that stands in for the philosopher: that is, that assumed voice or character through which the philosopher speaks. As is well known, philosophy begins with such a figure, in Plato, who spoke in the guise of his teacher Socrates (*WP?*, 9). But, as Deleuze and Guattari observe, philosophy is inseparable from these personae, exactly insofar as it is a form of 'constructivism' (*WP?*, 35), in which its concepts must be put together. That is, each actual philosophical system necessarily creates its own distinct and recognizable persona, from Plato's Socrates to Kant's 'bachelor and his stocking-suspender' (*WP?*, 72), from Nicholas of Cusa's 'Idiot' (*WP?*, 64) to Pascal's 'gambler' (*WP?*, 73), from Kierkegaard's 'Knight of Faith' (*WP?*, 74) to, indeed, Deleuze and Guattari's old men 'with nothing left to lose' (*WP?*, 1). However, for Deleuze and Guattari, it is undoubtedly Nietzsche who is the greatest inventor and exploiter of personae in the history of philosophy, from Apollo and Dionysus in *The Birth of Tragedy* to the Antichrist in *The Antichrist*, from the woman-hater in *Beyond Good and Evil* to Zarathustra in *Thus Spake Zarathustra*.

Each such persona, needless to say, is able to be analyzed biographically, sociologically and even historically. Obviously, at each stage in philosophy there is only a certain range of options open to the philosopher, from which he or she has to choose. But, as Deleuze and Guattari emphasize, the persona is not able to be reduced to, or to be explained by, these external factors. The persona is not directly biographical, autobiographical or in any way literally able to be identified with the philosopher. Philosophers have often put forward antithetical personae with which they do not agree, for example, Leibniz in his *New Essays on Human Understanding*; or staged dialogues between several personae, with all of whom they obviously cannot agree, for example, Hume in his *Dialogues Concerning Natural Religion*. And, indeed, Nietzsche towards the end of his life was able to write that 'The unpleasant thing, and one that nags my modesty, is that at root every name in history is I',[13] with the result that at once any position is able to be attributed to him and is always able to be contested by another. And even when a philosopher appears to have no persona, to be speaking directly, rationally and without intermediary, this is merely another persona: the philosopher as pseudo-neutral judge or legislator of all other positions (*WP?*, 72). In all these ways, philosophy is irreducible both to the 'history of philosophy' (*WP?*, 83) and to any analysis of 'psychosocial types' (*WP?*, 67). On the contrary, it is the very task of philosophy to wrest thought from the 'historical state of affairs of the lived experience of individuals in order to turn them into the features of conceptual personae or thought-events on the plane laid out by thought' (*WP?*, 70). And yet, if the persona is not mediated by either history or biography, it is also not a matter of directly identifying with the persona. This is why Deleuze and Guattari reject conceiving of the persona in terms of any kind of fictional character or aesthetic expression (*WP?*, 65), involving any interpretive method of 'logodrama' or 'figurology' (*WP?*, 66). Although the plane of composition of art and the plane of immanence of philosophy in some ways intersect, the concept of philosophy must absolutely be distinguished from the percept and affect of art. It is for similar reasons that Deleuze and Guattari reject seeing philosophy as any form of religious 'wisdom' (*WP?*, 52) and the philosopher as any kind of 'sage' (*WP?*, 3), as is the case in Eastern religions or even aspects of Ancient Greek thought. Again, it is never a matter of any 'revealed truth' that is to be attained by directly identifying with the persona, as though it exists outside the philosophical concept. As Deleuze and Guattari make clear in their analysis of the Christian philosophers Pascal and Kierkegaard, if their religious beliefs can be understood as involving a truly existential 'leap of faith' that takes place outside rational thought, this 'leap' is itself precisely a philosophical concept, not so much breaking with immanence as being a 'transcendence' that recharges or redoubles immanence (*WP?*, 74–5).

In fact, if we read *What is Philosophy?* closely, we will find that the persona does not just come between the plane of immanence and the concept as what selects and puts together components to make up the concept, but also before the plane of immanence. As Deleuze and Guattari write: 'The persona and the plane of immanence presuppose each other' (*WP?*, 73). And this is to make clear that – although again they should not simply be identified – the real origin of the persona, the real force or function it stands in for, starts with the third stage of the dynamic genesis of art. At the end of art, as we have seen, we are left with 'force', a sense of the 'future' and a withdrawn or nomadic figure that seeks to put sensations together. In the third passive synthesis, we have, after a first apprehension of discontinuous matter and a subsequent recording of appearance in a pure past of reproducibility, the attempt to bring these two together in a final synthesis of recognition. This would be as in Kant's Transcendental Deduction, in which, through apprehension, the unity of the object is matched with the unity of the subject, so that our representations can be recognized as our own, and we do not repeat them having once produced them. But, as we have seen, for Deleuze, this attempt at recognition fails, and instead of any unifying apperception the subject is unable to see an image of itself in the object. As Deleuze writes, for example, in *The Movement-Image*: '[With the crisis of the action-image] the first thing to be compromised everywhere are the linkages of situation-action, action-reaction, excitation-response, in short, the sensory-motor links' (*MI*, 206). Or, as he puts it in *Proust and Signs*, at a certain point any totality breaks down and we are left only with 'fragments that can no longer be restored, pieces that do not fit into the same puzzle' (*PS*, 101). In both cases, the subject of art dissolves, leaving its sensations to disperse, no longer able to be held together. And it is this that we have seen in *What is Philosophy?* with the 'hollowing out' of art and the 'dissolving of identity' (*WP?*, 187). However, as we have also seen, for Deleuze and Deleuze and Guattari, it is at this point that a new subject and principle of order emerges. In *Difference and Repetition*, it is the 'apprentice' who constitutes problems (*DR*, 164). In *The Logic of Sense*, it is the 'player of the game' who casts their dice to put together differential elements outside any pre-existing rules (*LS*, 75). And, of course, in *What is Philosophy?*, it is the philosophical persona.

Indeed, if it is Nietzsche who is the greatest thinker of the persona in philosophy, it is exactly because he understands it as this new principle that arises after the failure of the third passive synthesis. In *Difference and Repetition*, Deleuze makes a distinction, drawn from the writings of French novelist and essayist Pierre Klossowski, between the doctrines of the 'will to power' and the 'Eternal Return', which are usually thought to be the same. The 'will to power' – and here once more the question of the transition of art to philosophy we have been speaking of – is described as a 'feeling', and more particularly a feeling of 'distance' (*DR*, 243). And in this 'feeling', the self, or the one who experiences it, dissolves, leaving only an 'intensity' (*DR*, 243). They are unable any more to give an order to the world, and the elements put together disperse once more, and we fall back into an endless difference in which nothing returns or is recognized. As Deleuze writes: '[The event and the act] turn back against the self which has become their equal and smash it to pieces, as though the bearer of a new world were carried away and dispersed by the shock of the multiplicity to which it gives birth' (*DR*, 89–90). But, following this, in the Eternal Return, a new principle of order is introduced. What Deleuze calls a 'fractured I' arises in the wake of the dissolution of the self, and runs through the various fragments left behind and finds in them a hitherto unrecognized organization in which certain objects can be recognized or seen as coming back. The world is no longer simply different, or subject to a transformation without end, but instead there is a certain holding or gathering together of things. Again, as Deleuze writes: 'The I which is fractured according to the order of time and the self which is divided according to the temporal series correspond and find a common descendent whose scattered remains gravitate around the sublime image' (*DR*, 90). But it is very important to understand clearly how the Eternal Return introduces a new principle of order after the failure of the will to power. It does not actually introduce some new and overarching category on top of what is. It does not restrict what is to be recognized or what can come back. It does not make experience conform to what is already known or any a priori. Rather, if we can put it like this, it simply repeats the *failure* of recognition of the third passive synthesis. It recognizes that things are not recognized or repeated and makes of *this* a new form of recognition. Endless difference or transformation is grasped as such, and, in this grasping, another principle is brought about, one that is at once outside this difference while ensuring that nothing is outside it. (And this is as with the persona: after tracing the components of a concept for the first time and starting again at the beginning, the beginning is not the same because it can now only be seen through the persona that comes after it. With reference to the concept, nothing is repeated, insofar as each passage through its components produces something different, that is, its concept, which just *is* this passage through its components.)

We can see the difference between the will to power and the Eternal Return brought out in Deleuze's early monograph *Nietzsche and Philosophy* (1962). Deleuze will draw a distinction there between two of Nietzsche's best-known personae: Zarathustra from *Thus Spake Zarathustra*, who is associated with the will to power; and Dionysus from *The Birth of Tragedy* and *Thus Spake Zarathustra*, who is associated with the Eternal Return. Deleuze begins by suggesting that Zarathustra must be understood as the 'precondition' (*NP*, 192) of Dionysus, the one without whom Dionysus would not exist. But at the same time he emphasizes that Dionysus is also 'unconditioned' (*NP*, 193) and owes nothing to anybody but is apodictic and self-causing. What is at stake in this distinction and why is it unable to be strictly maintained? Why is it that Dionysus both follows on from Zarathustra and bears no relation to him, and why is this ambiguity crucial to our understanding of Dionysus? Zarathustra, as Deleuze makes clear, is a prophet or principle of 'transformation' (*NP*, 191). He is the first to make of the negative an affirmation, to make of the failure of meaning or the absence of higher values a new form of meaning and value (*NP*, 170). But, if Zarathustra formulates the rule of transformation, the failure of recognition, he also wants to remain finally outside it. He might see the world as destined, as lacking any higher order or future goals against which to judge it, but he nevertheless regards himself as the source or origin of that destiny. Or we might even say for Zarathustra that either he wills the world or the world is destined, but he cannot think the two together. It is just this that Dionysus is able to do. As Deleuze suggests, with Dionysus a first affirmation (either that he wills the world or that the world destines him) is always accompanied by a second (either that the world destines him or that he wills the world).[14] In other words, with Dionysus we get that Spinozan recursiveness, in which he cannot simply will the world from the outside without the world also destining him. As opposed to Zarathustra, who as Deleuze writes can operate only in a mediated way, with a certain 'delay' or 'entanglement' (*NP*, 193) between thought and its causes, with Dionysus there is no such delay. He is absolutely identical to the principle he enunciates; and thus in a paradoxical way, unlike Zarathustra, who ultimately disappears in the endless transformation of things in his attempt to state it from the outside, he lives on through his very disappearance, for he *is* his own transformation, which is always the relation between the thinker and his or her concept. It is only at this point, when the concept destines that world that destines it, that it becomes virtual, breaking with all context and being able to be explained only by itself. As Deleuze writes:

> Dionysus' determination is of another kind [from Zarathustra's], identical to the absolute principle without which the conditions would themselves remain powerless. And this is Dionysus' supreme disguise – to subject his products to conditions which are themselves subject to him, conditions that these products themselves surpass. (*NP*, 193)

However, if we read *What is Philosophy?* carefully, we can see that there is even a third possible position for the persona: not before the plane of immanence at the end of the third passive synthesis as what allows or leads to philosophy, not between the plane of immanence and the concept as what picks out which components to make up the concept, but what comes *after* the concept itself. As Deleuze and Guattari write, canvassing all these possibilities: 'The three actions making up constructionism continually pass from one to the other, one creating concepts as a case of solution, another laying out a plane and a movement on the plane as conditions of a problem, and the other inventing a persona as the unknown of a problem' (*WP?*, 81). In other words, sometimes the persona comes before the plane of immanence and the concept, sometimes the plane of immanence comes before the persona and the concept, and sometimes the plane of immanence and the concept come before the persona. But how are we to understand this? What does it mean that the persona is now seen as running all the way from before the plane of immanence to after the concept? In one way, the persona can be grasped as a certain 'intensity' (*WP?*, 66) or 'insistence' (*WP?*, 76) that drives the creation of concepts. This is to speak of the fact that, although not to be confused with any historically or biographically existing philosopher, the persona responds to the necessity that, once fully determined or differentiated, the concept needs to be incarnated or effectuated in actual bodies and objects. That is, insofar as we might characterize concepts as the 'structures' (*DR*, 47) or even 'mental objects' (*WP?*, 207) of experience, they need immediately after being generated to be put back into experience. To recall the continuously Kantian inspiration behind Deleuze's enterprise, the persona plays something like the role of the Kantian schema, which is how the a priori categories are applied to the objects given in intuition, after initially being deduced from the possibility of experience. In Deleuze's case, this might be understood as the philosophical concept being materialized again after originally breaking with the materiality of the third stage of dynamic genesis. But this 'intensity' that arises after the final stage of dynamic genesis, which drives the cutting out and selection of components from the plane of immanence, the putting of these components together to form concepts and finally the incarnation of these concepts in objects, is always missed. While the concept attempts to give form to it, this intensity is always outside those moments of genesis that at once drive it on and it drives on. And, in fact, we see this in Deleuze and Guattari's elaborations of various philosophical concepts in *What is Philosophy?* When we look at the diagram they produce of Descartes' Cogito, it is important to ask what exactly is the 'I' that runs between 'I think', 'I doubt' and 'I am'. It is not so much the Cogito as such as what precedes and underlies the Cogito. It is what we might call the 'persona' of Descartes' system, that place from where it is spoken, which is unlocatable as such, although nowhere outside the concept. And the same applies to Deleuze and Guattari's laying out of Kant's *Critique of Pure Reason*, in which – although each part of the system stands in for it – the question is raised of what it is that moves between the different elements, and that is indicated by the lines, wheels and dotted arcs of their diagram. In one way, it is the 'I' or transcendental subject that is the dotted line that connects the various parts of the system, and that the entire system is 'immanent' to (*WP?*, 57), but in another way it is precisely Kant's persona; and it is crucial to realize that Deleuze and Guattari speak of both the concept and the persona as 'events' that lay out components, in order to make the concept more distinct, include more differences, and 'survey', although outside any distance, more of what is.

* * *

There is no history of philosophy. Philosophical concepts do not meaningfully transfer complete from one system to another. Through the process of double genesis, each philosophical system creates its own conditions, so that no one of them can be compared to any other. But, despite all of this, Deleuze and Guattari can still speak of good and bad philosophy, or at least make the distinction between authentic and inauthentic philosophy, philosophy in the first degree and mere commentary, between philosophy and the history of philosophy (*WP?*, 96). Indeed, it is something like the difference between the two senses in which philosophy is actually used in *What is Philosophy?*: between the sense used by Deleuze and Guattari in the first four chapters of the book (philosophy as the creation of concepts) and the sense in which it is used in the chapter 'Prospects and Concepts' (philosophy as 'contemplation, reflection or communication' (*WP?*, 6)). As Deleuze and Guattari write, summarizing this distinction: 'Those who criticize without creating are the plague of philosophy. All these debaters and commentators are inspired by *ressentiment*. They speak only of themselves when they set empty generalizations against one another' (*WP?*, 28–9). But what is the basis of this distinction? Can it be strictly maintained? What are the criteria Deleuze and Guattari use for distinguishing good from bad philosophy, or philosophy from logic or mere opinion? Deleuze and Guattari certainly do not judge philosophy in terms of any truth or *adequatio ad rem* – this is exactly the realm of the prospect or proposition, in which the answer is found in the question, or the object is a projection of the subject – but rather in terms of such categories as the 'interesting, remarkable or important' (*WP?*, 82). And what is it that this 'remarkable' philosophy does? It does not so much provide solutions as create problems. And these problems are not anything that can be solved definitively, but a kind of inexhaustible 'doubling' of what is, which does not so much directly oppose or criticize the world – which for Deleuze and Guattari would constitute only another 'axiom' (*WP?*, 106) or 'relative deterritorialization' (*WP?*, 98), indebted to what it criticizes and able to be substituted for any number of equivalents – as propose another condition for it, for which there can be only one solution. This new condition would at once respond absolutely to the system it inhabits, completing it, and reveal that it comes about for an entirely other reason than its own. It is what Deleuze and Guattari call, following Nietzsche, a 'total critique' (*NP*, 89), which is Kant's method of immanent critique taken to its limit, so that not even the tools or values in the name of which this critique is undertaken (in Kant's case, those transcendental Ideas of the soul, the world and God) are exempt, and all conditions are shown to be conditioned. And yet all of this is only possible in turn – and here we must recall Spinoza's definition of an adequate idea – because this critique is absolutely unconditioned, brings itself about or is the cause of its own cause.

Of course, these 'doublings' make each system of philosophy incomparable in that it can be explained only by itself, but at the same time it is also a philosopher who has to create it. It is in this sense, as we have tried to explain, that it is not a matter of the philosopher's successively choosing particular concepts to put together, both because there is no choice as to what goes with what and because they all have to be chosen together – this, again, is why Deleuze and Guattari speak of the various components in a philosophical system as 'inseparable', and, indeed, why it is not a matter of choosing concepts from a preceding plane of immanence, as though they pre-exist in an undetermined state. And yet, for all the difficulty of judging any system of philosophy insofar as it creates its own conditions, Deleuze and Guattari repeatedly insist upon a certain 'taste' (*WP?*, 77) in the creation of concepts, inasmuch as its components nevertheless still must be selected. This 'taste' is to refer to the fourth of the five qualities Deleuze and Guattari associate with the philosophical persona: the pathic, the relational, the dynamic, the juridical and the existential (*WP?*, 70–3). By 'pathic', they mean to speak of what forces the thinker to think, the encounter that drives the persona 'mad' or 'crazy'. By 'relational', they mean to speak of the relation of philosophical systems with each other, mediated by the persona as either friend or rival. By 'dynamic', they mean to speak of the role of the persona in the dramatization or differenciation of the fully differentiated concept in order to actualize it in objects. By 'existential', they mean to speak of the relationship of the persona to the actual philosopher who incarnates it in their person. And by 'juridical', they mean to speak not only of the particular legal personae adopted by philosophers – Leibniz, Kant, even Nietzsche – but the fact that this persona is adopted because it is always a matter of judging what properly belongs to the concept. Again, however, there is raised the question of what is the basis on which this judgement might take place, insofar as the plane of immanence, concept and persona all depend on another, and are even the limit to one another, paradoxically incomparable only inasmuch as they are in a relationship with other. As Deleuze and Guattari write of what they call the 'well-made concept': '"Well-made" meaning not merely a moderation of the concept but a sort of stimulation, a sort of modulation in which conceptual activity has no limit but only in the other two limitless activities [persona and plane of immanence]' (*WP?*, 77–8).

In *What is Philosophy?*, Deleuze and Guattari set out the task of philosophy in terms of the three Kantian faculties: it is the laying out of the plane of immanence that corresponds to Reason, the invention of the persona to Imagination and the creation of concepts to Understanding. But, as we know, Deleuze and Guattari differ from Kant or subject him to a re-reading, insofar as Kant in his project of critique does not subject these faculties themselves to critique. Although he breaks with Descartes' notion of a merely 'external error' (*WP?*, 52) in proposing a kind of permanent 'illusion' or 'inability' (*WP?*, 54) inherent to philosophy, he does not draw the proper consequences from this in proposing a still 'harmonious' (*DR*, 133) exercise of the faculties in which each has its proper place and finality. In Kant, starting with an initial spatio-temporal diversity or manifold, we pass initially through a synopsis or reception of this manifold through sensibility, a putting together of this data through the synthesis of Imagination and a formal unification of this synthesis through the categories of the Understanding, with the whole process overseen by the

Ideas of Reason, which allow the categories of the Understanding to apply to the synthesis of the Imagination in a kind of shared 'common sense'. For Deleuze, by contrast, there is no spontaneous coming together of the faculties guided by any natural order or any higher faculty or 'speculative interest' (*KCP*, 27). On the contrary, beginning from an initial intensity, a first shock of sense is passed on through three successive passive geneses, each involving an attempt to make up for the failure of the previous one, before ending not with a coming together of subject and object in a unity guaranteed by apperception, but with a 'fractured I' and its 'scattered members' that arise out of the recognition of the failure or dissolution of the passive self (*DR*, 90–1). It is often asked by commentators how seriously Deleuze takes the Kantian doctrine of the faculties, with a number suggesting that he uses them only for heuristic purposes or when he is paraphrasing Kant in his well-known 'free indirect' style. But, crucially, we can see in *What is Philosophy?* that when Deleuze and Guattari as old men are speaking in their own voice they go on to suggest that at the 'end' of philosophy with the failure of recognition what is needed is precisely a vocabulary of 'great beauty' (*WP?*, 8). Undoubtedly, what Deleuze and Guattari mean by 'great beauty', here, is a more-than-beautiful or 'sublime' (*WP?*, 8) faculty in which, as they say, 'even monsters and dwarves must be well-made' (*WP?*, 78). And by this, they might be meaning to suggest that, as with Kant's sublime, philosophy as the succeeding moment in the genesis of representation is not merely the result of the failure of art but the acknowledging of this failure, the making of a faculty out of the 'failure' of the other faculties.

It is certainly this sublime or greatly beautiful faculty that we see in the relationship between the plane of immanence, the persona and the concept in *What is Philosophy?* Deleuze and Guattari will speak of the 'transcendental' (*DR*, 143), by which they mean the highest or most superior exercise of the faculties in the creation of philosophical concepts. In philosophy, there is no 'harmonious' relationship between faculties, as in Kant's Beautiful, in which each faculty is given in advance and takes its place within an overall finality, but what Deleuze calls a 'discordant harmony' (*DR*, 146), in which nothing is prefigured and each faculty takes on its identity only in its relationship with the others. In the 'discordant harmony' of philosophy, each faculty – and not just the Imagination, as in

Kant's *Critique of Judgement* – is forced to its limit in its encounter with the formless, incomprehensible or unrecognizable, which takes it beyond any relationship with the others. The respective faculties are thus not directly comparable but comparable only in their mutual incomparability. And this is what we see in *What is Philosophy?* when Deleuze and Guattari speak of a taste for the 'undetermined' (*WP?*, 78) that characterizes philosophy. This taste, they go on to suggest, is like the 'rule of correspondence of the three instances [Reason, Imagination and Understanding] that are different in kind ... The three activities are strictly simultaneous – have only incommensurable relationships' (*WP?*, 77–8). And all of this is to be seen in Deleuze's early monograph on Kant, *Kant's Critical Philosophy* (1963). Deleuze similarly makes the point there that Kant's *Third Critique*, which is meant to serve as a 'bridge'[15] between the first two, does so not by means of a comparison between pre-existing faculties, but rather by driving each respective faculty to its limit. The faculty of the Imagination that is the subject of the *Critique of Judgement* does not merely add itself to the faculty of Understanding that is the subject of the *Critique of Pure Reason* and the faculty of Reason that is the subject of the *Critique of Practical Reason*, but at once is able only to be given in terms of them and transforms them completely. More specifically, that sublime discovered at the end of the 'Critique of Aesthetic Judgement' at the same time can only repeat what has already been laid down in the other two *Critiques*, occupy a place set for it within Kant's overall 'architectonic', and means that Kant's entire critical project must be rewritten from the end, that those first two *Critiques* must be understood for reasons entirely other than their own. As Deleuze writes in the essay 'The Idea of Genesis in Kant's Aesthetics', which appears in the same year as *Kant's Critical Philosophy* and draws out further the argument first suggested there: 'This means that the *Critique of Judgement*, in its aesthetic part, does not simply complete the two others; in reality, it grounds them. It discovers a free accord of the faculties as the presumed *ground* of the two other critiques' ('G', 60).

To say all of this more slowly, in the *Critique of Pure Reason*, the faculties enter into an 'accord' (*KCP*, 21) under the legislation of the Understanding in relation to an overarching 'speculative' interest. In the *Critique of Practical Reason*, the faculties enter into a new 'harmony' (*KCP*, 34), this time under the legislation of

Reason in relation to a 'practical', we might say a moral, interest. We might therefore think that, according to a certain 'common sense' (*KCP*, 21), whereby the duties of the various faculties would be evenly spread, it would now be the turn of the Imagination to legislate over the other two, perhaps in the name of a certain faculty of feeling or aesthetic pleasure (*KCP*, 47). However, Deleuze insists that what Kant discovers in the *Critique of Judgement* is not so much the completion of his critical project as that the regulated accord or harmony of the first two *Critiques*, in which different faculties enter into a relation by way of a third, is possible only because they are first of all able to enter into a 'spontaneous' ('G', 60) relationship between all of them, in which no single faculty is in charge. First of all, in the 'Analytic of the Beautiful', there is a relation between the Imagination as 'free' and the Understanding as 'indeterminate' (*KCP*, 49). Then, in the 'Analytic of the Sublime', Kant draws up a relationship between Imagination and Reason, but this time in terms not of any simple accord between them but a 'dissensus', in which the only unity between them is 'suprasensible' (*KCP*, 51). And this sublime therefore opens up a true principle of genesis, in which any accord between the faculties is not assumed or even 'subjective', as it is in the *First* and *Second Critiques* and even in the 'Analytic of the Beautiful', but actually has to be engendered from the beginning. As Deleuze writes in 'The Idea of Genesis': 'This, in effect, is the meaning of the *Critique of Judgement*: beneath the determinate and conditioned relations of the faculties, it discovers a free, indeterminate and unconditioned accord [that makes it possible]' ('G', 68). And the location where this unity occurs – what makes possible this undetermined and suprasensible connection between the faculties – is the 'soul'. The soul is 'the point of "concentration", the vivifying principle from which each faculty is "animated", engendered in its free exercise and in its free accord with the others' ('G', 68). And it is this soul or even 'genius' ('G', 66) that will become Deleuze and Guattari's persona.

All of this is to say that Kant's sublime – at least as interpreted by Deleuze – is an allegory of philosophy itself. The coming together of the various components (Understanding, Reason and Imagination) to make up the concept of the sublime is like the coming together of the components in the philosophical concept. Indeed, we might even say that *every* philosophical concept is an allegory of philosophy. The putting together of its components to form its particular concepts – no matter what their actual contents or their attitude towards philosophy – always involves a certain 'adjunction' or 'coadaptation' (*WP?*, 77), in which each component at once determines and is determined by another. And this can be seen in Deleuze and Guattari's other treatment of Kant in *What is Philosophy?*: in the first *Critique* the transcendental subject is understood to stand outside genesis, but what we see in Deleuze and Guattari's diagrammatic reconstitution of it is that it cannot be grasped outside the synthetic activities of the passive self, which it is said to lead to. And this is undoubtedly the case for Deleuze and Guattari's own conception of philosophy in *What is Philosophy?*, in which each of its components (the plane of immanence, concept, and persona, but also art, philosophy and science) are at once comparable and incomparable, determining of and determined by the others. But, in another way, no philosophical system – even Deleuze and Guattari's own – is ever entirely able to embody this abstract 'diagram' (*WP?*, 51) or 'machine' (*WP?*, 55–6), is ultimately able to reflect or reflect upon this sublime indetermination that lies at its genesis. We can never speak of this sublime directly but only indirectly or allegorically, as precisely that plane of immanence it produces. This sublime indetermination with which philosophy begins necessarily remains, as Deleuze and Guattari put it, the 'preconceptual' or 'prephilosophical' condition of philosophy. It is that which philosophy not so much thinks as 'shows that it is there, unthought in every plane'. Philosophy always tries to think the immanent behind the transcendental; but it always turns it into another transcendental, thus allowing another to think its immanent condition and the process to begin all over again. So that it is not so much anything philosophy says as what philosophy *does* that indicates the immanent. In a paradoxical way, it is the very continued taking up and recreation of philosophy that testifies to the immanent. The immanent, as Deleuze and Guattari tell us in their personae as old men in *What is Philosophy?*, is always a matter of 'weariness' (*WP?*, 214). Or, as Deleuze writes in an essay on Samuel Beckett, another great thinker of the connection between immanence and a certain exhaustion:

> There is therefore a language, which no longer relates language to enumerable or combinable objects, nor to transmitting voices,

but to immanent limits that are ceaselessly displaced – hiatuses, holes or tears that we would never notice, or would attribute to mere tiredness, if they did not suddenly widen in such a way as to receive something from the outside or from elsewhere.[16]

CHAPTER FIVE

Science and Logic

In this chapter, we look at the two chapters devoted to science and logic in *What is Philosophy?*, 'Functives and Concepts' and 'Prospects and Concepts'. They come after the chapters devoted to philosophy and before the chapter devoted to art. The first point to be made here is that these two chapters are not merely a third attempt to 'cast a plane over chaos', following those of art and philosophy. Rather, they correspond to a third and concluding moment in the long process of genesis we have been tracing throughout this book, which we call active or static genesis, after the passive or dynamic genesis of art and the sense or virtuality of philosophy. In fact, there are two distinct and successive moments of active or static genesis in *What is Philosophy?* It is science in 'Functives and Concepts' that corresponds to static *ontological* genesis, and logic in 'Prospects and Concepts' that corresponds to static *logical* genesis. Across the two chapters, Deleuze and Guattari themselves divide up science and logic into three distinct orders of what they call 'prospects': a first prospect of functives, which are 'scientific functions presented in discursive systems' (*WP?*, 117); a second prospect of logical propositions, which are 'acts of reference' with regard to 'already constituted states of affairs or bodies' (*WP?*, 138); a third prospect of opinions, which are 'subjective evaluations of judgements of taste' (*WP?*, 141). Indeed, it might even be suggested that, with the third prospect of opinion and the arrival of fully-formed representations and conscious subjects able to share them, the process of genesis the book outlines is complete and its justification retrospectively given (although, as we will discover, the process of genesis is never able to be completed).

In other words, as we have previously seen with art and philosophy, Deleuze and Guattari's concept of science and logic in these two chapters is fundamentally *metaphorical* or at least *positional*. Before being used to speak about anything recognizable as science or logic, it is employed to indicate a certain moment in the progression of genesis. (However, at the same time there is a complex methodological question raised here, insofar as science and logic are not simply philosophical concepts but correspond to that moment in genesis when referentiality in that objective sense we are used to arises for the first time.) This positionality can be seen in the way in which the 'referent' of science and logic changes throughout Deleuze's and Deleuze and Guattari's writings. In *The Fold*, calculus is used to speak of the first dynamic genesis, in which perception is formed from 'millions of differential microperceptions' (*F*, 81). In *Difference and Repetition*, as we have seen, it is used to speak of that successive moment of genesis, in which the Idea is made up of 'reciprocally determined' (*DR*, 183) components. And in *What is Philosophy?*, finally, it is used to speak of that concluding moment of static genesis, in which the virtual singularities left behind by philosophy are 'differenciated' (*WP?*, 126) to bring about actualized bodies.[1] Indeed, in the posthumous collection, *Desert Islands*, Deleuze speaks of the way that maths and science constitute 'technical models' (*DI*, 220), while in *Difference and Repetition* he speaks of science allowing 'correspondences without resemblance' (*DR*, 184) with other, non-scientific fields. And it is just this that complexifies, without entirely disqualifying, efforts by various commentators to produce a Deleuzian-inspired 'minor' maths or science, insofar as it is not exactly really-existing maths and science he is speaking about.[2] The inclusion of the word 'concept' in the titles of the chapters dealing with maths and science in *What is Philosophy?* indicates that, before all else, maths and science are to be understood *philosophically*, are components of the particular concept of philosophy that Deleuze and Guattari are attempting to construct.

In fact, what both 'Functives and Concepts' and 'Prospects and Concepts' trace is a progressive actualization. They follow a movement from the virtual singularities and internal relationships of the philosophical concept through the fully extended and individuated bodies of science and on to the general classes and categories of logic and opinion. To this extent, the overall trajectory *What is Philosophy?* outlines is from the preindividual intensity without subject of the passive syntheses of percept and affect through the sublimation and symbolization of concepts that form the rules for the production of objects and on to the final match between subject and object in the active syntheses of perception and affection. Deleuze and Guattari can be seen to be following an arc from the undifferenciated actuality of the first moment of genesis through the dematerialized virtuality of the second moment of genesis and back to the now fully differenciated actuality of the third moment of genesis. Science and logic return us to where we began with art. However, all of this is too simple. The actual of art is not the same as the actualized of science and logic. The former is unindividuated and disordered, while the latter is individuated and ordered. The former starts with that chaotic diversity with which the process of genesis begins, while the latter finishes with conscious and reproducible representations. In the end, as we will come to see, there *is* a real continuum between art and science and logic. The intensity that is produced at the end of the third passive genesis is what drives the process of individuation that runs through active genesis. The three successive stages we observed in passive genesis – coupling, resonance and forced movement – are repeated in a way in active genesis. It is for this reason that Deleuze and Guattari are able to suggest in *What is Philosophy?* that art and science 'intersect' (*WP?*, 198). But this intersection can take place only through the mediation of philosophy. The disordered sensation without idea of art and the idea without object of philosophy come together to make up the subject and object of science and logic.

Indeed as we have already indicated, the whole genesis of representation set out in *What is Philosophy?* broadly repeats the trajectory of Kant's *Critique of Pure Reason*, which similarly attempts to account for the conditions of experience. The three passive geneses of art replay Kant's Transcendental Deduction and its three syntheses of apprehension, reproduction and recognition. The virtual concept of philosophy replays Kant's Transcendental Analytic, in which the concepts necessary for thought are attempted to be deduced. And the active synthesis of science and logic through which virtual ideas are actualized replay the Kantian process of schematization, in which those concepts deduced from the possibility of thought about experience are now applied to the actual objects of experience. In other words, we see in Kant at first a move away from experience towards the concepts that make it possible and then a move back from these concepts towards the imaginatively schematized objects in which they can be seen. As Kant will remark of the structure of his book, it does not matter 'whether we proceed from the smallest element to the whole of pure reason or reverse-wise through its final end to each part'.[3] However, if Deleuze sets himself in his work the same task as Kant of accounting for the possibility of experience immanently, on the basis of experience itself, he also differs from Kant in several crucial regards. First of all, as we have seen, Kant does not understand the faculties associated with the syntheses (understanding, imagination and apperception) as arising in a genetic relationship with each other. Or, if he begins to do so, he ultimately installs a supervening transcendental faculty (apperception) that sits above and judges all the others. And this is not unrelated to Deleuze's other major criticism of Kant, which is that his method of Transcendental Deduction does not provide the conditions of real experience but only of possible experience. The 'categories' in Kant, which are meant to derive from experience, merely impose upon experience a pre-existing logic, to which experience in turn must conform. As Deleuze writes in *Kant's Critical Philosophy*: 'The understanding's legislative acts (categories) therefore constitute *general* laws, and are exercised on nature as objects of *possible* experience' (*KCP*, 62). As opposed to this, if in active synthesis there is a certain application of philosophical concepts to empirical reality, Deleuze is also very particular to insist that these concepts must be responsive to this reality. Deleuzian concepts do not pre-select experience or seek to determine what form it must take, but rather are conditioned at the same time as they condition in being the rules by which real experience is brought about. Or, as Deleuze says: 'Both terms of the difference [determinable intuition and determinant concept] must be conceived as pointing towards a principle of reciprocal determination' (*DR*, 173). This is exactly that 'double becoming' (*WP?*, 109) of Ideas, in *What is Philosophy?* and elsewhere, in which the philosophical concept at once entirely repeats reality and entirely makes over reality.

Deleuze follows the immediate post-Kantian thinker Salomon Maïmon in making his critique of Kant here, a critique to which it can be seen that Kant responds in his subsequent *Critique of Judgement*. But Deleuze's other resource in thinking the conditions of real experience in a way beyond Kant is Leibniz. It is in Leibniz's doctrine of sufficient reason that Deleuze finds a mutual coming together of the world and the categories used to think it. Leibniz substitutes the usual analyses of things in terms of essence, which treat only those qualities sufficient to distinguish the general category of a thing, whether it actually exists or not, with an analysis in terms of existence, which includes in principle everything that actually happens to a thing as part of its definition. As a result, there is an unprecedented breaking down of experience to its absolute singularities, because at once everything that happens to something is included in the definition of that thing and everything that happens is potentially itself able to become a thing. This is Leibniz's reciprocal doctrine of indiscernibility, in which every single thing, such as a leaf or a drop of water, has its own concept, so that if every concept includes everything it is also true that every concept corresponds to an individual thing.[4] And yet, as with Kant, if Leibniz approaches immanence in thinking the granular conditions of real experience, he also turns away from what he opens up. At the very moment he countenances the possibility of a non-selective and non-hierarchical concept, coming as close as it can to the singular individual it nominates, he introduces the notion of 'vice-diction', whereby God chooses only the 'best' of all possible worlds to pass into existence, by which Leibniz means a world of maximum of continuity and clarity, in which monads for all their differences and divergent points of view all 'converge' upon the same consistent world. It is exactly against this that Deleuze will insist on the crucial generative capacity of an incompossible 'vague' or 'ambiguous' object that would be forbidden by Leibniz, such as an Adam who does not sin or the various irreconcilable fates of the Roman king's son Sextus Tarquin (*F*, 61), which allows us to begin to think beyond the individuality of singular monads, and construct more general classes and categories.

In this chapter, we trace a progression from the fully differentiated but virtual concept through the individuation and differenciation of objects and on to the wider logical categories and subjects able to think them. In fact, it is an end point – and Deleuze and Guattari acknowledge this – that is shared with Kant. As they write in the 'Conclusion' of *What is Philosophy?*, repeating Kant's example from the *Critique of Pure Reason*: 'If cinnabar were sometimes red, sometimes black, sometimes light, sometimes heavy ... my empirical imagination would never find opportunity when representing red colour to bring to mind heavy cinnabar' (*WP?*, 202). But, as we will discover, their respective ways of getting there are different, and for Deleuze and Guattari the problem of genesis does not end even with the familiar notion of cinnabar, as it does for Kant. In *Difference and Repetition*, Deleuze draws a distinction between 'living' and 'dead' representations (*DR*, 262–5), and in *The Logic of Sense* and *What is Philosophy?* he speaks of the way in which philosophy 'counter-actualizes' (*LS*, 171–3) or 'counter-effectuates' (*WP?*, 159–60) the actual. And this is to say that, if Deleuze and Guattari are not directly opposed to representation in *What is Philosophy?*, they nevertheless understand it as part of an ongoing genesis that does not come to a halt with logical categories and subjects endowed with consciousness. Rather, the conclusion of genesis leads to further genesis or returns us to the beginning of genesis, which is to suggest that all three stages of genesis occur at the same time as reciprocally defining components of the concept of philosophy. And we pursue this analysis here through a reading of Deleuze and Guattari's notion of 'functives' in terms of Leibniz's monads, as outlined in the chapter 'Sufficient Reason' of Deleuze's *The Fold*. We then look at how the 'intensity' that is left over at the end of the third passive synthesis selects singularities and relationships from the philosophical concept to become individuated or actualized in a process Deleuze calls 'dramatization', as elaborated in the essay 'The Method of Dramatization'. We then identify the movement from science to logic or from the functive to the prospect in relation to the passage from good to common sense in the static ontological genesis and then from common sense to logical proposition in the static logical genesis through a reading of Deleuze's *The Logic of Sense*. Finally, we characterize the 'opinion' or 'signification' that comes after logic as a third prospect or culminating moment in genesis, through a reading, perhaps surprisingly, of Deleuze and Guattari's first collaboration, *Anti-Oedipus*.

* * *

In 'Functives and Concepts', Deleuze and Guattari speak of what they call 'functives' (*WP?*, 117), which are scientific propositions presented in discursive form. Functives, we might say, deal not so much with actual fact, as in real science, as with *facticity*, the constitution of fact or how fact comes about and is grasped in the world. Indeed, functives can be scientific, mathematical or even biological in character, but what strictly defines them is their attitude towards 'chaos'. The chaos that confronts functives is spoken of as 'containing all possible particles and drawing out all possible forms, which spring up only to disappear immediately, without consistency or reference, without consequence' (*WP?*, 118). It sounds like the chaos that comes before art – which also disappears as soon as it appears – but, crucially, it is a chaos that is also described as 'virtual' (*WP?*, 118). Deleuze and Guattari speak of it as the same chaos that philosophy confronts, but we might better describe it as the chaos *of* philosophy. In an understanding that very much goes against the independence of art, philosophy and science, but that on the contrary points to the genetic connection between them, what seems clear is that science begins with what is left behind by philosophy. The chaos science inherits is not the appearing and disappearing chaos of art but the chaos rendered 'consistent' (*WP?*, 118) of the virtual singularities and internal relations of philosophy, arriving in any order and at infinite speed. And what is it that the functives of science seek to do with these singularities and relations? In the first instance, they seek to slow them down, separate them and put them in an ordered sequence. As opposed to philosophy, which attempts to make chaos consistent and self-referential without losing its original intensity, functives begin the process of distinguishing its various parts, laying them out next to one another, and cancelling its intensity, so that it might form a bounded object. As Deleuze puts it in *Difference and Repetition*: '[Intensity] is cancelled by extension, extension being the process by which intensive difference is turned inside out and cancelled' (*DR*, 233). And it does this in the first instance by drawing a limit between two things, so that there is something inside and something outside. Or, to put this otherwise, this limit *is* something. That is, although the limits of functives introduce a limit into the world, they also constitute this world. Again, as Deleuze writes in *Difference and Repetition*: 'Good sense essentially distributes or repartitions: "on the one hand" and "on the other" are characteristic formulations' (*DR*, 224). And functives in *What is Philosophy?* similarly have – and even in a way allow – this extension-giving and boundary-drawing capacity. As Deleuze and Guattari write: 'The first functives are therefore the limit and the variable, and reference is a relationship between values of the variables, as abscissae of speeds, with the limit' (*WP?*, 118–19).

For those without mathematical training, functives here might be imagined as that line running across and either up or down a gridded graph, matching values on the *y*-axis (the limit or ordinate) with values on the *x*-axis (variables or abscissae). The line of a functive in a mathematical differential equation puts together values that not merely values that proportionally change (say, $^2/_3$ in relation to $^4/_6$), but values in which one is of a higher power than the other ($^{y^2}/_x = P$). Thus the derivative as the quotient of the two differentials that form a relation of the type d*y*/d*x* allows two otherwise incommensurable quantities to be determined precisely as their relationship to each other. Indeed, in the vanishingly small quantities of differentials or in something like the cusp of an inflected curve, in which the values on the *y*-axis move from positive to negative across a single point, there is implied a kind of infinity. And Deleuze and Guattari use this to suggest that in the functives of something like a differential equation infinity is able to be represented. Intensive change or velocity as limit or input on the *y*-axis is able to be matched with – or rather cancels itself out in giving rise to – extensive values as variables or output on the *x*-axis. In this regard, Deleuze and Guattari are able to suggest that the true post-calculus revolution in mathematics is not so much the discovery of infinitesimals as being able to work with infinity in order to give it a comparative value. As they write of the nineteenth-century German mathematician Georg Cantor's notion of transfinitude: 'What [Cantor's] theory of sets does is inscribe the limit within the infinite itself, without which there could be no limit: in its strict hierarchization, it installs a slowing down' (*WP?*, 120–1). And, more generally, the whole vocation of science is to give apparently absolute forms or forces a numerical value or limit: 'The speed of light, absolute zero, the quantum of action, the Big Bang' (*WP?*, 119). Hence the defining quality of mathematical functives is that at no point do they simply break off or have a gap or lacuna within them. Everything can be represented and given a value somewhere on their *x*- and *y*-axes. Or, if something cannot be represented in one functive, it can be in another, which begins where it breaks off. In this sense, the whole world can be understood as an endless series of functives, each one starting where another ends, almost like individual perspectives onto the world (and the world for its part would be nothing outside these functives).[5] It is for this reason that the 'plane of reference' (*WP?*, 118) of maths and science – that which the functives form and to which they refer – is not single and united like the plane of immanence of philosophy, but rather made up of innumerable limits that are always splitting, reforming and multiplying. And, against the common understanding, the project of maths and science is not to unify or gather everything together under a single overarching equation, but always to invent, create, produce new functives, thus breaking with any possible unity (*WP?*, 206–7).

In fact, Deleuze and Guattari describe three different functives, which correspond to three successive stages of individuation. The first is the 'state of affairs' (*WP?*, 122), which arises not from the simple matching of limit and variable, but – because the intensive limit can be seen only through its corresponding variable, in a kind of reciprocal determination – the intersection of two independent variables, which produces in turn a third variable as the 'state of affairs'. In a sense, the state of affairs represents a first 'touching down' (*WP?*, 119) of the intensity and virtual singularities of philosophy. The intensive ordinate selects which values are to be represented as abscissae, while these extensive abscissae are the form in which the intensity of the ordinate is expressed. Deleuze and Guattari speak of states of affairs in terms of 'ordered mixtures' that come out of 'closed' systems (*WP?*, 123), that is, each particular state of affairs does not take into account any other, and they compare them to 'derivative' functions in mathematics (*WP?*, 122) because, like a derivative, in states of affairs two 'differentials' of potentially infinite different powers are compared and placed in relation to each other. The next type of functive Deleuze and Guattari call a 'thing' (*WP?*, 122). Here, by contrast, the variables that make it up are not merely mixtures but combine to form relations, even if as we will see what is produced remains at the same level as the variables that make it up. As Deleuze and Guattari write: 'A thing is always related to several axes at once according to variables that are functions of each other, even if the internal unity remains undetermined' (*WP?*, 122). They speak of things in terms of the 'interactions' between 'coupled' systems

(*WP?*, 1234), which is to suggest that things form relations with other things (and this echo of the 'coupling' that characterizes the first stage of passive genesis is significant here), although they also later speak of this second stage of the functive as transitory, a 'passage' from the state of affairs to the body through the 'intermediary of a potential or power' (*WP?*, 154). And the third and final functive Deleuze and Guattari describe as a 'body' (*WP?*, 122), which as opposed to the simple 'undetermined' unity of the thing involves an 'invariant and a group of transformations' (*WP?*, 122). With the body, indeed, the possible substitution of elements that make it up, as opposed to the thing, becomes increasingly limited, until there is, as Deleuze and Guattari say, a 'perfect individuation' (*WP?*, 123). Deleuze and Guattari describe the body in terms of the 'communication' between 'separated, unconnected' systems (*WP?*, 123), which implies that bodies take the form they do in relation to other bodies.[6] Examples of the body Deleuze and Guattari provide are the forms of Euclidean geometry such as a triangle, which is made up of three vertices or singular points and ordinary points stretching between them, and biological species, which grow and develop in response both to internal (endo-referential) and external (exo-referential) factors (*WP?*, 123).

What Deleuze and Guattari are implicitly speaking of here with functives is the Leibnizian theory of monads. What we find in this passage from states of affairs through things to bodies is a vocabulary to describe how we move from the infinite and self-identical attributes of God through to the infinitely divisible and discernible monads that are his earthly expression. But, if this passage is narrated in *What is Philosophy?* as a movement from a single undivided concept through to perfectly individuated and distinguishable bodies, in fact what Deleuze and Guattari find in Leibniz is an alternative to the long-running Aristotelian argument that individuals are formed by the 'breaking down' of more general categories. On the contrary, in Leibniz, individuals are built up from smaller predicates and differences, and it is on the basis of these individuals that wider categories are formed. As Deleuze writes in *Difference and Repetition*: 'There is a differenciation of differenciation which integrates and welds together the differenciated' (*DR*, 217).[7] And we see this also in 'Functives and Concepts'. We begin with the state of affairs, which is the first cancellation of intensity in its spacing out or extension as points along a line. But the state of affairs is merely the first emergence of order out of chaos, so that, although the variables that make it up intersect, they are 'independent' of each other and produce only other variables. Each functive is 'closed', bearing no relation to any other, but tracing only a momentary limit or series of stopping points that soon break off to be replaced by another functive that has no memory of it (*WP?*, 153). Then on the next level we have the thing, in which the sometimes several variables that make it up are not simply independent, but related to each other without anything beyond that relation. Finally, we have the fully individuated body, which is 'invariant' although taking different forms. Here we can see, in a kind of extension of the logic of the thing, that each body is at once 'separate and unconnected' and that each 'communicates' with all the others. And all of this is like the logic of the Leibnizian monad, in which each monad expresses the entire world, including all the other monads that make it up, but only expresses clearly that portion of it closest to its own body. In other words, each monad is composed of a singularity that extends over all the other ordinary points that make up its body, which represents the way in which it dominates or offers a perspective onto these points, up to that point where another singularity begins, which equally extends over a series of ordinary points, including that original singularity, that make up *its* body.[8] And overseeing all these monads, ensuring that they converge on the same world, for all their different perspectives onto it, is God, who chooses the 'best of all possible worlds', by which Leibniz means a maximum continuity and compossibility of monads. And in all of this, as we can see, what Deleuze and Guattari are tracing is a progressive building up or 'integration' of monads from those original singularities of states of affairs through a repeated differenciation.[9]

It is in the chapter 'Sufficient Reason' of Deleuze's *The Fold* that we can find a similar passage to that from the concept through to the individuated body in 'Functives and Concepts', described in terms of that from the auto-inclusive 'infinity' (*F*, 44) of the Identical through to the infinitely divisible 'individual notion' (*F*, 67) of the monad. The whole trajectory Deleuze characterizes as going from 'inflexion' to 'inclusion', that is, from the 'event' that happens to the line or point to the incorporation of this 'event' in the line or point (*F*, 41). The first stage in this procedure of sufficient reason that would make the event equal to its predicates is the 'Definable'. This is the initial connection between predicates or parts, which takes the absolutely simple notion, A, B and so on, of the Identical and expresses it in the form AB, which breaks the whole of the Identical into extensive parts, thus rendering everything comparable, insofar as it is submitted to a principle of similitude (F, 46). Then comes the 'Conditionable', in which there arise for the first time 'relations' between the various parts that make it up (F, 46). Here there is no longer an extension without limits, as with the Definable, but an 'intension' (F, 47) converging towards a limit. And this intension or intensity produces what Leibniz calls a 'texture', as something like the 'sum' of the Conditionable's inner qualities (F, 47). It is this that allows Leibniz to speak of the 'characteristic' with regard to the Conditionables, as opposed to the mere 'combination' formed by the Definables (F, 47). But this same characteristic is to be found in several Conditionables (or, inversely, each Conditionable has several characteristics), insofar as they only tend towards limits (F, 49). As Deleuze writes of Leibniz's conception of gold: 'We have more than one notion of the same subject, for example weight and malleability for gold' (F, 50). The final stage Deleuze outlines from Leibniz is the 'Individual', which is marked by an 'infinite convergence' (F, 49), so that, unlike the Conditionable, there can be no two identical Individuals. Each Individual, again in a difference from the Conditionable, which comprises several characteristics, lies at the intersection of an infinite number of characteristics or qualities, but its absolutely singular identity is given by which particular combination of qualities it expresses clearly and which confusedly. (Again, each Individual expresses the same world, including that expressed by other Individuals, although clearly only that part of it closest to its body.) Another Individual begins when *its* singularity is able to offer another perspective onto the world, expressing clearly what its neighbours can express only confusedly.

Throughout, we can observe an intricate series of parallels between the process of 'inclusion' that Deleuze outlines in 'Sufficient Reason' and those successive stages of 'individuation' that Deleuze and Guattari set out in 'Functives and Concepts'. In the Definables, there is a shift from 'primary or indefinable Identicals' to 'simple derived beings, defined by two primary beings in a simple relation' (F, 45), and this is like the state of affairs, which comes about as a result of the intersection not between a limit and a variable but between two variables, which produces a third variable. In the

Conditionables, the extended parts of the Definables, which were previously without relation, 'acquire relations by becoming requisites or the [reciprocal] definers of the derived' (F, 46), and this is like the thing, which is related to several axes at once, axes which are functions of each other, even if their internal unity remains undetermined. In Individuals, the singular substance of the monad can be 'interior to movement, or a unity of change that can be active' (F, 55), and this is like the body, which is constituted by an invariant in relation to a group of movements. Similarly, in terms of the process of individuation itself, with the Definables, it is an 'infinity by way of cause that constitutes wholes and parts' (F, 46), like that infinity of the intensive limit that allows the extensive values of the variable to be selected to form a state of affairs. With the Conditionables, it is not a matter of simple definers or limits, as with the Definables, but of 'designating conditions, limits and differential relations among the limits' (F, 47), and this movement towards convergence is like the division into individuated bodies from the subsisting state of affairs that is the thing. And with Individuals, something is 'no longer defined either by itself [as with the Identicals] or by the "limit" of a series [as with both the Definables and Conditionables, in different ways], but by a law of order or continuity that classifies limits or transforms series into a "totality"' (F, 50), and this is like bodies, whose perfect individuation comes about as a result of their being in communication with other Individuals in a convergence guaranteed by a pre-established harmony or law of continuity.

* * *

However, we might pause at this point and ask how it is that we can pass from Identicals to Individuals or from the concept to the body? What drives this process of individuation whereby the disordered virtual singularities and internal relations of philosophy are turned first into ordered and extended points and then into integrated bodies? And what continues to drive this process of actualization beyond individual bodies or monads through to more general classes and categories and ultimately into logical propositions and opinions? For, as Deleuze and Guattari write in 'Prospects and Concepts', the interaction of bodies in individuation already conditions a 'proto-perceptibility' and 'proto-affectivity' that we will see in the 'perceptions' and 'affections' of opinion (*WP?*, 154). In fact, as Deleuze makes clear in *Difference and Repetition*, it is not a direct passage from Ideas to individuated bodies. Differenciation, the externally determined elaboration of points and qualities in empirical objects, does not immediately follow from differentation, the internally determined production of singularities and relations between elements in the virtual Idea. Rather, it is mediated by a process of 'dramatization', which Deleuze compares to the Kantian 'schemata', whereby the categories of Understanding are applied to appearances. We have already seen the equivalent of Kantian synthesis in the passive syntheses of art, in which we pass from diverse sensation to a certain thought of time. In the third synthesis of art we get the dissolution of the subject and the production of intensity. Then arises the virtual of philosophy, which contains the rules for the determinability of experience. Now in the three active syntheses of science we get a putting together of the passive syntheses of art with the virtual of philosophy to lead us towards the actual representation of objects and a subject able to think them. In a way, as we will see, we have a repetition of the three passive syntheses of art, but mediated through the virtual idea or concept of philosophy. Just as in Kant, the virtual Idea is worth nothing in itself, but must be taken outside itself, in order to become an object. And what takes the idea out of itself is intensity in a process of dramatization (*DR*, 245). But, equally, intensity merely loses itself unless guided by the rule or blueprint of the Idea. As Deleuze writes, in echo of Kant's famous 'Thoughts without content are empty, intuitions without concepts are blind',[10] of the mutual coming together of Idea and intensity in the three active syntheses: 'A concept alone is completely incapable of specifying or dividing itself ... However, the [Kantian] schema does not account for the power with which it acts. Everything changes when the dynamisms are posited no longer as the schemata of concepts but as dramas of Ideas' (*DR*, 218). The virtual singularities and internal relations of the Idea are taken out of themselves by the progressive playing out of intensity, while intensity itself is progressively cancelled or explicated in the form of extended points and the relations found between them. In a sense, intensity comes first. It is obviously already there in the passive geneses before the Idea, and as we have seen it is what literally creates the space in which differenciation takes place. But, in another sense, intensity can be seen only through the actualized forms in which it is found. It does not exist outside those individuated bodies it makes possible, although it is not to be reduced to them. Intensity is, as Deleuze says, 'transcendent': it is not so much given, as that by which the given is given (*DR*, 222). And yet – and this is Deleuze's difference from Kant – if intensity is that by which the given is given, it is also at each point only the given.

We see all of this in 'Functives and Concepts' in the initial functive that constitutes the state of affairs. For if it can be understood as a simple matching up of the intensive values of the ordinates with the extensive values of the abscissae, it also represents a certain *selection* by ordinates of abscissae. If intensity can be seen only through extensity – which is why the state of affairs is composed of two variables rather than a limit and a variable – it is nevertheless intensity that decides where these extensities will be, where the limit will be drawn (or, more simply, just *is* this extensity and limit, insofar as space itself does not exist before it). As Deleuze and Guattari write in 'Functives and Concepts': 'A state of affairs does not actualize a chaotic virtual without taking from it a potential that is distributed in the system of co-ordinates' (*WP?*, 122). And this is to suggest that this intensity is not entirely exhausted by this formed limit. With the result that, even as we move through the successive stages of individuation, and this intensity is progressively explicated, it nevertheless remains. The successive stage of the 'thing', between the first extension of the state of affairs and the fully integrated or individuated body, is precisely described as an 'intension', made up out of the 'sum of its inner qualities' (*F*, 47). It is undoubtedly with the thing that we see most clearly intensity beginning to gather up points or predicates in a continuity or convergence on the way to becoming an individuated body. (The mathematical analogy would be that 'power series' or repeated 'differentiation of differentiation' that would also bring about an integration.[11]) Finally, if with the fully individuated body there appears for the first time a certain internality or self-selection, insofar as it does not merely interact but actually communicates with the outside, there is nevertheless an equivalent external selection or selection by another that makes this possible. If the external factors that will count can be chosen by the body, the body also takes the form it does because of a principle greater than it (in Leibniz, for example, God). This is what Deleuze and

Guattari mean in 'Functives and Concepts' by speaking of bodies in terms of both endo- and exo-reference. And it is why, with regard to evolution and embryology, Deleuze opposes the doctrines both of epigenesis, in which the embryo is simply the outcome of external forces, and preformism, in which the development of the embryo is merely the playing out of a predetermined process (*DR*, 251). Rather, the true enigma of the living creature's growth is that the 'egg', even at the earliest stage of its development, at once shapes the world and is shaped by the world. As Deleuze writes in *Difference and Repetition*: 'The vital egg is already a field of individuation, and the embryo is a pure individual, and the one in the other testifies to the primacy of individuation over actualization – in other words, over both organization and the determination of species' (*DR*, 250). And this is also to be seen in Leibniz's monadology, in which monads are at once able to select which world they are the outcome of and are the infinite outcome of this world: 'The world is in the monad, but the monad lives for the world. God himself conceives individual notions only as a function of the world that they express, and chooses them only through a calculus of the world' (*F*, 50–1).

It is this intensity and the question of selection it opens up that Deleuze and Guattari speak of in 'Functives and Concepts' in the guise of a discussion of the role of scientists' names in science. As we have already seen, Deleuze and Guattari analyze the way in which the world is actualized through a series of splits or bifurcations, a boundary drawn between two things that were previously regarded as the same. And this can be understood as akin to the monadic process of selection, insofar as the monad is the decision as to what to make clear and what to leave confused – and the agent or intensity behind this process in science can be called the scientist's 'proper name' (*WP?*, 128). Examples of this split or bifurcation Deleuze and Guattari give in 'Functives and Concepts' are brought about not only in the elements, as in nineteenth-century Russian chemist Dmitry Mendeleyev's periodic table, but also between rational and real number and even between Newtonian and Einsteinian conceptions of the universe (*WP?*, 123–4). Indeed, in the light of this split – and this is important in terms of the relationship between differenciation and integration, and perhaps even, as we will see, good and common sense – it is not merely pre-existing unities that are prospectively split, but such unities can themselves now be regarded only as splits-to-come, in effect, only the putting-back-together of what is already split. As Deleuze and Guattari write: 'But in the other simultaneous direction, from after to before, the whole number appears as a particular case of the fractional number, or the rational as a particular case of a 'break' in a linear set of points' (*WP?*, 124). (It is for this reason that Deleuze and Guattari speak of integration and differenciation as the 'two poles' (*WP?*, 126) of functives, which is ultimately to say that integration is only an effect of differenciation, a certain taking further of differenciation. And this is just as Deleuze in *Difference and Repetition* says that in biological classification it is not individuals that are an illusion in relation to species, but species that are an illusion in relation to individuals (*DR*, 250).) It is for this reason, finally, that scientist's names work differently in science from how philosophers' do in philosophy. In philosophy, as we have seen, philosophers' names (or the philosophical systems that they nominate) *double* what they speak of, which is to say the prior philosophical system, and through it the world, that is their subject. That is, when one philosophical system adds a component to the one before it, it does not so much refute it as propose another entirely different explanation for it. Thus when Kant adds the component of time to Descartes' Cogito, it is not that Descartes is suddenly wrong or outmoded, but that henceforth what he is saying can be grasped only for the reason that Kant himself provides: the equivalence of the 'I' to itself can now only be understood as taking place through the invisible medium of time (*WP?*, 31–2). By contrast, a scientific system does not leave the previous one intact, but either introduces a split within it or shows that it is only the putting together of a previous split. It does not repeat it as whole and only able to be doubled, but as merely a 'particular case' (*WP?*, 126) and the effect of a split either in the past or yet to come. Thus real does not simply break with rational number, but reveals rational number as a subset of real. Einstein does not simply break with Newton, but reveals Newton's classical as a subset of Einstein's quantum mechanics, applicable only in particular circumstances. It is for this reason that Deleuze and Guattari are able to characterize science as existing in a 'serial, ramifying' rather than a 'stratigraphic' time, and the history of science as 'paradigmatic' rather than 'syntagmatic' (*WP?*, 124), insofar as each successive scientific system breaks with what comes before, meaning that we do not continually have to go back to it, as opposed to philosophy, where it is always a matter of re-reading the same texts differently (*WP?*, 124–5).[12]

Crucially, however, scientists play another role in 'Functives and Concepts'. For, immediately after speaking of them in terms of 'proper names', Deleuze and Guattari go on to speak of them as 'ideal intercessors' or 'partial observers', in which they no longer function as 'total observers' (*WP?*, 129), like a monad or better the God behind all monads. Indeed, the expression 'partial observer' is particularly appropriate with regard to this second conception of the role of scientists because, above all, it is a matter here of 'seeing' (*WP?*, 128), which implies a certain going beyond of the strictly numerical limits of functives, but not necessarily a seeing of everything. Indeed, an example of this 'seeing' that Deleuze and Guattari provide, originally in Deleuze's *The Logic of Sense* (*LS*, 64–5), lies in the field of mathematics itself, when mathematicians 'indicate the course of calculation and anticipate the results without ever being able to bring them about' (*WP?*, 128). But perhaps the most important example of this second type of functive or second kind of relationship to the functive that Deleuze and Guattari provide – which also appeared before in Deleuze's *The Fold* (*F*, 21–2) – is the problem of the geometric cone, as originally set out by Leibniz and then by the seventeenth-century French mathematician Girard Desargues. Here it is precisely a matter of a 'partial observer', insofar as every observer of the cone sees something different and irreconcilable about it. Even an observer standing at the point of the cone, who is notionally in a position to see everything about it, in fact only sees some things about it and not others. As Deleuze and Guattari write: 'But perspective fixes a partial observer, like an eye, at the summit of the cone, and so grasps contours without grasping reliefs or the quality of the surface that refers to another observer position' (*WP?*, 129). However, as Deleuze and Guattari insist, this inability to see everything or necessary generalization is not at all a simple limit to knowledge. Rather, it represents a different kind of knowledge. In their words, this scientific perspectivism or even relativism represents not so much the 'relativity of truth' as the 'truth of the relative' (*WP?*, 130).[13] Or, as they elsewhere put it – against the common understanding of science, but also against Leibniz' principle of sufficient reason, which is directed by an all-seeing God – what is properly at stake in science is a 'demon' of the kind spoken of by the nineteenth-century British experimental physicist James Maxwell. In a way, it is because this demon cannot be grasped that all else can be (or, to put this otherwise, this demon must remain unknown because it accounts for so many incompatible and yet really existing results). As Deleuze and Guattari write: 'It is not a question of what [the "subjects" of science] can or cannot do, but of the way in which they are perfectly positive, from the point of view of concept or function, even in what they do not know and cannot do' (*WP?*, 129).

It is in the essay 'The Method of Dramatization', originally delivered as a lecture to the French Society of Philosophy in 1967, during the writing of *Difference and Repetition*, that Deleuze addresses the question of what exactly it is that drives this stage of active genesis, what takes the Idea away from the virtual and leads it towards an object with extension and qualities. It is what Deleuze calls the 'spatio-temporal dynamism' of 'dramatization' ('D', 94), describing it in the following terms: 'Beneath organization and specification, we discover nothing more than spatio-temporal dynamisms: that is to say, pure syntheses of space. The most general characteristic of branching, order and chaos, right on up to generic and specific characteristics, already depend on such directions of development' ('D', 96). It is a process that, as we have seen, Deleuze compares to Kantian schematism, which similarly takes the abstract concept and gives it to the objects of intuition. However, consistent with Deleuze's critical method, if this moment of active genesis is consistent with schematism, there are also important differences between them. In Kant, for all his emphasis on the creativity of schematism – 'This schematism of our understanding ... is an art concealed in the depths of the human soul, whose real modes of activity nature is hardly ever likely to allow us to discover'[14] – the concept still passes largely unchanged from the faculty of Understanding, where it originates, through the mediation of Imagination and into the object. Experience in effect is seen through, and arises as an effect of, a prior logical concept, meaning that it can be recognized only insofar as it conforms to this concept. By contrast, if in Deleuze it is the virtual singularities and relations of the Idea that are directed towards the object, this Idea also does not exist outside the object and can be seen only through it. The dramatization of active genesis, whereby through a process of differenciation the virtual singularities and relations of the Idea are progressively actualized, is not merely passive as in Kant's schemata but precisely active, insofar as it brings about something that was not already present in the Idea. Again, as Deleuze emphasizes in 'Dramatization': 'However, we must emphasize the absolute condition of non-resemblance [between the Idea and its actualization]: the species or the quality do not resemble the differential relations that it incarnates, no more so than the singularities resemble the organized extension which actualizes them' ('D', 100). And it is this that is implied, we would say, in the essential 'I don't know' (*WP?*, 128) to be seen in the sciences. But, again – and this is another distinction from Kant – for all the emphasis on the 'activity' of dramatization in Deleuze, it is nevertheless not the activity of a conscious agent. The first stage of active genesis, individuation, is brought about through either a proper name or a 'necessary reason' (*WP?*, 126). And a second stage, which we have begun to elaborate, is a brought about by an 'ideal intercessor' or 'partial observer'. And this is as Deleuze speaks in 'Dramatization' first of a 'larval' or 'embryonic' subject ('D', 94) that brings about individuation or good sense and then a 'difference operator' or 'obscure precursor' ('D', 97) that brings about a second moment of differenciation or common sense.

In 'Dramatization', Deleuze sets out the process by which intensity 'dramatizes' or differenciates Ideas in three successive stages. These three stages of active genesis echo the three similar stages of passive genesis (with the difference that they are spatial and operate through the Idea and larval subject, whereas the passive syntheses are temporal and lead up to the Idea and dissolve the subject): 'coupling', 'internal resonance' and 'inevitable movement' ('D', 97). It is the first of these, 'coupling', that has largely been spoken of so far in the context of 'Functives and Concepts', and it is described in 'Dramatization' in terms recognizable to us as, 'even when we cannot [yet] distinguish actual parts, we still single out remarkable regions or points' ('D', 96). But Deleuze goes on in 'Dramatization' to outline two subsequent stages of differenciation that we have already seen hinted at in 'Functives and Concepts', in which we have no longer simply fully individuated bodies or monads made up of extended points and the sum of their predicates but independent actualized objects made up of differential qualities. The first is 'internal resonance', in which, as opposed to the divisible parts of 'coupling', there is a 'synthesis of qualification or specification' ('D', 96), which differenciates not the singular points but the relationship between qualities of the Idea. And the second is 'inevitable movement', in which, beyond both coupling and resonance, but arising out of them, there is a kind of 'amplitude that goes beyond the most basic series themselves' ('D', 97). (Deleuze will say that the quantitative differences of coupling and the qualitative differences of resonance are not possible without each other – 'There is no quality without an extension underlying it, and no species without organic parts or points' ('D', 96) – and in some ways 'inevitable movement' is the putting together of these two processes.) This progression from 'coupling' through 'internal resonance' and on to 'inevitable movement' can sound merely like that 'individuation' we have already looked at in 'Functives and Concepts' – and in some respects it is – but we want to suggest that what is also at stake is something that takes us beyond individual monads, which are defined by the rule of convergence of sufficient reason. In fact, we want to suggest that when Deleuze speaks of the 'internal resonance' produced by putting 'intensive series', we might say monads, into relationships, this is no longer ruled by convergence but opens up a certain *divergence*. This 'divergence' ('D', 102) is only hinted at towards the end of 'Dramatization' – and Deleuze generally has trouble working it into his discussion of monadic individuation, as in the separate chapter devoted to it that comes after 'Sufficient Reason' in *The Fold* – but it seems to be implied by his description of what he calls the 'difference operator' or 'obscure precursor' there ('D', 97), which again we would want to relate to the 'ideal intercessors' and 'partial observers' of 'Functives and Concepts'. Here is how Deleuze describes the actions of the 'obscure precursor' in 'Dramatization', in a way that suggests that they go beyond that extension of points and summation of predicates of individuation, understood as a kind of good sense, and begins to explain how it is that the differenciation of the Idea is able to produce something that is not already in either its singularities or qualities: 'A lightning bolt flashes between different intensities, but it is preceded by an obscure precursor, invisible, imperceptible, which determines in advance the path as in a negative relief, because this path is first the agent of communication between series of differences' ('D', 97).[15]

* * *

Deleuze, as we have seen, outlines in 'Dramatization' three distinct stages of active synthesis: coupling, internal resonance and inevitable movement. The first, coupling, we have already looked at in some detail. It is the process Deleuze and Guattari call 'individuation', in which that intensity deriving from the end of passive genesis is cancelled, first as single points extended along a line and then as the coming together of these points in an individual body. But the crucial aspect of this individuation, even though it is not immediately apparent, is that the final body or monad produced is nothing more than the 'sum' of the predicates that make it up (*F*, 47). In other words, as Leibniz emphasizes in his doctrine of sufficient reason, the predicates that make up a monad are 'analytic' (*LS*, 131) or 'non-attributive' (*F*, 53). Each applies with an equal directness or immediacy to the world they make up, only more or less clearly. There is no wider generality, when two monads are defined by the same quality or the same quality can be seen in two different monads, or perhaps only in the transitional stage of the 'thing', in which the final individuation is not complete. As Deleuze puts it in the chapter 'Incompossibility, Individuality, Liberty' of *The Fold*: 'We begin with the world as if with a series of inflections or events: it is a pure emission of singularities. Here, for example, are the three singularities [that make up Adam]: to be the first man, to live in a garden of paradise, to have a wife created from one's own rib. And then a fourth: sinning' (*F*, 60). The second moment of active genesis, internal resonance, is what we might think of as the succeeding stage of actualization. It precisely puts qualities or predicates together that do not usually belong together to produce something that is not simply to be found in them or not merely to be reduced to them. That is, predicates here are not analytic but *synthetic*, in that they are not equivalent to the object in which they are found, but help to create a new object. Leibniz's famous example – which he ultimately rejects – is an Adam, hitherto defined by the predicates first man, living in the garden of paradise, out of whose rib Eve is created and sinner, to whom the predicate 'resistance to temptation' is added (*F*, 61). What is produced is not so much a contradiction, insofar as it is not, to the extent that it is predicate of existence not essence, a matter of opposition, but what Leibniz calls a 'vice-diction', insofar as it points, against an order in which monads are defined by a continuity in which the difference between them is meant to disappear, to the possibility of other worlds. Now we have a world in which it is possible that the 'same' Adam both sins and does not sin or, put otherwise, different worlds that do not converge towards but diverge from each other. Nevertheless, it is this moment of putting irreconcilable qualities together that Deleuze insists is a necessary part of genesis, the process by which objects become not merely the analytic sum of their predicates but a generality that can be used in different circumstances, that can cross unconnected worlds and still be understood. As he puts it with respect to *an* Adam, who is not perhaps *the* Adam we know but who can still be called the same name: 'It is not simply that the fifth singularity [that Adam resists temptation] contradicts the fourth, "sinning", such that a choice has to be made between the two. It is that the lines of prolongation that go from this fifth to the three others are not convergent, in other words, they *do not pass through common values*' (F, 61).

The third and final stage of 'Dramatization' – again, repeating in a way what we have already seen with the passive geneses of art – is 'inevitable movement', in which, through the operation of the 'dark precursor' of the second stage, both a recognizable object and a subject able to recognize it are produced. If resonance involves a certain object = x or 'communication between differences' ('D', 97) and subject = x or 'difference operator' ('D', 97), both of which are incompossible, unable to be rendered consistent or reduced to their constituent parts, it is also true that each is possible only because of the other. The incompossible subject = x able to span different worlds arises only because of a certain object = x it is able to recognize, and this incompossible object = x arises only because of a subject = x able to recognize it. This is again Deleuze's version of the transcendental object = x in the Transcendental Deduction of the *Critique of Pure Reason*[16], but unlike Kant Deleuze does not understand it as ready-made. In Kant, the object = x is simply a pre-existing object or object-form that underwrites the unity of the subject by providing the empty form under which different cognitions can be synthesized. In Deleuze, by contrast, it is only as a result of the relationship between the two that object and subject come about, in a process Deleuze describes as an 'amplitude that goes beyond the most basic series [we might say coupling and even resonance] themselves' ('D', 97). Indeed, it is both the 'obscure' subject and the 'incompossible' object that are in a way done away with to produce the final actualized subject and object, as is apparent in this otherwise obscure passage in *What is Philosophy?*, in which Deleuze and Guattari speak of the way that in Heisenberg's uncertainty principle in quantum mechanics an 'objective state of affairs' is able to be attained, provided the 'respective positions of two of its particles are outside of the field of actualization' (*WP?*, 129). And it is just this separation of subject and object after their momentary coming together in resonance that Deleuze calls 'inevitable movement' in 'Dramatization'. It is precisely through this 'inevitable movement' that we end up not simply with an individuated body made up of extended parts and qualities, but a fully actualized object not defined by the sum of its qualities and able to be used in different contexts. (As Deleuze makes clear in 'Dramatization', the first moment of active synthesis, coupling, can be understood as the drawing out of the virtual singularities of the Idea in extension, and the second moment of active synthesis, internal resonance, can be understood as the differenciation of the virtual relations between parts of the Idea. As he also makes clear, this extension of singularities in extension is not possible outside of the differenciation of quality, just as this differenciation of quality is not possible outside the extension of singularities. Additionally, it is this coming together of the first and second moments in the third moment of inevitable movement that makes both of those previous movements possible. However, the truly difficult interpretive question is the suggestion here that these spatio-temporal dynamisms Deleuze speaks of in 'Dramatization' do not just bring about individuation but take us beyond individuation to fully actualized and differenciated objects and subjects. To the extent that bodies in *The Fold* and *What is Philosophy?* appear to be defined by convergence, we would say we are not yet at that stage of the second active synthesis or what Deleuze calls 'common sense'. However, in another way, along the lines of the retrospective nature of active synthesis itself, where later stages explain earlier stages or earlier stages already contain later stages, perhaps bodies can also be the name for the outcome of that third stage of 'dramatization', inevitable movement, that Deleuze describes in 'Dramatization'.[17])

It is in *The Logic of Sense* that Deleuze traces in greatest detail this relationship between coupling and resonance, individuation and differenciation and convergence and divergence. In the chapter 'Static Ontological Genesis', he outlines a trajectory from what he calls 'good sense', in which individuals are made up of 'singularities', laid out next to each other, each of which expresses a world that is ultimately consistent with others, through to 'common sense', in which we are confronted with a 'single ambiguous sign' that crosses worlds that are 'divergent' from each other (LS, 131). But, again, the crucial aspect for us here is how this movement proceeds by means of a certain 'incompossibility' (LS, 130), brought about by what we have seen Deleuze call in 'Dramatization' an 'obscure precursor' and in *What is Philosophy?* a 'partial observer'. In asking how we pass from 'good' to 'common' sense, that is, from individuated bodies to differenciated objects and then to wider classes and categories, Deleuze at first canvases Husserl's post-Kantian solution of a 'sense-bestowing Ego' that 'transcends the monad' (LS, 129). However, as we have seen, Deleuze rejects this 'objective transcendency' (LS, 129), whereby a pre-existing subject simply imposes its ready-made categories, so that experience becomes immanent to it. Rather, for him, it is only *within* the difference or divergence of experience that the possibility of something transcending it arises. As he writes: 'The Ego as a knowing subject appears only when something is identified inside worlds which are nevertheless incompossible and across series which are nevertheless divergent' (LS, 130). (All of this is perhaps what Deleuze and Guattari mean in *What is Philosophy?* when they suggest that science is 'inspired less by the concern for unification in an ordered actual system than by a desire not to distance itself too much from chaos, to seek out potentials in order to seize and carry off a part of that which haunts it' (WP?, 156).) It is again what Deleuze speaks of in 'Static Ontological Genesis' as an object = x that is identified between divergent series or between incompossible worlds that is more than any individual monad; and the Ego that identifies it would similarly be more than any particular monad, thus giving rise to something that is not to be found in either of them. Again, Deleuze puts it in terms of an irreconcilability of sinning and not sinning that can nevertheless belong to the 'same' Adam, or the various diverse appearances – ellipse, hyperbola, parabola, straight line – that are nevertheless properties of the 'same' cone (LS, 130). Deleuze then turns to a famous short story by Argentine writer Jorge Luis Borges, one of the key exponents of a contemporary aesthetic of the Neo-Baroque he outlines in *The Fold*, 'The Garden of Forking Paths', in which various possibilities are suggested for the main character – 'Fang can kill the intruder, the intruder can kill Fang, both can be saved, both can die' (*LS*, 131) – without any way of deciding which actually takes place, and yet all occurring in 'similar' worlds and to the 'same' character. In each case here, as opposed to the individuation of the first level of actualization, in which predicates describe bodies analytically, predicates synthetically define 'persons' (*LS*, 131), who are more than the mere sum of the qualities that make them up and who run across worlds that would otherwise be irreconcilable. It is at this point that the possibility of more general classes and categories arises, based on these singular yet ambiguous persons, 'essentially affected by an increasing or decreasing generality in a continuous specification against a categorical background' (*LS*, 131). That is to say, instead of the individual being an effect of the predicates or worlds that make it up, breaking off only when another expresses more clearly what they express confusedly, with persons it is the predicates or worlds themselves that become variables. It is *they* that change or even appear or disappear, while the person remains the same.

To say all this more slowly, at the end of the ontological genesis we have persons, on the basis of which we have 'classes with one single member that they constitute and properties with one constant which belongs to them' (*LS*, 132). And we might think of this single-member class as a certain 'signified' to go with the previous 'denoted' of good sense and 'manifested' of common sense. (In 'Static Logical Genesis', Deleuze speaks of individuated bodies in terms of a 'denoted' and the object = x brought about by its conjunction with a subject in terms of a 'manifested' (*LS*, 137).) But, almost immediately after speaking of these classes with only one member and one constant, Deleuze cuts short his discussion, saying that at this point ontological genesis comes to an end and logical genesis begins. For, in fact, these classes with only one member and one constant not only open up the possibility of more extensive classes with variable properties, but are inseparable from them. Indeed, as Deleuze goes on to say, it is these wider logical classes and categories that are the retrospective condition of signified objects and subjects (*LS*, 138). And we can see this argument repeated in *What is Philosophy?* where, after speaking of 'partial observers' and a 'perspective belonging to things themselves' (*WP?*, 131) towards the end of 'Functives and Concepts', as something like the equivalence of subject and object in common sense, Deleuze and Guattari point to an entirely other order of 'prospects' at the beginning of 'Prospects and Concepts'. And in the same way as with ontological and logical genesis, the prospect is revealed as the retrospective condition of the function, or put otherwise the functive is merely the first of the prospects (*WP?*, 155). But before we turn to the prospect in more detail, we might return to the relationship between good and common sense, the individual who marks a convergence and whose predicates are analytic and the person who marks a divergence and whose predicates are synthetic and, indeed, the wider classes and categories that result from these. We might seek to explain what Deleuze means by that incompossible object = x common to all or several worlds and why it depends on a certain subject = x that is able to recognize it, and furthermore why there is not a simple relationship of resemblance between the fully differentiated Idea and the fully differenciated object that is its actualization. And we might attempt to do all this through a reading of that author who, more than any other, Deleuze draws on to develop a post-Leibnizian metaphysics in both *The Fold* and *The Logic of Sense*: Borges.

It is not a Borges story we take up here, but an essay, 'Kafka and His Precursors'. The essay, in an imitation or parody of classic literary method, seeks to identify that particular quality that defines Kafka by looking at six 'precursors' to his work, in each of whom we can 'recognize his voice, or his habits'[18]: the Ancient Greek philosopher Zeno, the nineth-century Chinese essayist Han Yu, the nineteenth-century Danish theologian Søren Kierkegaard, the nineteenth-century English poet Robert Browning, the twentieth-century French novelist Léon Bloy and the twentieth-century Irish writer Lord Dunsany. After setting out and justifying the case for each precursor, Borges then concludes in difficult and complex words: 'If I am not mistaken, the heterogeneous pieces I have listed resemble Kafka; if I am not mistaken, not all of them resemble each other'.[19] How are we to understand this? On first reading, it cannot but seem wrong. Indeed, the truth can appear almost the opposite of what Borges asserts: that each of these precursors has something in common with the others (some 'Kafkaesque' quality), but nothing in common with Kafka (Kafka is a great and singular author, whereas they are merely his 'precursors', of interest only in light of Kafka himself). However, let us consider this process of comparison or the adducing of successive examples of precursors more carefully. A first comparison to Kafka is made, say, to Zeno. Zeno's paradoxes of motion, we feel, capture something of the particular Kafkaesque quality we are trying to put our finger on, but not perhaps all of it. In order to indicate what of Kafka has been left out, thus introducing a kind of split into our Zeno comparison, we put forward our second precursor, Han Yu, and his fable about unicorns. And so on. Each successive precursor – this how we are able to keep on adding names to the list – is an attempt to speak of what has been left out from the comparisons before, to show that they do not speak for all of Kafka. Exactly as Borges suggests, then, the list is composed of authors who have nothing in common with one another – each is given as an attempt to speak of what has been left out from the previous comparisons – and yet all nevertheless have something in common with Kafka. Even more profoundly, we might say that each precursor does not so much seek to say what Kafka is as attempt to point to what all of the previously provided precursors have in common. Each attempts to speak of that real 'Kafka', left out, who allows all of those others to speak of Kafka. Each attempts to speak of that difference between Kafka as a general quality and that particular series of qualities said to define Kafka. And the real 'Kafka' of Borges' story, the real 'Kafka' all those various precursors are endeavouring to locate, is precisely this difference, the difference that allows the 'Kafkaesque' or the resemblance between Kafka and his precursors. And the list ends, no more precursors can be evidenced, when we can no longer speak of that 'difference' that allows us to speak of Kafka, when there is no other quality that has been left out from the previous series of precursors, which would be the 'real' Kafka they all have in common.

To put all of this in terms of Deleuze, we might say that this set of precursors in extension – that sequence of authors laid out one after another in historical time – is an attempt to explicate Kafka as a kind of common sense. What explains the quantitative stretching out along the line of good sense is an explication of quality in common sense: the attempt to bring out the distinctive quality of Kafka in terms of the relationship between his various precursors. But, equally, there can be no common sense without good sense: there is no other way to describe this 'Kafkaesque' quality except through that historical sequence of his precursors. However, more profoundly, what we see here is that the finally differenciated class or category of the 'Kafkaesque', which implies something compossible or in common to its various parts, is not possible outside a 'Kafka' that is incompossible or has nothing in common to its various parts. The various precursors to Kafka *do* obviously have something in common with each other, each has something of the 'Kafkaesque' about them; and yet this is only because of a 'Kafka' that is nothing but the difference between its various parts, nothing but the sequence in which each of his precursors has nothing in common with the ones before and after. Indeed, to recall the coming together of incompossible object and the subject able to recognize it, it is obvious that it is *Borges* who sees the commonality between Kafka and his various precursors, who is in effect the difference between Kafka and the Kafkaesque that allows them to resemble each other. And, to come back to Deleuze's perhaps under-theorized distinction in 'Static Ontological Genesis' between an object = x that is common to several worlds and an object = x that is common to all worlds (*LS*, 131), we might say that the 'Kafka' we are speaking of as the difference between his precursors is to be found in *all* literature. With the very greatest of authors, those who have established a quality that is named after them, we might suggest that all literature is their precursor or has to be read through them (perhaps, in fact, the list Borges draws up in 'Kafka and His Precursors' can be continued forever). But, again, it is also true that, although that fully differenciated object = x must be a nothing in common to all worlds, we can only ever see it as a *something* in common to several worlds, insofar as it is always some actual quality that it must be perceived through. It is undoubtedly for something like this reason that, although Kafka represents an entirely 'new value' (*LS*, 130) without precedent in the history of literature, he can only ever be understood through his precursors, that is, those who are already like him. And all of this is not unrelated to another complex distinction we might make in terms of the relationship between differentiation and differenciation, which is that, while each successive precursor might be understood to 'double' the virtual Idea of Kafka, speak of that 'difference' they all have in common, on the level of the actual they rather 'split' or 'bifurcate' him, indicate the next particular quality or difference that has been left out. It is for this reason that we are able to say, finally, that the process of differenciation does not follow or resemble differentiation, that we cannot simply 'read off' the empirical reality of Kafka from his virtual Idea, although the two are not in any way separable.

* * *

At the beginning of the chapter 'Static Ontological Genesis', Deleuze makes the point that the 'multiple classes and variable properties, which in turn depend on persons are not embodied in a third proposition that would again be ontological, but send us over to another order of the proposition, and constitute the condition or the form of possibility of the logical proposition' (*LS*, 136). We can see this also in *What is Philosophy?* where, in a similar move, we go from the scientist's name or even 'partial observer' at the end of 'Functives and Concepts' to the more general classes and categories at the beginning of 'Prospects and Concepts'. As Deleuze and Guattari make clear, these more general classes and categories are not another and final type of functive, but represent a whole other order, which they call the 'prospect' (*WP?*, 155). The prospect is defined as the 'logicization of the functive that thus becomes the prospects of a proposition' (*WP?*, 137), in which – and this is undoubtedly a continuation of the 'inevitable movement' of the third and final stage of dramatization – a kind of distance or 'disjunction' (*WP?*, 136) is introduced into the functive. That is, as opposed to the functive, which directly constitutes the state of affairs as a third variable as a result of the intersection of two variables, the prospect only indirectly refers to its referent as something that is outside it but without which it is incomplete. Or, again, as opposed to the individuated monad, which is nothing outside its predicates, and the object of common sense, which does not exist outside the subject perceiving it, both different objects can fill the same referent (depending on other conditions being met) and the particular personal relationship to the referent is not determinative (it can be any person, in principle). The prospect, we might say, takes the single-member class produced at the end of ontological genesis and generalizes it, so that there can be any number of members of that class. The example of the prospect Deleuze and Guattari provide in 'Prospects and Concepts' is the logical proposition 'x is human', in which 'being human' is not the functive, but merely the value f(a) for the variable x. Here it is not any particular functive that is at stake but the very processes and procedures of the functive itself, how it refers to its object x – f(a) and not a. As Deleuze and Guattari write: 'The propositional function "x is human" clearly shows the position of an independent variable that does not belong to the function but without which the function is incomplete. "Being human" is not itself the functive, but the value of f(a) for the variable x' (*WP?*, 135).

In fact, Deleuze's point in *The Logic of Sense* is that the three stages of logical genesis repeat those of ontological genesis. Although we have already seen that any final order is more complicated than this, just as we move through a denoted, manifested and signified in relation to the functive on the level of ontological genesis, so we now move through an equivalent denotation, manifestation and signification in relation to the prospect on the level of logical genesis. Indeed, as we have suggested, that first example of the prospect we looked at – 'x is human' – could be said to correspond on the level of logic with the state of affairs. That is, the whole first order of logical prospects, corresponding to denotation, repeats the steps we saw with individuation in functives. With regard to these prospects, Deleuze and Guattari begin by speaking of their 'extension', which is the series of values or objects that satisfy its definition, each of which is evaluated on the basis of 'true or false' (*WP?*, 136). This is followed by a consideration of the prospect's 'intension', which are the circumstances under which those values or objects of denotation are true or false (*WP?*, 136). If extension involves a certain 'exoreference' of the prospect, its relation to something outside it, then intension involves a certain 'endo-reference', its dependence on certain internal conditions (*WP?*, 130). The well-known example of intension Deleuze and Guattari give is Venus as alternately the 'evening star' and the 'morning star' (*WP?*, 136), when of course it is the same Venus each time, according to when it is seen. And, finally, we have what Deleuze and Guattari call the referent's 'comprehension' (*WP?*, 137), which is the series of 'essential predicates' by which it is defined. Here Deleuze and Guattari make a distinction between what may be said of something, which is not one of its necessary qualities, and what is strictly part of its definition. Thus, 'Victor at Jena' is a description or presentation of Napoleon, while 'general' is a predicate of Bonaparte, insofar as the referent here is the military figure. 'Emperor' is a predicate of Napoleon, while general or holy emperor are descriptions, insofar as the referent here is the king.

However, the crucial thing in all of this is that what we see in this first order of prosects, for all of its suggestion of a later manifestation and signification, is a certain repetition of the individuation we saw at the beginning of 'Functives and Concepts'. What we have in this passage through extension, intension and comprehension is a successive movement through states of affairs, things and bodies. This becomes clear when Deleuze and Guattari write of the process of logical 'identification or individuation that takes us from states of affairs to the thing or body (object), through operations of quantification that also make possible attribution of the thing's essential predicates' (*WP?*, 136–7); and later they will describe this second order of prospects (after the functives of science itself) as 'functions of things, objects or individuated bodies', on which logical descriptions or even logical 'states of affairs' are 'brought to bear' (*WP?*, 155).

In this sense, we might describe this whole sequence of extension, intension and comprehension as making up denotation as the 'first' of the prospects or the second of the functives.[20] But one of the things we notice about the set of qualities attributable either to Napoleon or Bonaparte as part of the referent's comprehension is that, like the body in individuation, they are only compossible 'predicates' and not incompossible 'descriptions' or 'presentations'. Indeed, as has been noted by several commentators, Deleuze and Guattari's outlining of the notion of reference in logical propositions in 'Prospects and Concepts' is indebted to Gottlob Frege, the late nineteenth-century German logician, whose work is extensively cited in the footnotes to the chapter (*WP?*, 227–8). But in *The Logic of Sense*, certainly, Deleuze is critical of Frege for overlooking the element of 'sense' in logic, that 'genetic element' (*LS*, 139) that grounds both knowledge and the known.[21] And, indeed, although Deleuze and Guattari are not overtly critical of Frege in 'Prospects and Concepts', they again seek to install something that goes against or beyond Fregean reference, in a way providing a 'power of creation' (*WP?*, 140) for it. It is precisely a transitory moment that does not have a settled place in their argument, as so often it or its equivalent does not in Deleuze's model of active genesis. It is a moment that must be understood as a 'hinge' (*WP?*, 143) between the second prospect of the logical 'states of affairs' of things, bodies and objects and a third prospect of opinion or signification. It is a moment that we might call 'manifestation' in logical genesis, which is a kind of replay of the 'resonance' between subject and object = x on the level of the manifested in ontological genesis. And its position as hinge or half-way point indicates that it is that principle of genesis or sense that makes not only Fregean reference retrospectively possible but also the general classes and categories of signification prospectively possible, even though it eventually disappears into them. For after outlining those three moment of the referent or individuation on the level of logical propositions and before setting out opinion and signification, Deleuze and Guattari speak of what they call concepts or propositions of the 'third zone' (WP?, 140), which, as they say, are unlike both scientific and logical functives, insofar as they do not constitute the clearly demarcated or well-defined sets that we find in either mathematical states of affairs or logical propositions. Here, by contrast, we have only 'vague' or 'fuzzy' sets of the kind we face all the time in the 'lived' or everyday life (WP?, 141). The examples Deleuze and Guattari provide are the categories of 'redness' and 'baldness', which they describe as 'qualitative' or 'intensive' multiplicities (WP?, 141), in which we cannot unequivocally decide whether a particular element or instance belongs to the set or not. Indeed – and Deleuze raises the similar problem of the 'redness' of a flower in *The Logic of Sense* (LS, 131–2) – this should again remind us the problem of incompossibility in static ontological genesis, insofar as there are no strict or unequivocal criteria that would unambiguously mark something as either in or out. We can only say such things as this is 'already red' or he is 'nearly bald' (WP?, 141), thus being either too late or too soon. The solution, Deleuze and Guattari suggest, is a kind of subjective evaluation or judgement of taste (WP?, 141), but one that is perhaps not unilateral, insofar as it also gives rise to the subject that makes it. In this, we should see an echo of the actions of that 'dark precursor' or subject = x of ontological genesis, which similarly discerns something in common to a series of objects or qualities that appear to have nothing in common and in doing so also brings itself about.

As we suggest, Deleuze and Guattari characterize this moment of the concepts of the 'third zone', like its equivalent moment in ontological genesis, as intermediary. These concepts do not still deal with the states of affairs, things and bodies of the second prospect, but they are not yet the opinions of the third prospect, although they can be classified this way (WP?, 155).

Instead, they constitute a 'hinge' and pose an alternative: either 'we end up reconstituting scientific or logical functions for these variables, which would make the appeal to philosophical concepts definitively useless,' or 'we will have to invent a new, especially philosophical type of function, a third zone in which everything seems to be strangely reversed, since it will be given the task of supporting the other two' (*WP?*, 141). However, although Deleuze and Guattari favour the second of these alternatives, it is only the first that they follow because immediately following this they trace – undoubtedly echoing the procedure of 'inevitable movement' in ontological genesis – a separation of subject and object following their coming together in 'resonance' or manifestation. Here it is no longer 'fuzzy' or 'intense' categories like 'redness' or 'baldness', which are unable to be separated from the subjective act that constitutes them, but a kind of putting back together of what is already separated. (In a way, it is like a doubling or repetition of that separation and putting back together of subject and object that leads to the signified.) We definitively shift to a fully-formed subject with conscious perceptions and affections, leaving behind any sense of a presubjective and unconscious percept and affect that we had in previous orders of prospects. As Deleuze and Guattari describe this third and final order of prospects: 'What opinion proposes is a particular relationship between an external perception as state of a subject and an internal affection as passage from one state to another. We pick out a quality supposedly common to several objects that we perceive, and an affection supposedly common to several subjects who experience it' (*WP?*, 144). We are now absolutely in the realm of opinion or signification. And perhaps the crucial aspect about it is that it is not a specific subject and a particular object or quality (either the extensive individuation of denotation or the intensive multiplicities of manifestation), but rather a generic subject and general objects or qualities. In the examples Deleuze and Guattari give of it, we have not merely the supposedly widely shared sense of the 'foul smell' of cheese (*WP?*, 145), but a more and more aggressively pursued universality that speaks of all others for all others: 'As a man, I consider all women to be unfaithful', 'As a woman, I think all men are liars' (*WP?*, 145). With this third and final order of prospects, as we say, genesis appears to come to an end and the 'sense' that underpins opinion is written out. These opinions would arrive ready-made, a matter of mere recognition, of stating a pre-existing and unchallengeable consensus. But, for Deleuze and Guattari, this 'recognition' has always been a poor model for philosophy (*WP?*, 145–6). The subject is never actually universal, but always particular: white, male, European (*WP?*, 149). The strict criterion is always lacking, insofar as those wider classes based on pre-existing objects and subjects are never able to be stated without falling into paradox. Indeed, the very truth of these philosophical functions or logical propositions is simply not able to be explained as coming from these classes and objects, unless it can also be shown how it gives rise to them, in that manner of which Deleuze and Guattari speak.

Deleuze and Guattari throughout *What is Philosophy?* oppose this model of thought as recognition. They contest all transcendental categories – such as subject and object – that can be understood to lie outside of genesis. The book is an extended diagnosis not only of recent Anglo-American analytic philosophy, which is absolutely erected on this model – as we have seen, they evoke humorously, even if a little unfairly, a dinner party at Richard Rorty's at which the guests exchange such opinions (*WP?*, 144–5) – but the entire history of philosophy as complicit with this model of recognition: from Plato's test of the 'beautiful in nature and good in minds' (*WP?*, 148), to Kant's 'a priori propositions or judgement as functions of a whole of possible experience' (*WP?*, 142), to Husserl's notion of the 'lived as immanent to a subject' (*WP?*, 143) and beyond. And yet the first difficulty for Deleuze and Guattari's argument here is that they acknowledge that all philosophy – including presumably their own – is written in sentences of a 'standard language' (*WP?*, 80), by which we might mean involving objective reference and opinion. And the second difficulty is that, if their book is in part a long genealogy of the forgetting of genesis in the erection of these transcendental categories in philosophy, it also shows just as convincingly that the history of philosophy – and perhaps philosophy as such – is the attempt to challenge this model, including many of the same philosophers who originally propagated it. Plato, in a world already characterized with the Sophists by the buying and selling of opinion, sought to go back by means of reminiscence to an 'original' or 'proto' opinion that would be beyond change: 'To reach true opinion, perception had to be taken as far as the beauty of the perceived and affection as far as the test of the good' (*WP?*, 148). Or Husserl, in a manner similar to Plato, although in the opposite direction, attempted to transcend opinion through recourse to everyday life. That is, Husserl, like Plato, sought to ascend to a kind of ur-doxa or underlying condition for things: 'Phenomenology too goes in search of original opinions which bind us to the world as to our homeland (earth). It also needs the beautiful and good so that the latter are not confused with variable empirical opinion' (*WP?*, 149). And Deleuze and Guattari suggest that this is the case also for a contemporary thinker like Alain Badiou, who, similarly, in his philosophy attempts to name that 'void' for which the symbolic order, or what Badiou likes to call the 'count-for-one', stands in. In other words, Badiou, like Plato (an acknowledged inspiration) and Husserl, seeks to identify, as opposed to partial and contingent opinion, an invariant and unchanging truth, which would be attained, also like Plato and Husserl, in an almost mystical or apophantic fashion: 'Finally, the event appears (or disappears), less as a singularity than as a separated aleatory point that is added to or subtracted from the site, within the transcendence of the void or the truth as void' (*WP?*, 152). And Deleuze and Guattari are in no sense simply dismissive of these respective philosophical projects. For, after all, the fundamental project of philosophy is to break with opinion. Each attempts to think the underlying conditions of reality, that for which it stands in. Each attempts to think the genetic constitution of reality, how it came about. And yet for Deleuze and Guattari at some point each project also stops and imposes a new and transcendental condition, that which cannot be explained but must be assumed or recognized: in Plato, the Beautiful; in Husserl, the subject; in Badiou, the void. If each philosophical system is critical of opinion, then, it is only to replace it with another (and perhaps it is even the attempt to do away with opinion that leads to opinion in the first place). Each philosopher is in effect merely that 'man of paradoxes' (*WP?*, 146), who, if they contest the prevailing doxa does so only in the name of another doxa, secretly hoping that their own criticism will in time constitute a new doxa.

It is undoubtedly at this point that we can discern a certain 'politics' in *What is Philosophy?* Opinion is not only a philosophical but also a political and even economic problem. Although this is a methodologically complex position, opinion is not merely a matter of philosophical genesis (or its denial), but corresponds both to a certain socio-political organization and a particular historical epoch. As Deleuze and Guattari make clear, if the confusion of philosophy and opinion was already present at the very beginning of philosophy, it is nevertheless particularly characteristic of our time. 'We are the ideas men!', say the creatives (*WP?*, 10). 'We, the conceivers', declare the marketers (*WP?*, 146). And it is in their *Anti-Oedipus* that Deleuze and Guattari first addressed opinion and how to go beyond it in a way that does not simply remain within opinion. In that book, there is a detailed social and historical 'allegory' of the various stages of genesis, producing an account that was much criticized on factual grounds at the time, but without commentators realizing that what Deleuze and Guattari were advancing was a 'universal' history (*AO*, 140), along the lines of Marx: a history that is true, regardless of the 'facts', that is no longer a matter of opinion.[22] The first period they identify is 'territorialization' (*AO*, 184), which marks the beginning of human history and articulates for the first time the family couplings or alliances between generations that 'forge a system in extension (representation), based on the repression of nocturnal intensities' (*AO*, 185). This corresponds with the 'good sense' of static ontological genesis, in which borders are drawn and bodies individuated. The second period they identify is 'despotism' (*AO*, 192), associated with the barbaric state, and organized around charismatic leaders, in which the extensive alliances of that first territorialization are now 'overcoded' onto the body of a despot in a new 'disjunctive synthesis' (*AO*, 198). This corresponds to the 'common sense' of static ontological genesis, in which an emerging subject puts together otherwise incomparable objects to form more general classes and categories. Finally – and this is the period that interests us here – we have 'capitalism' (*AO*, 222), beginning with the collapse of the despotic, 'Asiatic' state, but equally present from the beginning of history, in which an originally deterritorialized form of capital and desire is subsequently captured by an 'axiomatic' that returns them to value and meaning (*AO*, 224). This corresponds with static logical genesis and particularly to its final stage of opinion or signification, which also takes an unlocatable intensity and maps it onto wider unities, and can be understood to have to have underwritten genesis from the beginning.

The self-described task of *Anti-Oedipus* is to 'decode' (*AO*, 246) capitalism, in a process Deleuze and Guattari describe as pushing capitalism to the limit, giving in to its 'deepest tendency' (*AO*, 246).

But what would this mean? In *Anti-Oedipus*, Deleuze and Guattari recognize that, precisely like opinion, capitalism works through the proposing of exceptions or alternatives to itself. In their words, 'it axiomatizes on the one hand what it decodes on the other' (*AO*, 246). Undoubtedly reacting against the political debates of the day, they put forward a number of these 'reterritorializations' or things or values that supposedly go against capitalism: the underdeveloped Third World (*AO*, 231), the limits of human exploitation (*AO*, 232), the 'pure' knowledge of maths and science (*AO*, 233), the antiproduction of the State (*AO*, 235). But, again, their point is that, far from resisting or inhibiting capitalism, it is just on these exceptions that capitalism starts up and expands. (It is for this same reason that Deleuze and Guattari describe 'human rights' as 'axioms' in *What is Philosophy?* (WP?, 107). In fact, far from offering any kind of a critique of capitalism, they come merely to confirm it: it is only through capitalism that we can guarantee human rights.) This is the great lesson Deleuze and Guattari take from Marx, and the profound interpretation of Marx they offer in their own work. Against many readings of him, their Marx does not assert any external or higher value against capitalism, classically something like the unalienated or surplus value of labour. Rather, it is another moment from Marx that they pay attention to: the 'tendency to a falling rate of profit' (*AO*, 228) that Marx noted in the first volume of *Capital*. Marx's point is that this tendency has 'no end, but reproduces itself while reproducing the factors that counteract it' (*AO*, 228). In other words, what Marx is remarking upon is the very cycle between re- and deterritorialization that we saw above: the fact that every deterritorialization leads to a further reterritorialization, but also that this reterritorialization leads to a further deterritorialization. It is exactly in this regard that we might say that Marx thinks the genesis of capitalism, the fact that it is total only insofar as it is incomplete. And it is this – this inseparability of re- and deterritorialization – that Deleuze and Guattari ultimately call 'deterritorialization' (*AO*, 231). However, the power of philosophy – we might even say 'pure' thought – beyond capitalism is that it is able to think *this*, the ground or plane of immanence that makes capitalism at once possible and impossible, never-ending because it is never completed.

* * *

An enigma is posed when we come with logical propositions and conscious representations to the end of genesis. A challenge is raised with Deleuze and Guattari's statement that philosophy is written only in something like opinions (*WP?*, 202). It is: why is everything not yet actualized? Why is not all opinion? Or to state this from the other end of genesis, why is there still art? Why is there still philosophy? In what way are we still able to create concepts and not merely exchange opinions? And the answer cannot be that there is still more to be actualized, more to go before we get to the end. (And, certainly, while Deleuze and Guattari refer to the event as 'pure reserve' (*WP?*, 156) in *What is Philosophy?*, they do not mean it in this sense.) It cannot simply be that there is something left to be actualized because, by the terms of Nietzsche's Eternal Return, which Deleuze and Guattari evoke towards the end of 'Prospects and Concepts' (*WP?*, 159–60), everything has already happened, we are already at the end. It cannot be that something remains to be actualized, therefore, because if this were so this actualization would already have taken place. Rather, we might say that everything is not already actualized, not because something is left out that comes before the actual, but because it is this actualization itself that leads to what must be actualized. We can see this in *What is Philosophy?* when Deleuze and Guattari speak about going down a line that 'descends from the virtual to the state of affairs' and up a line that goes from the 'state of affairs to the virtual' (*WP?*, 155–6). Although the two directions are opposed – going down indicates a progressive actualization and going up a counter-actualization – they are in fact inseparable. We cannot have one without the other. That is, just as the virtual leads to the actual, so actualization produces the virtual. This is also that difficult Leibnizian theme, in which we say that not only can we only see the world through the monad, but the monad also points to something beyond it. This is to be seen in Deleuze's use of the 'frightened face' in *Difference and Repetition* (*DR*, 260) and *The Logic of Sense* (*LS*, 346), an example that is repeated in *What is Philosophy?* (*WP?*, 17). If in one way here, the expressed is only the expression of something, in another way it is also the expression of a nothing that is in excess of anything: a 'frightened face', as it were, that is in excess of any actual world it might be thought to refer to. (All of this might be compared to that moment in Hitchcock's *Lifeboat* (1944) – this is precisely that moment in cinema when we get expression without its necessarily being an expression of anything in the time–image – when we have a shot of the frightened face of a rescued German sailor without the matching reverse shot showing us what he is frightened of, the former as it were more frightening than anything that could actually be shown.)[23]

It is undoubtedly in *Difference and Repetition* that Deleuze develops this theme at greatest length, with an extended discussion of the relationship between explication and implication (*DR*, 228–30). Deleuze's argument there – and it is very much an argument against Leibniz – is that actualization does not fundamentally proceed in one direction from implication to explication. It is not that what was once implicated is now forever explicated. Rather, it is that explication leads to implication, to what has to be explicated. As Deleuze writes in the chapter 'Asymmetrical Synthesis of the Sensible', which is, as we have seen, where Deleuze outlines the parallels between passive and active synthesis and the intensity that runs through both: 'It is an extension or 'explication' which is implicated as such in intensity, which does not exist outside the implication or except as implicated, and this because it [implication] has the function of making possible the general movement by which that which is implicated explicates itself or is explicated' (*DR*, 229; see also *DR*, 243). Deleuze speaks of an 'asymmetrical synthesis' (*DR*, 244) there, insofar as the reciprocal synthesis dy/dx of the components of Ideas is continued in the 'asymmetrical synthesis' that combines the x and y of different intensities in the first functive of the state of affairs; but we might also speak of a certain 'asymptotic synthesis', insofar as what brings any final actualization closer is also what moves it away, the more genesis completes its task of explicating all intensities the further there is to go. And all of this is not unconnected with the other major theme of the chapter, which might at first appear unrelated, and that is Deleuze's elaboration of the relationship between Nietzsche and thermodynamics – which we might even restate as the relationship between philosophy and science (*DR*, 223–4, 242–3). Deleuze begins by making the point that both Nietzsche's doctrine of the Eternal Return and the discovery of the second law of thermodynamics took place at about the same time in the second half of the nineteenth century. In fact, Deleuze insists, Nietzsche actually knew of the scientific theory of entropy, with its prediction of the eventual 'heat death' of the universe, and knew moreover that it appeared to go against the possibility of the Eternal Return, in which the same events occur over and over, without appearing to run out of energy or come to an end (*DR*, 243). And, Deleuze again asserts, Nietzsche went even further, understanding the two doctrines as inseparable and implying each other without exception. The Eternal Return can take place only within a horizon set by thermodynamics, just as thermodynamics for its part is made possible by the Eternal Return. How can this be so? The answer is perhaps suggested by asking why has this predicted heat death of the universe not yet occurred? Why is it still taking place? And why will it continue to take place forever? Is it not to indicate that it is subject to a form of Eternal Return, that this progressive 'running down' will carry on forever without coming to a definitive end? That the same thing that results from entropy is the same thing that continues to feed it? As Deleuze writes, pointing out the coincidence between the doctrines of thermodynamics and the Eternal Return:

> Are we not led to distinguish two states of quality along with two signs of extension? One in which extension remains implicated in the enveloping order of differences; the other in which extensity explicates difference and cancels it out within a qualified system. This distinction, which cannot be drawn within experience, becomes possible from the point of view of the thought of Eternal Return. (*DR*, 243–4)

All of this is to indicate that the Eternal Return is not simply a form of voluntarism or an effect of the will. Or, to put this in its equivalent terms in *What is Philosophy?*, that 'counter-effectuation' Deleuze and Guattari speak of as a 'vapour' (*WP?*, 159) is not so much an alternative to the actual, which either might or might not take place, as what necessarily accompanies actualization, outside which actualization is not possible. It is in this sense that we might say that counter-effectuation is fated, which is also to say that it has already occurred, insofar as there is actualization. As Deleuze and Guattari write: 'Not willing what happens, with the false will that complains ... but taking the complaint and rage to the point where they are turned against what happens' (*WP?*, 160). And yet at the same time – and this is the complex position of the subject in

Deleuze and Guattari's work – this necessity is not possible unless it is willed. In counter-effectuation, will and what is willed come together. One wills once for all time and all times come together to produce this single act of will. And this is perhaps even what Deleuze and Guattari mean when they speak in 'Functives and Concepts' of the partial observer as that which does not act but simply perceives and experiences (*WP?*, 130). The 'subject' that is is not the usual transcendental subject that is outside what is – here again is why Deleuze and Guattari reject both Husserl's notion of reality as 'immanent to' a subject (*WP?*, 45–6, 142) and Badiou's finally voluntaristic conception of a subject that comes to a situation from outside (*WP?*, 152) – but is part of the reality that it makes possible. And, finally, this is what Deleuze and Guattari mean by speaking of the 'event' as a certain 'meanwhile' (*WP?*, 158): something neither in the past nor future but always missing, that passes by in the present unnoticed. 'Meanwhile', we might say, is a kind of 'entre-temps' or 'between-times', not so much what separates one moment from the next as what separates one moment from itself, what means that things are the only way they can be only insofar as they stand in for something else.

To this extent, we might say that virtual genesis or becoming is at once what allows the actual to become actual and what means that the actual can never become actual. At the end of genesis, when all is actual, there is still a genesis, which in a way is the thought of how things became the way they are. (Nietzsche's Eternal Return is only the very *thinking* of the Eternal Return. To think the Eternal Return *is* the very Eternal Return we would think.) And where do we see examples of this virtuality at the end of genesis in *What is Philosophy?* Undoubtedly inspired by Maurice Merleau-Ponty's posthumous *The Visible and the Invisible*[24] and Jacques Lacan's Seminar XI on the gaze,[25] Deleuze speaks in 'Asymmetrical Synthesis' of a certain distance that allows appearance (*DR*, 230, 253). And beyond this – and this will return us to that reciprocal implication of implication and explication that Deleuze speaks of there – he will speak of a certain depth that allows distance (*DR*, 229). In Merleau-Ponty and Lacan, depth is frequently figured as a kind of gaze from the side of things, as it is in the famous anamorphic skull of Holbein's *The Ambassadors* (1533). And the point both Merleau-Ponty and Lacan make is that this depth or gaze from the side that is usually invisible to us is the symbolic guarantor of the everyday three-dimensional space we inhabit. Moreover, Lacan suggests, if we were actually to shift to the side of Holbein's painting and look at the skull 'head on', we would be shocked not only by the realization that we were being looked at before we saw, but also by the thought that at this very moment there must be yet another gaze looking on from the side, allowing us to see what we see.[26] It is *this* that Deleuze means by the depth that allows distance: depth is that always implicated virtual dimension that allows everything to be explicated, including itself. And we find something similar in Deleuze's famous short text on the French novelist Michel Tournier's *Friday*, his version of Daniel Defoe's *Robinson Crusoe*. Deleuze in his essay, through Tournier, speaks of the way that, even when Robinson is alone, there is a certain 'other' (*LS*, 344) necessarily present, a 'possibility' (*LS*, 347) that allows Crusoe to represent the world to himself. Indeed, Crusoe would become 'psychotic' (*LS*, 353) if fully actualized representation was all that there was and there was no other.[27] Or, more precisely, even when the island on which he is shipwrecked is all that there is, this solitariness or self-possession would not be possible without something 'outside' it – and it is this 'other' that is the true Man Friday in Crusoe's novel. Indeed, the actual Man Friday whom Crusoe befriends in Tournier's novel merely comes to take the place of this necessary possibility, and yet he could never entirely take its place, there never can be only this fully realized Man Friday.

It is in the same manner that Deleuze and Guattari insist in 'Prospects and Concepts' that signification does not exist outside 'possibility' and the notion of the 'Other person' (*WP?*, 138). It is 'possibility' here in the technical sense that logical propositions attempt to replace the inseparability of philosophical components and 'combination' of elements we see in ontological genesis with 'arithmetical number', the 'intensity' or even 'intensionality' of manifestation with the requirement that what is held together there eventually be distinguished according to the requirements of reference. Possibility, as Deleuze puts it in *The Logic of Sense*, is the 'nonsense' necessary for sense, the incompossibility necessary for universal logical categories (*LS*, 131–2). But Deleuze and Guattari also mean possibility to speak of the fact that we could not actually have representation and communication unless they could be carried beyond themselves, go against the empirical facts.

(It is here that we might see the analogy between Deleuze and Guattari's theory of language and that of someone like Kripke, who is getting at something similar with his 'counter-factual' notion of 'baptism', alluded to in *What is Philosophy?* (*WP?*, 8).) But also, beyond this, the very ability to represent what is entails a certain otherness or not-all. To represent something is necessarily also to counter-effectuate it, to open it up to the possibility that it could be other. And this is the case for the entire philosophical project of Deleuze and Guattari here. In one sense, what they say is true: all philosophy, including their own, is able to communicate only in sentences of 'ordinary language'.[28] However, in another sense, this book they have written in this language both allows us to think and is already a certain virtuality. Genesis is the question of how things have become as they are, and this question itself – insofar as it suggests that things were once otherwise – is *already* a certain otherness. The process of genesis always ends with the actual, but the question or problem of genesis is always virtual. The book *What is Philosophy?*, as we have been trying to suggest throughout, *is* the very philosophy Deleuze and Guattari speak of in it. Of course, it can only take the form of ordinary language, opinions, actualized representations, but it also constitutes an irrefutable doubling of what is, in which the only way things can be at any particular moment can be explained only by the possibility that they were once different, a difference that can never be realized, never be completed, except at the price of beginning again. (And here, of course, the paradox of a certain *not otherwise* that insists that things could be otherwise.)

In this sense, *What is Philosophy?* is a failure, always falling short of what it points to. It can never actually speak of what it wants to. Like all philosophy perhaps, it can only ever indicate what it stands for. For, even looking at things from the oblique angle they do, they necessarily miss the depth that makes this possible. However, as Deleuze and Guattari suggest of philosophy, as opposed to logic, what it cannot speak of it 'shows' (*WP?*, 140). Or, as we have been suggesting here, perhaps even in an argument Deleuze and Guattari would not endorse, it metaphorizes or allegorizes what it wants to say. Art, philosophy and science are components of the philosophy Deleuze and Guattari construct, and the philosophy they speak of is the philosophy that is *What is Philosophy?* In this regard, the book is, precisely as they say of philosophy, 'auto-poetic', 'self-reflexive' and 'self-referential'. But, in another way, all of this is also the sign that *What is Philosophy?* cannot speak directly of the philosophy it wants to. It always misses it, and it is in this miss that philosophy comes about. As Deleuze suggests in *Nietzsche and Philosophy*, the attempt to grasp genesis, which we might call the sublime, always fails, but what comes about as a result of this failure is philosophy as such: 'Not the Overman, who is the positive product of critique itself. But man, insofar as he wants to be gone beyond, overcome' (*NP*, 94). Deleuze and Guattari go on to make the point that Kant could write the *Critique of Judgement*, in which he theorized the sublime and completed his own philosophical system, only in an 'unrestrained old age' (*WP?*, 2). And in a subtle sign that they understand *What is Philosophy?* as following its 'critical' project, they note that they too have come to write their book in a 'moment of grace between life and death, when all the parts of the machine come together' (*WP?*, 1). For them, *What is Philosophy?* is a book that can be written only at the end of their own careers and perhaps at the end of philosophy itself with its replacement by 'opinion' and the 'ideas men'. And yet, as Kant shows, if the sublime represents a necessary failure by the Imagination, it also represents a necessary success by Reason in being able to think this (*KP*, 51). In other words, Deleuze and Guattari arrive at the end of *What is Philosophy?* only to begin again. They can no sooner think that all is actualized and there is nothing left to think than all is counter-actualized in thinking *this*. This is why they can speak of art, philosophy, science and logic in a book called *What is Philosophy?*, why all can simultaneously be components of the concept of philosophy they construct: because philosophy is what holds all of these components together, is their mutual genesis, is the fact that we are at once at the beginning (art), middle (philosophy) and end (science) of things.

CHAPTER SIX

The Brain and Geophilosophy

In separate chapters, *What is Philosophy?* deals with art, philosophy, science and logic. And, although it is not narrated in the proper sequence, we would say that each of these corresponds to one of the successive moments of genesis: art corresponds to the dynamic genesis that takes off from the primary order, philosophy to the sense and virtual that make up the secondary order and science and logic to the static genesis that leads to the tertiary order. The process of genesis starts with an undifferentiated chaos that disappears as soon as it appears and ends with a conscious and individuated proposition or opinion that can be repeated and shared with others. And, in the Conclusion to *What is Philosophy?*, 'From Chaos to the Brain', Deleuze and Guattari summarize and explicitly relate to each other for the first time the separate moments of genesis they have previously elaborated. They compare the 'varieties' (*WP?*, 204) of art, which form a being of the sensible and aspire to the infinite, to the 'variations' (*WP?*, 202) of philosophy, which are inseparable and infinite, to the 'variables' (*WP?*, 203) of science, which are independent and represent a slowing down from the infinite. They compare the 'aesthetic figures' (*WP?*, 216) of art, which are the conditions under which the art produces affects, to the 'conceptual personae' (*WP?*, 216) of philosophy, which put together components through a survey without distance, to the 'partial observers' (*WP?*, 216) of science, which are the perception and experiencing of functives. They compare the 'plane of composition' (*WP?*, 203) of art, from which artistic materials and techniques are drawn, to the 'plane of immanence' (*WP?*, 202) of philosophy, which is made up of consistent and inseparable philosophical components, to the 'plane of reference' (*WP?*, 202) of science, on which functives at once connect and break apart. And, finally, they compare the 'force of sensation' (*WP?*, 216) of art, which preserves percept and affect outside any original subject and object, to the 'form of concept' (*WP?*, 216) of philosophy, which grasps heterogeneity or becoming in pure form, to the 'function of knowledge' (*WP?*, 216) of science, which actualizes perceptions and affections in relation to an external referent.

The obvious question raised by *What is Philosophy?* is how these different orders of genesis relate to one another. As we suggested at the beginning here, this is undoubtedly the major interpretive question raised by the book. Such readers of *What is Philosophy?* as Elizabeth Grosz in *Chaos, Territory, Art: Deleuze and the Framing of the Earth* and Rodolphe Gasché in *Geophilosophy: On Gilles Deleuze and Félix Guattari's What is Philosophy?*[1] speak of them as distinct and unrelated throws over chaos, while others such as in Joe Hughes in *Deleuze and the Genesis of Representation* and Mathias Schönher in 'The Creation of the Concept through the Interaction of Philosophy with Science and Art'[2] understand them as inseparable and successive stages of an overall genesis in what is essentially a reworking of Kant's Critical project. And, as we have already tried to make clear, there is evidence in *What is Philosophy?* for both points of view, particularly in this last, summary chapter. On the side of the idea that art, philosophy and science are unrelated, Deleuze and Guattari frequently treat the genetic sequence of art, philosophy and science out of order in *What is Philosophy?*, not only in the actual sequence of chapters of the book but in the linking or connecting of them in this final chapter. They speak there of the way that the 'three planes are irreducible' (*WP?*, 216), and earlier of the way that the 'three routes are specific, each as direct as the others' (*WP?*, 198). On the side of the idea that art, philosophy and science are related and part of a single, continuous genesis, there are moments in the Conclusion where Deleuze and Guattari do treat the three faculties in the correct order and do allow relations between them. They speak there of the way that it is 'their succession that makes it possible to speak of "progress"' (*WP?*, 203) and earlier of a 'sensation of concept or function', a 'concept of function or sensation' and a 'function of sensation or concept' (*WP?*, 199). They allow that we can speak of the 'intrinsic beauty of a geometric figure, an operation or a demonstration' or that a function can be grasped 'within a sensation that gives it percepts and affects' or on a 'specific plane of creation that wrests it from any reference' (*WP?*, 217).

But this latter series of examples is not exactly evidence of a unified genesis and can even go against the idea that these orders are successive. The connections Deleuze and Guattari speak of are not always posited in the appropriate order of genesis but seemingly in any sequence, between any two faculties, either across an intervening moment of genesis (a sensibility of function or a function of sensibility) or in a reverse order from philosophy to art (a concept of sensation) or from science to philosophy (a function of concept). But these kinds of relation, for all their heuristic usefulness, are merely the 'extrinsic' (*WP?*, 217) connection between faculties, which still retain their fundamental identity. It is immediately after this that Deleuze and Guattari posit another, 'intrinsic' (*WP?*, 217) relationship between the faculties, in which particular *elements* from each actually become part of another: for example, the concepts and conceptual personae of philosophy becoming the sensations and aesthetic figures of art or the functives and partial observers of science (*WP?*, 217). But even this more 'intrinsic' connection between faculties is not the final moment in the relations between art, philosophy and science. Beyond this – although Deleuze and Guattari leave the suggestion undeveloped – there is a deeper connection that cannot even be 'localized' (*WP?*, 217). It occurs, they explain, insofar as each faculty is related to a certain 'no' or 'nonphilosophy' (*WP?*, 218) that occurs not just at its beginning or end where it touches another, but at 'every moment of its becoming or development' (*WP?*, 218). It is this 'no' that allows us to think of Deleuze and Guattari's entire project in *What is Philosophy?* in terms of Kant's sublime, and how each of the faculties of art, philosophy and science arises only in a relation with the others in an overall genesis, which nothing is outside.

Deleuze and Guattari, as part of their understanding of philosophy as genesis, speak of a certain 'taste for the undetermined concept' (*WP?*, 78). And we have previously detailed the relationship of the various faculties in Kant in relation to the sublime. According to Deleuze, there is a kind of genesis at stake in Kant, in which, more than an extrinsic or even an intrinsic relation between faculties, there is a 'unity' or even mutual 'engendering' (*KCP*, 51) of faculties that comes about in response to the sublime or that which cannot be thought (and which we might call, after Deleuze and Guattari, a certain 'no' or 'nonphilosophy'). In Kant's first two Critiques, *Critique of Pure Reason* and *Critique of Practical Reason*, the faculties of Reason and Imagination and Imagination and Understanding are brought into a relationship with each other under the legislation of Understanding and Reason respectively. And in the first part of Kant's Third Critique, *Critique of Judgement*, with respect to the Beautiful, there is a similar relationship between the Imagination and Understanding that, although 'free and indeterminate', is nevertheless 'harmonious' and 'universally valid' (*KCP*, 49). But in the next section of *Critique of Judgement*, 'The Analytic of the Sublime' – and it is this that it shows retrospectively about 'The Analytic of the Beautiful'[3] – it is not a matter of a joining of preformed faculties in any kind of harmony under the direction of one, but rather of each faculty in its encounter with the sublime object at once stretched to its limit and coming about only in its relationship with the others. That is, if in one way in the sublime it is Reason that pushes Imagination to the limit of its ability to grasp the infinity of the sensible world, in another way it is Imagination that merges with Reason in the attempt to think the suprasensible substrate to this infinity of the sensible. As Deleuze writes in 'The Idea of Genesis in Kant's Aesthetics':

> At the very moment the Imagination believes it has lost its freedom, through the violence of Reason, it is freed from all the constraints of the Understanding, it enters into an accord with Reason to discover what the Understanding had hidden from it, namely, its suprasensible destination, which is also like its transcendental origin. ('G', 63)

And the crucial thing for our purposes here is that it is just at this point that Kant discovers what he calls the 'Gemüt' or 'mind', which both is the transcendental 'origin' for the various faculties and is brought about by them as the place where they meet. This mind at once comes out of the genesis of the faculties and is the very figure for this genesis, indeed, is a kind of reflection upon this genesis.[4]

It is something like this that is to be seen in Deleuze and Guattari's Conclusion. At the end of the story of genesis that is *What is Philosophy?*, where the relationship between the various faculties for the first time becomes explicit, Deleuze and Guattari discover a principle that is equivalent to Kant's 'Gemüt' or 'mind'. It is the 'cerveau' or 'brain' (*WP?*, 208). It is the brain that both arises out of the relationship between art, philosophy and science and is the 'unity' or, better, 'junction' (*WP?*, 208) that thinks this. That is to say, the brain is at once only the relationship between art, philosophy and science and the name of their relationship, that stands somewhere outside them. It is perhaps in this sense that Deleuze and Guattari can describe the brain in terms of both a 'horizontal connection' and a 'vertical integration' (*WP?*, 208), although they will also admit that this kind of objectification is insufficient: the brain is 'horizontal', insofar as it arises out of its faculties and is on the same level as they are; and it is 'vertical', insofar as it is what remains outside them, giving them a unity and finality they do not possess themselves. In a way, we might say that the brain is that *concept* made out of the individual components of art, philosophy and science. We will trace the parallels out in more detail in a moment, but for the moment we might suggest that the brain is the answer to the question not only of where philosophy occurs but of what philosophy is. It is the brain that is – and is the figure of – the philosophy that lies at the junction of all of its faculties. This is to make philosophy a component of its own concept, as Deleuze and Guattari allow (*WP?*, 39), but it is always philosophy in the form of the brain that is the concept made up of philosophy as a component. The word Deleuze and Guattari employ for philosophy as what is common to art, philosophy and science, the ongoing process of genesis that brings them about, is the *brain*.

But how is all of this actually played out in *What is Philosophy?* If we read the chapter 'From Chaos to the Brain' closely, we will see that the brain is involved at every stage of the genesis that we see as making up the argument of the book. The brain is identified with the first dynamic genesis, insofar as it is the fundamental 'contraction' and 'preservation' (*WP?*, 211) of vibrations that would otherwise disappear. The brain is like the plant that 'contemplates' (*WP?*, 212) by contracting the elements out of which it is composed. Or it is like the eye that 'binds light and is itself a bound light' (*DR*,

96). However, even at this stage, the brain is not just contraction and contemplation but also what contracts and contemplates. As Deleuze and Guattari write, one 'contemplates oneself to the extent that one contemplates the elements from which one originates' (*WP?*, 212). There is then the next stage of genesis, which is that of the virtual sense or cerebrality of philosophy, in which the brain at once breaks with reality and produces the Ideas that become reality. Here, by contrast with the first dynamic genesis in which the brain is inseparable from reality, the brain becomes 'subject' at the same time as the concepts it produces become an 'object' (*WP?*, 211). Finally, corresponding first with science and then with logic, the brain is not an 'inject' (*WP?*, 212), as in art, nor a 'subject', as in philosophy, but an 'eject' (*WP?*, 215), insofar as its fundamental task is now that of discriminating or drawing limits that exclude or render impossible the kinds of immersion or reversibility that mark art and philosophy. Here the brain is characterized not by contraction or creation but by a 'branching and individuation' (*WP?*, 215). The brain is neither in the world, as in art, nor at once inside and outside the world, as in philosophy, but definitively outside the world, able to put words to things so that they can be represented. As Deleuze and Guattari write: 'Causalities, associations and integrations inspire opinions and beliefs in us that are ways of expecting and recognising something' (*WP?*, 214). And the brain is all of these, so that what we are tracing here is the genesis of the brain itself through these different faculties, which crucially at this point in the argument are outlined in the correct order (*WP?*, 213–16). The brain, as opposed to Kant, is not a higher immaterial soul or a pre-existing consciousness, but emerges out of nature while also bringing this nature about. This is precisely the insight Deleuze gets from Bergson (and, before that, Hume) in his earliest books: the brain is neither inside and part of nature nor outside and beyond nature, but at once inside and outside nature. We have neither simply nature nor the brain but rather a mutual 'becoming' in which each comes about (*WP?*, 207). We are thus not able to ask Deleuze and Guattari, as with Slavoj Žižek, how the brain or thought arises in an otherwise 'flat' nature,[5] not only because the brain does not arise outside of nature but also because nature is never entirely flat. If, as commentators remark, drawing upon Deleuze's cinema books and monograph on Leibniz, what the brain introduces is a certain delay between things,[6] then nature itself – this is what we have previously seen with regard to art – does not exist before this delay. At the same time, nature exists only in the brain and the brain exists only in nature.

It is this 'doubleness' that is the crucial aspect of the brain for Deleuze and Guattari. In fact, as is evident from their other writings – but it is especially so for Guattari, and this brain chapter is undoubtedly the place in *What is Philosophy?* where his influence or at least his expertise is most evident – Deleuze and Guattari were amongst the first major philosophers to take the then-emerging discipline of neuro-science seriously. And by this we mean that they do not dismiss it or attempt to render it in philosophical terms, but see it as engaged in the same investigation as their own.[7] The proto-vitalist Alfred Whitehead, who argued for the priority of events over substances, was a long-term influence on Deleuze, and the work of English biologist Steven Rose is everywhere present, although barely cited, in *A Thousand Plateaus*. And Guattari wrote several solo-authored texts that would touch on the brain and neuro-science, including *L'inconscient machinique* in 1979 and *Cartographies schizoanalytiques* in 1989. But *What is Philosophy?* is also marked by the distance Deleuze and Guattari take from the two then-prevailing conceptions of the brain, which they describe as the 'mechanical' and the 'dynamical' (*WP?*, 209). The first understands the brain as a single centre that issues commands, and is associated with such neuro-scientists as Charles Sherrington and Edward Tolman. The second understands the brain as having a series of centres with commands able to be issued from anywhere, and is associated with a succeeding generation of neuro-scientists, such as Antonio Damasio and Francisco Varela. In the first, thought is seen as following 'ready-made paths' that are 'followed step by step along a pre-established track' (*WP?*, 209). In the second, thought is seen as opening up 'self-producing' paths that are constituted within a 'field of forces proceeding through the resolution of tensions acting step by step' (*WP?*, 209). But Deleuze and Guattari take a distance from both of these models, or in a way combine them, understanding the brain as a 'fold' (*WP?*, 215) that both follows and breaks with pre-existing forms. And, if 'thought' is to be located – and it is here that Deleuze and Guattari object to the usual conceptions, which treat the brain as an 'objectified' (*WP?*, 209) organ, capable merely of opinion and recognition – it is only in the deepest 'fissures, intervals and meantimes' (*WP?*,

209) of a certain folding of the brain upon itself (metaphorizing or allegorizing the creases of the actual cerebellum), which is also that of the brain upon the world and, indeed, that of the world upon itself – which is ultimately to make both the brain and thought unlocatable altogether.

But what ultimately is at stake in this conception of the brain as a fold; and how does it break with the prevailing models of neuro-science? In what ways does it allow Deleuze and Guattari to conceive of the brain not as objective or locatable, and thought not as opinion or recognition? The answer, we might say, is that, if the brain is a fold, is somehow folded upon itself, it also does not exist before this fold. In a kind of philosophical *petitio principii*, it is the very folding of the brain upon itself that leads to the brain's being folded. It is this that goes against the models both of thought coming from a locatable centre that runs along pre-existing paths and thought coming from a series of centres and breaking with pre-existing paths. In both cases, there is still a pre-existing brain, even if decentred, still a pre-existing path, even if broken. By contrast, in conceptualizing the brain in terms of a folding, it is not that there is no centre but that this centre does not exist before a decentring. It is not that there is no path, but that this path does not exist before it is broken. The brain is constantly being split, a split that can never be made up because the brain *is* this split or difference from itself.[8] And what this means is that, even when the brain just is the contraction of what it contracts at the beginning of genesis, it is also something else. Because, if the brain is simply the contraction of the colours, odours and varieties of the world (*WP?*, 212), these colours, odours and varieties would not exist before this contraction. The brain is not only contracted but also what contracts. And the same goes for the world itself. If the brain is split, it also introduces a split into the world – a split that *is* the world, before which the world would not exist. In a sense, the brain – the brain as philosophy, as a figure for the counter-actualization of philosophy – simply follows the world, but the world now exists only for a completely other reason, because it is thought by the brain.[9]

It is this that Deleuze and Guattari mean by speaking of the brain as a 'self-survey without distance' (*WP?*, 210), which crucially is the same description they propose for the relation of the concept to its components in philosophy (*WP?*, 20). And it is survey in this sense, as self-survey, that Deleuze and Guattari oppose to both mechanical and dynamic conceptions of the brain, or is what is implied by both of them. It is this gap or delay, they suggest, that allows both the idea of thought proceeding from a centre along pre-existing tracks and from a series of centres breaking with pre-existing tracks. It is this fold or self-difference that precedes both identity and difference.[10] And all of this is another way of thinking the question that is often put to the brain by such theorists as Catherine Malabou, who in a series of important books has extended Deleuze and Guattari's initial taking up of neuro-science explicitly into the social. This 'folding' is what she calls the 'plasticity' of the brain, a notion that she acknowledges comes from Deleuze and Guattari, but that is also an answer to the necessary Deleuzian requirement that the conditions of possible experience are no wider than those of real experience.[11] That is to say, the brain does not exist outside and is entirely moulded by the social and historical conditions surrounding it. As Malabou writes: 'Neuronal functioning and social functioning interdetermine each other and mutually give each other form, to the point where it is no longer possible to distinguish them'.[12] But, again, the brain and its conditions are also not the same – and this is not what Deleuze and Guattari mean by immanence – because the virtual is always wider than the actual, insofar as it thinks its conditions, how it comes about. And this is the other aspect of 'plasticity' that Malabou emphasizes: the fact that, if the brain always does take an actual shape, it is also what allows it to take such a shape. This is because thinking the real conditions of things, what actuality is or does, *is* to think otherwise. It is to think becoming as the world's own difference from itself. In Deleuze and Guattari's words from *What is Philosophy?*, philosophy is the 'diagnosis of becoming in every passing present' (WP?, 113). And this again is the profound connection between the brain and philosophy and why the brain constitutes the real concept of the book: not merely because at certain points in its becoming the brain is capable of philosophy, but because the brain both is and thinks its own genesis across art, philosophy and science. The brain, insofar as it lies at their 'junction', is not simply to be identified with any one of them, but always with a certain becoming across them, a becoming that – this is ultimately the wager or challenge of philosophy – does not simply end with science and logic and the final emergence of the brain as something that is capable of conscious representations outside nature, for the brain also thinks the *concept* of science and logic, which is to say how science and logic become science and logic.

* * *

We have already seen how the brain is the paradoxical coming-together of the inside and outside. The brain is only its relation to itself and yet it is a relation to itself as other. It is at the same time self-referential (creation, conception) and merely the tracing of what is around it (contraction, contemplation). And we might put this coming-together in another way. For – and this is an unavoidably Hegelian theme, echoing Hegel's famous declaration that 'the being of spirit is a bone'[13] – if thought occurs only in the 'deepest of the synaptic fissures' of the 'non-objectifiable' brain, this brain is also absolutely historically and geographically situated on the surface of the world. As Malabou puts it in her *What Should We Do with Our Brain?* with regard to our present: 'How could we not interrogate the parallelism between the transformation of the spirit of capitalism and the codification, brought about in approximately the same period, of our view of cerebral structures?'[14] But, again, this is only to follow Deleuze and Guattari, who in *Anti-Oedipus* identify the brain with a certain moment of history, and more particularly that of the *Urstaat* that underlies our entire modernity. As they write: '[The State] appears to be set back at a remove from what it transects and from what it resects, as though it were giving evidence of another dimension, a cerebral ideality that is added to, superimposed on the material evolution of societies' (AO, 219). And in the subsequent *A Thousand Plateaus*, Deleuze and Guattari go even further in casting the brain as breaking with the State and belonging instead to a later period of human development, which we might call capitalism. As they write, contrasting the new 'private' thinker of capitalism with the old 'public' thinker of the State: 'He does not ground himself in an all-encompassing totality but is on the contrary deployed in a horizonless milieu that is a smooth space, steppe, desert or sea' (*TP*, 379).

Deleuze and Guattari say exactly the same thing in *What is Philosophy?* in the chapter 'Geophilosophy', which concludes the first section on philosophy and comes before the chapters on science, logic and art. They ask there the question of when philosophy (by which they can also be understood to mean the human brain) arises. And the answer they give, following the contemporary French philosopher Jean-Pierre Faye, is Ancient Greece. Of course, in one way, this is an obvious answer. It is the answer of almost the entire history of Western philosophy (Hegel, Husserl, Heidegger). But Deleuze and Guattari mean it in a different sense, in that, unlike those others, they do not mean to imply some necessary connection of language, culture or *Weltgeist* linking philosophy to its birthplace. Rather, the connection is contingent, or rather it was precisely in Ancient Greece that thought first broke with its historical, linguistic and even spiritual determinants. Philosophy first arose in Ancient Greece, write Deleuze and Guattari, because it was in Ancient Greece that the essential conditions for philosophy were first met: opinion, friendship and rivalry, and the trade between countries (*WP?*, 87–8). To elaborate further, in Ancient Greece there was the free exchange of opinion because of a certain 'democratization' or levelling of the social order so that increasing numbers of citizens were able to discuss things without sanction, a kind of 'milieu of immanence' (*WP?*, 87) in which each opinion is hypothetically equal to any other, or at least able to contest any other. There must also be friendship and rivalry, both of which in various ways break with this *doxa* or opinion, in the attempt either to put together a new consensus or to break with the existing one. Finally, there is the necessary presence of trade, putting Greece, as a country on a peninsula surrounded by the sea, in touch with other cultures, including the non-European ones of North Africa and Asia Minor, so that from the beginning philosophy – against both its own understanding of its origins and the accusations frequently made of it – was not an exclusively 'European', let alone a Greek, undertaking (*WP?*, 88).

In each case here, there is a certain breaking with culture and context. Democracy breaks with the inherited classes or factions, friendship breaks with the existing philosophical schools or associations and free trade breaks with the political and geographical boundaries of the Greek state. Even opinion, which Deleuze and Guattari will later come to criticize, is first of all a breaking with the specific, a kind of generalization beyond the particular. In a sense, as they suggest, each of these is a precondition for philosophy. It is their presence that explains why the Greeks, uniquely, were able to produce philosophy.[15] And this is ultimately to suggest that philosophy is inseparable from capitalism, that the levelling of distinctions that Marx observed as a result of capitalist exchange – his famous 'all that is solid melts into air' – is both necessary for philosophy and analogous to what philosophy does. In capitalism, there is always a kind of 'decoding' (*WP?*, 106) or overcoming of established limits. Or, as Deleuze and Guattari put it in *What is Philosophy?*, in an analysis that is also to be found in *Anti-Oedipus*: 'The social field no longer refers to an external limit that restricts it from above, as in the empires, but to immanent internal limits that constantly shift by extending the system, and that reconstitute themselves through displacement' (*WP?*, 97). That is to say, as opposed to any overcoding or holding of one element above the others – this, as we have seen, is exactly the difference of the third order of capitalism from the previous order of despotism – there is the putting of the transcendental among the others, the seeing of it as just one of many like it. And this capitalism is understood as always being there – again perhaps against the historical evidence – or there at least from the beginning of philosophy. In *Anti-Oedipus*, for example, the 'capitalist' order that allows 'cerebral ideality' is understood to date back to the time of the first State, which is to say at least back to Ancient Greece (*AO*, 218–20). In *A Thousand Plateaus*, the 'plateau' that most extensively deals with capitalism is for some reason dated 7,000 BC (*TP*, 448–73). In Deleuze and Guattari's conception, capitalism constitutes a kind of 'becoming' that at once is outside of and leads to history (*WP?*, 96), just as in Marx.

But all of this, in Deleuze and Guattari's terms, constitutes only a 'relative deterritorialization' (*WP?*, 98). Capitalism, if it decodes, also immediately recodes. This is again Deleuze and Guattari's point in quoting the celebrated passage from Marx's *Capital*, in both *Anti-Oedipus* and *What is Philosophy?*, that 'capitalist production seeks continually to overcome these immanent barriers, but overcomes them only by means which once again place these barriers in its way' (*AO*, 231; *WP?*, 224). They precisely analyze in *Anti-Oedipus* and *A Thousand Plateaus* capitalism's endless generation of 'axioms' (*AO*, 246–53; *TP*, 453–73), which we might say are capitalism's authorized exceptions to absolute exchangeability, in effect making immanence immanent to a transcendent. (Examples of these axioms in *Anti-Oedipus* and *A Thousand Plateaus* include such things as linguistics, psychoanalysis, southern nations and worker's struggles (*AO*, 246; *TP*, 462–3).) And equally, as we have also seen, in *What is Philosophy?*, soon after paraphrasing that passage from *Capital*, Deleuze and Guattari speak of 'human rights' as an axiom (*WP?*, 107), which ultimately is to understand them as an exception to capitalism, a way of ameliorating its injustices, but a 'higher' value that does not change anything and even enables capitalism. Capitalism is only a 'relative deterritorialization' in the sense that it is an endless critique of itself, but only in its own terms (*WP?*, 106). Within it we can do anything we want, except undertake a fundamental critique of its own conditions. In a way, it is even its own exception. And we see the same thing for 'democracy', which is the political form of capitalism. In *What is Philosophy?*, Deleuze and Guattari speak of both Russia and America as failed experiments in 'democracy' (*WP?*, 98–9); but we understand by this – admittedly, against other readings[16] – not that democracy must be judged against some true model of the form, that democracy is perfectible, but that democracy itself is a necessarily failed form. It endlessly reforms itself, attempts to improve itself, but it never actually contests democracy in any terms but its own. It is not against *democracy* that we should judge democracy, but against something other than itself. Deleuze and Guattari do not see their work as an internal reform or even critique of the democratic project, and themselves as Rortyesque 'gadflies', who would merely seek applause and approbation from those they are criticizing (*WP?*, 146), but seek to overthrow democracy altogether.

Deleuze and Guattari see the equivalent of this relative deterritorialization in certain forms of both Western and non-Western philosophy and religious thought. In them, in an analogy to the positing of axioms or designated exceptions in capitalism, we have a kind of 'rotation' of the 'transcendent element' (*WP?*, 89), so that what was originally underneath is put on top and what was on top is moved below. Thus in Chinese hexagrams we have 'combinations of continuous and discontinuous features deriving from one another according to the levels of a spiral' (*WP?*, 89). Or in the Hindu mandala there is a 'projection on a surface that establishes correspondences between divine, cosmic, political, architectural and organic levels as so many levels of one and the same transcendence' (*WP?*, 89). Equally, there have been throughout the long history of Western philosophy attempts to free thought from its material conditions and attain absolute deterritorialization. In Plato, there is the weighing up and going beyond of rival opinions through the contemplation of the Beautiful (*WP?*, 79–80, 147–8). In Kant, there is the selection and distribution of opposed opinions thanks to the universals of reflection (*WP?*, 79–80). In Hegel, there is a dialectic that generalizes even further in taking the contradictions between rival opinions and using them to exhaust the absolute (*WP?*, 80). In Husserl, there is a search for the underlying knowledge or *Urdoxa* that goes beyond lived experience and breaks with common opinion (*WP?*, 142). However, as Deleuze and Guattari emphasize, each of these attempts also fails; and the very sign of this failure, at least for Hegel and Husserl, is that they do not break with the assumption of the 'Greek' origins of philosophy, are not finally able to 'de-actualize' its original conditions and see them as not determinative. In Plato, if there is a certain passage opened up from opinion to knowledge, this knowledge is 'immanent to something transcendent, to ideality' (*WP?*, 148). In Kant, if there is a reaching towards philosophical truth, his concepts are related back to lived experience 'through a priori propositions or judgements as functions of a whole of possible experience' (*WP?*, 142). In Hegel, if the dialectic claims to go beyond opinion, it does so only by 'linking opinions together' (*WP?*, 80). And in Husserl, if we can go beyond opinion through the reality of the lived, this reality in the end will be revealed as 'constituted by the subject' (*WP?*, 142). In each case here, even Plato, the aimed-at immanence of philosophy still only takes place within the overarching category of the subject. Its deterritorialization is inevitably accompanied by an equal and opposite reterritorialization. In capital, as we have seen, there is always a certain overcoding or axiomatic by means of which transcendence is preserved, and in many ways the same thing can be seen in philosophy: the subject in philosophy is another version of human rights in capitalism. As Deleuze and Guattari write, criticizing the transcendental subject that remains in Husserl and the phenomenological tradition in terms that would also apply to the partiality and selectivity of supposedly 'universal' human rights in capitalism:

> The lived turns the concept into nothing more than an empirical opinion as psychosociological type. The immanence of the lived to a transcendental subject, therefore, must turn opinion into a

proto-opinion in whose constitution art and culture are involved and that is expressed as an act of transcendence of this subject within the lived, so as to form a community of friends... Are we not led back in this way to the simple opinion of the average Capitalist, the great Major, the modern Ulysses whose perceptions are cliches and whose affections are labels, in a world of communication that has become marketing? (*WP?*, 149)

As opposed, then, to the relative deterritorialization of capitalism and certain forms of religious thought and philosophy, Deleuze and Guattari speak of the 'absolute deterritorialization' (*WP?*, 88) that characterizes authentic philosophy. But what exactly do they mean by this? How is philosophy able to break with its context and have no historical or geographical determinations in the counter-actualization it brings about? In fact, the example – the political example – they speak of is revolution, and more particularly Kant's much-discussed response to the French Revolution in his *The Conflict of the Faculties*, in which he speaks of the 'enthusiasm' with which he greets the 'historical sign'.[17] And by this 'enthusiasm' – which Deleuze and Guattari repeat (*WP?*, 100) – Kant means to refer not so much to any actual revolution as to the 'sympathy' it manages to arouse in the spectator.[18] It is a 'spirit' that is shared, which Kant and the onlooker have in common with the original revolutionaries, and that makes them and their reception of it part of the original event. Indeed, in a certain way, the actual revolution – and Kant acknowledges this – always fails; but the spirit of the revolution, the 'enthusiasm' it both is and incites, is not to be confused with this (and this 'revolution' judged against 'enthusiasm' is different in principle from capitalism judging capitalism or democracy judging democracy). This enthusiasm, we might say, hovers over the actual events of the revolution in the same way as the 'Event' of a battle hovers over the real incidents of the battlefield (*LS*, 116; *WP?*, 159). It is the very embodiment of a philosophical 'event', in that it is immaterial, incorporeal, at once 'still to come and having already happened' (*WP?*, 158). Enthusiasm is not only a philosophical concept – at least in Kant – but is able to be grasped only from a philosophical perspective, insofar as it is a 'self-referential' and 'self-positing' doubling of the world, in which 'thinking and being are said at the same time' (*WP?*, 38). Enthusiasm is not some expression of an immortal world-spirit that is waiting to be awakened, but a singular event that is each time different, existing only in its narration, its transmission to another (*WP?*, 16–19).

This is what Deleuze and Guattari mean by the absolute deterritorialization of philosophy: virtual, breaking with its historical context or occasion (again, it is not the actual French Revolution that Kant identifies with, which soon turned into terror and later mere democracy), eluding its own actualization in everything that subsequently happens (*WP?*, 156). This is the real image (or, better, abstract or non-image) of thought, the counter-effectuation that philosophy performs. And yet even here the difference between absolute and relative deterritorialization is very small. A moment ago, we drew a distinction between philosophy and capitalism, in that in capitalism any deterritorialization is always accompanied by a corresponding reterritorialization, and between philosophy and religious thought, in that in religious thought there is always a transcendence that allows immanence. But, as we have already seen, both of these are how Deleuze and Guattari characterize authentic philosophy: it, too, is not entirely distinguishable from the transcendental. It never actually attains immanence as such, but is only ever on a perpetual path towards it. Precisely, it is a kind of 'movement' (*WP?*, 47) that, if not a simple rotation, nevertheless attains immanence through transcendence or thinks an immanence that allows transcendence (*WP?*, 73). Or as Deleuze and Guattari put it, there is a reversibility between the earth (deterritorialization) and the territory (reterritorialization), in which each is possible only because of the other (*WP?*, 85–6). In other words, the event enters into the state of affairs and therefore must be extracted from this state of affairs. And this is undoubtedly the other way of reading their taking up of Kant on the French Revolution: the revolution, as in 'The Analytic of the Sublime', is not to be directly presented but only in the very failure to think it. That immanence that is Kant's sublime is not to be directly thought, but thought only as the failure to think it, the fact that we can think our failure to think it.

So what, finally, is the difference between the philosophy Deleuze and Guattari propose and religious thought or the non-philosophy of other philosophers? Indeed, how are we to put into practice their philosophy, if we cannot actually think it? Why is it not merely a 'figure' or 'metaphor', if what they advocate can never be realized? And how can we say that philosophy breaks with its surrounding context if it can never be seen to do so? Let us start with *Anti-Oedipus*. How is it that the 'schizo-analysis' Deleuze and Guattari propose is able to break with capitalism? They write there of desiring-production: 'This interpretive field will continue to survive and work, even through Oedipus, even through myth and tragedy, which nevertheless mark the reconciliation of psychoanalysis with representation' (*AO*, 300). And how does the similar concept of 'deterritorialization' work in *What is Philosophy?* They write there: 'Absolute deterritorialization can only be thought according to certain still-to-be-determined relationships to relative deterritorializations that are not only cosmic, but geographical, historical and psychosocial' (*WP?*, 88). In fact, by schizoanalysis and deterritorialization Deleuze and Guattari do not mean – this is a common misreading of their work, even encouraged by them – a simple disordering or disaggregation, some other actual order. On the contrary, in *Anti-Oedipus*, schizoanalysis is described as making 'escaping escape' (*AO*, 341). And in *What is Philosophy?* deterritorialization is described as an 'erewhon' or 'no-where' (*WP?*, 100). By schizoanalysis and deterritorialization Deleuze and Guattari do not mean to oppose some actual alternative to what is but rather to think its conditions of possibility. Or, to put it otherwise, the genesis of how it came to be. This is exactly Deleuze's point regarding the way we determine 'the conditions of real [as opposed to possible] experience, which are not larger than the conditioned and which differ in kind from the [Kantian] categories' (*DR*, 68): that it is not a matter of some possible as opposed to the actual. That is, against Kant's transcendental categories of experience, which Deleuze argues, for all of their supposed transcendentality, are always in fact too much based on or a reflection of what is, his 'conditions of real experience' are not merely the inversion of or counter-image to the actual, but at once are nothing different from the actual and have nothing to do with it. This is Deleuze's breaking with the 'image' of philosophy, and more particularly from the Kantian 'image' of philosophy, which is not to propose another image but no image, the world itself and not the image of another world. It is Nietzsche's 'amor fati' as opposed to Kant's 'critique', a 'mime' or 'mimicry' as opposed to judgement and legislation (*WP?*, 159).

This is the particular power of philosophy. It is not so much to think difference as what is different from itself. Indeed, it is to think the actual as the virtual, as what is different from itself.

For even to think that there is only the actual *is* to think how the actual became the actual. It is this that Deleuze and Guattari mean by speaking of philosophy as the 'diagnosis of our actual becomings' (*WP?*, 112), by which they mean the endless becoming of the actual. For it is true, as they themselves admit, that every virtual ends up becoming actual. And in a way there is only ever this continual rotation or substitution of actuals. There is only ever the transcendental. But, as Deleuze and Guattari insist, this transcendental, if it is necessarily the failure of immanence, also serves to 'recharge the plane of immanence with immanence itself' (*WP?*, 73).[19] And all of this is to say that what the immanence of philosophy makes us think – in the sublime or enthusiastic manner of Kant thinking the failure of the French Revolution – is how the actual became the actual. And, in doing so, it introduces a gap between the actual and itself, makes the actual different from itself. Deterritorialization, as Deleuze and Guattari say, is not a final stopping point but only the continual movement of stopping points (*WP?*, 158). Deterritorialization is only this continual motion or substitution that each time ends in – and can only be seen through – reterritorialization. Deterritorialization is what is different from itself. It is why Deleuze and Guattari say that philosophy only ever thinks in opinions or can only ever use the sentences of a 'standard language'. But in a sense this, too, like Kant's thinking of the French Revolution, attests to the sublime power of thought: to think the actual, that there is only the actual, is also to think the 'transcendental', that is, immanent conditions that allow this. It is something like this coincidence of the Revolution and Kant's thinking of it, the actual and the virtual, that Deleuze and Guattari call the 'utopic' (*WP?*, 99): not only does the Revolution call forth this enthusiasm in Kant, but this enthusiasm leads to, insofar as it allows us to think, the revolution. This would be that immediate bringing together of Being and Thought that Deleuze and Guattari say is the very definition of philosophy (*WP?*, 38).

CHAPTER SEVEN

Reception

What is Philosophy? [*Qu'est-ce que la philosophie?*] attracted widespread media attention when it was first published in France in September 1991. Deleuze was the recently retired Professor of Philosophy at Vincennes University and author of a long series of monographs. Guattari was well-known as the assistant at La Borde clinic and for his involvement in French politics at the highest levels. Their collaboration was now retrospectively hailed for having produced *Anti-Oedipus*, one of *the* books of theory and radical politics of the 1970s. As well, the French press was in the admirable habit of giving coverage to the products of the nation's leading thinkers, playing its part in what it saw as the country's proud cultural tradition. The book was reviewed in the pages of *Libération* on 12 September by Robert Maggiore, who wrote: 'It is with great quietness and a most exquisite courtesy that Deleuze and Guattari place their bomb under philosophy'.[1] It was also reviewed some four days later in *La Quinzaine littéraire* by Xavier Delcourt, who offered a contrasting view, perhaps more in accord with the newspaper's conservative readership: 'How to take seriously trouble-makers who design for Tinguely a Kant-machine in the middle of their arguments?'[2] It was then given a more 'considered' opinion – again, following the immutable laws of the public reception of cultural products, in which daily newspapers and monthly magazines unofficially divide up opinion – in the monthly *Magazine littéraire* by Raymond Bellour, who offered: 'And as the difficulty [of philosophy] cannot be shared, but resolves itself by insistence, we understand that *What is Philosophy?* is the pedagogical instrument we have been lacking, and should be on the syllabus of what remains of philosophy courses'.[3]

What is Philosophy? was also given, both in its untranslated form and when its first translations started appearing, considerable coverage in European journals and magazines. The work of Deleuze and Guattari was by now widely known, and various 'experts' in other countries competed to get out their 'advanced' opinions on this important new book from France. In Germany, the task of reviewing the 1996 German translation was given to Andreas Platthaus, who rather nationalistically said of it: 'It's nice to see how with this obsession with the number three [art, philosophy, science], which is reminiscent of the basic triadic pattern of the dialectic (thesis, antithesis, synthesis), we find Hegel's shadow, against which Deleuze has been fighting for so long'.[4] In Italy, where Guattari had worked with the *autonomia* movement throughout the 1970s, the book was given a predominantly left-wing reading, as in Toni Negri's review for *Futur Antérieur*: 'This philosophy is actually the strongest example of a "philosophical communism" presented in our modernity as an alternative to capitalist modernity. Through its rigorous materialism, it presents itself as a philosophical communism, as part of its insistence upon an absolute immanence by which it would liquidate post-modernism'.[5] In England, which prided itself on its early pick-up of French theory, which was also used in academic circles as part of the struggle against the official analytic philosophy, it was extensively reviewed after its translation into English in 1994, for example, by James Williams, who wrote: 'Deleuze's ability to grasp and develop themes from the history of philosophy is brought to the fore in a balance of standard and impressively clear presentations allied to highly controversial, but convincing, speculative statements'.[6] In America, where Deleuze and Guattari had been introduced into subcultural circles by the publishing house Semiotext(e), *What is Philosophy?* was given a review more befitting a rock record by Erik Davis in *Voice Literary Supplement* review: 'The heavy dazzle of the language makes some folks just toss their book down, muttering about wacky frogs who have lost their politics'.[7] In England again, perhaps as part of a delayed backlash by analytic philosophers against the perceived 'irrationalism' of French philosophy, it was given a scathing review by Roger Caldwell in *New Statesman and Society*: 'Given that reason is here downplayed as an obsolete idol, philosophers seem to be placed in a position of delirious irresponsibility'.[8] And, in faraway Australia, the book spoke to a younger generation of Francophile intellectuals, who again took it up as part of a struggle against Anglo-American analytic philosophy, but this time overlaid with a certain anti-colonialism, as in this review by Robyn Ferrell in the long-running *Australian Journal of Philosophy*: 'It has the characteristics of earlier Deleuze and Guattari collaborations, such as the inventive use of metaphor and of rebuke. But in the simple vigour of its style and the energy of its theoretical solutions, *What is Philosophy?* is a singular pleasure'.[9]

Undoubtedly, however, the best-known response to *What is Philosophy?* – and certainly the one most often quoted – is that of Jean-Jacques Lecercle, who reviewed the translated version for *Radical Philosophy*. There he conjured up the image of a 'yuppie' perplexedly reading the book on a train: 'The underground train is taking you, rather fast, towards the skyscrapers of La Défence and, a little further west, the University of Nanterre. On the seat facing you, a bespectacled yuppie, complete with tailored suit and regulation tie, is reading Deleuze and Guattari's *What is Philosophy?* The incongruity of the scene induces a smile – after all, this is a book explicitly written against yuppies'.[10] And Lecercle's vision here is testament to the fact that, as we have suggested, Deleuze and Guattari were already at the time minor celebrities, their work widely known and their ideas commodified. *Anti-Oedipus* had introduced a whole new vocabulary into critical discourse. *A Thousand Plateaus*, published eight years later, for all its daunting length and encyclopaedic breadth of reference, was a comparative bestseller. And *What is Philosophy?*, appearing some eleven years after that, almost immediately topped the lists after release in France. However, the liberatory hopes of the late 1960s out of which *Anti-Oedipus* was written and Guattari's experiments in alternative politics throughout the 1970s had come to an end during the 'winter' decade of the 1980s; and by the early 1990s when *What is Philosophy?* came out Deleuze and Guattari could already be seen to belong to a recent past, thus embodying a nostalgia that was able to be indulged. Their theories of 'desire', 'nomadism' and 'schizophrenia' were now being used widely and increasingly subjected to the usual procedures of academic evaluation, or, to put it the other way round, it was increasingly being seen that Deleuze and Guattari's 'desiring theory', for all its initial reception as a form of anarchism, was no longer opposed to contemporary forms of capitalism, but on the contrary complicit with or even arising out of them.

It is all of this that Lecercle implies in his review with his evocation of the yuppie bemusedly reading *What is Philosophy?* on the way to work, before (hypocritically) rejecting it. But it is, indeed, something like this conception that many of the readings of *What is Philosophy?* and the work of Deleuze and Guattari more generally begin to suggest. It is the new forms of 'soft' capitalism emerging out of the tech industries of Silicon Valley, which were no longer directly coercive but on the contrary exploited their employees' interests, that were seen to be predicted by Deleuze and Guattari's notion of 'desiring production'. It is a critique that was taken up and developed at greatest length by Slavoj Žižek in his *Organs without Bodies: Deleuze and Consequences*, which contains a long set-piece restaging Lecercle's original.[11] But it is a possibility that several early reviews of *What is Philosophy?* were quick to point to and that even comes up in a review of a 1998 novel by Douglas Coupland, inventor of the notion of 'Generation X': 'Coupland has effectively paraphrased, in a testament to the power of Deleuze and Guattari's ideas, *What is Philosophy?* in his latest educational and philosophical solution'.[12] It is an argument implicit even in a book that is indebted to the work of Deleuze and Guattari, Michael Hardt and Antonio Negri's *Empire*, which wants to argue that its move beyond Deleuze and Guattari in thinking through biopower and the society of control was motivated by its sense that their original critique was becoming increasingly 'subsumed', that it could not have predicted what would happen to it in the new conditions that capitalism would throw up.[13] And something like this is also to be seen in one of the most developed and often-cited critiques of Deleuze and Guattari in English, Peter Hallward's *Deleuze and the Philosophy of Creation: Out of this World*. There, Hallward's argument that Deleuze errs in positing a virtual that is disconnected from the actual undoubtedly comes out of a more fundamental dissatisfaction with the political consequences of Deleuze's thinking, or it could even be suggested that the future political reception of Deleuze's thought reveals for Hallward this more fundamental error.[14]

But, in fact, for all the critique of Lecercle and those who come after him, Deleuze and Guattari in many ways foresee themselves this future. Already in *What is Philosophy?*, there is a diagnosis of a new 'permissive capitalism' that concerns ideas and not materials and that speaks in the language of free flows, communication and creativity. There is already an identification of the emerging class of the yuppie or knowledge worker, who are more than happy to admit their affinity with radical forms of philosophy, and even aspire, themselves, to be philosophers. As Deleuze and Guattari mimic in humorous, if scathing, lines: 'We are the creative ones, we are the ideas men!' (*WP?*, 10). And, more generally, in *What is Philosophy?* we find a diagnosis of that realm of endlessly circulating speech that is the contemporary world of books reviews, TV panel discussions and even the 'referenda' of those stars that are awarded to books of philosophy on websites like Amazon. It is a world of 'opinions' that, although appearing free and freely given, are secretly determined by a whole series of factors, from an unavoidable bad or common 'taste' (*WP?*, 80) to the illusion that they are neutral (*WP?*, 145) to the hegemony of capitalism itself. Indeed, as we see, it is something like this marketplace of opinion that has characterized philosophy from the very beginning. And, again, all this reflection on the context in which their work is received is another aspect of what Deleuze and Guattari speak of as their 'growing old', which is how they are finally able to summarize not only their work but the conditions in which it is undertaken. Or, alternatively, that 'fatigue' or 'weariness' they speak of, in which we are no longer able to contract concepts and sensations but offer only 'readymade' opinions (*WP?*, 213–4), would be not merely biological or even biographical but ultimately civilizational (although in another way it has also been the case since Ancient Greece).

However, *What is Philosophy?* not only foresees its reception, but also *responds to* it. And it is just this that defines philosophy as an event or counter-actualization that occupies not so much a present that is actual as a future that is always yet to come (*WP?*, 112). At the very moment it acknowledges that this is how it is taken up, it also thinks the conditions for this and thus opens up a certain outside onto them. We start perhaps with their point, which can now seem so much like a form of contemporary feminism or post-colonialism, that behind any 'neutrality' or 'universality' of opinion there is always a highly culturally and historically determined context: 'But does not the Husserlian transcendental subject hide European man whose privilege it is constantly to 'Europeanize', as the Greeks 'Greekized', that is to say, to go beyond the limits of other cultures that are preserved as psychosocial types?' (*WP?*, 149) We then move to a more general critique of opinion or commentary as not constituting a real philosophy, insofar as it does not produce a new image of thought or propose itself the real conditions of thought: 'What is naturally uninteresting? Flimsy concepts – or, on the contrary, concepts that are too regular, petrified and reduced to a framework' (*WP?*, 83). Finally, we have the project of *What is Philosophy?*, itself, which is to think the real genesis of opinion or how opinion comes about. We have in all of this a certain rising up from the logical propositions of opinion towards that which makes opinion possible. Philosophy, although it is always able to be mistaken for opinion and is never entirely able to break with it, is not to be identified with opinion. It is not to be identified with opinion because it is not exhaustively able to be assessed, evaluated or corrected. Rather, insofar as its concepts can never be grasped in themselves but only in their difference from themselves, any proposed criticism of philosophy is possible only because of it. In an impossible act of self-prophecy, it foresees all possible criticism made of it and responds to it in advance.

We have two telling examples of this phenomenon, involving two of the most important receptions of Deleuze's and Deleuze and Guattari's work over the years. And both show that that this 'self-prophetic' quality of philosophical concepts is not put there by their creators, but is rather part of the logic of the philosophical concept itself, something that does not exist in advance of any criticism as some unrealized potential in the future, but at once exists in advance and only after its criticism in that 'infinite past' and 'infinite awaiting' (*WP?*, 158) that marks the particular temporality of the philosophical concept. The first example of this that we would recall concerns Alain Badiou's critique of Deleuze, first put in a review of Deleuze's *The Fold*, and then in more extended form in his *Deleuze: The Clamour of Being*. In The *Clamour of Being*, Badiou suggests that Deleuze's philosophical concept is too virtual, that he 'retains from Plato the universal sovereignty of the One, but sacrifices the determination of the Idea as always actual'.[15] It is, as we have seen, a critique later extended by Hallward in his *Out of this World* and, to some extent, by Žižek in his *Deleuze and Consequences*, and now itself the subject of any number of academic papers and even books evaluating the merits of the respective sides in the 'debate'. But what is often forgotten in these commentaries is that Deleuze and Guattari had already made a similar criticism of Badiou in *What is Philosophy?*, where they accuse his 'axiomatic' method of reintroducing the transcendent in its belief that it can directly attain the 'void' or the 'truth as void' (*WP?*, 152) outside any genesis, in a philosophy that would literally be 'outside of this world'. This is what Deleuze and Guattari write with regard to Badiou in the chapter 'Prospects and Concepts' in *What is Philosophy?*:

> Philosophy thus seems to float in an empty transcendence, as the unconditioned concept that finds the totality of its generic conditions in the functions (science, poetry, politics and love). Is this not the return, in the guise of the multiple, to an old conception of the higher philosophy? (*WP?*, 152)

We have another example of this taking into account in advance of criticism with regard to perhaps *the* intellectual movement that understands itself as coming after Deleuze, and in some ways based on a critique of his work: Speculative Realism. The movement, of course, begins with an important book by a student of Badiou, Quentin Meillassoux, *After Finitude: An Essay on the Necessity of Contingency*. Meillassoux's book seeks to break with what it calls 'correlationism', in which the world can be seen only as it is 'for us' and we cannot have access to reality except insofar as it can be thought. But in its desire to think on the contrary how things are 'in themselves', it understands itself as having to go back before Kant, with whom this constitutive gesture of philosophy refusing to think noumenal reality begins. Indeed, as part of this, Meillassoux attempts to revive the thought of the English empiricist David Hume, against whom Kant formed his critical project as a rejection of Hume's 'scepticism' or refusal of a priori metaphysical principles through which reality would have to be mediated.[16] And, in perhaps the best-known English-language elaboration of Meillassoux's theoretical gesture, one of the founders of the school of Speculative Realism, Ray Brassier, in his *Nihil Unbound: Enlightenment and Extinction*, accuses Deleuze of this correlationism.[17] For Brassier, there is a confusion in Deleuze between the conditions of real experience and the conditions of possible experience, brought about by the fact that Deleuze commits the correlationist mistake of reducing the empirical world (the 'the conditions of real experience') to an effect of how we think about it (the 'conditions of possible experience'). As Brassier writes: 'He is constantly equivocating between the claim that he is providing an account of the genesis of actual experience and the claim that he is giving an account of the genesis of actuality *tout court*'.[18]

But, in fact, Meillassoux, in turning to Hume as an attempt to outflank Kant, repeats the same philosophical gesture as Deleuze himself. After all, Deleuze begins his own philosophical apprenticeship, his putting together of philosophers from the margins to form a distinctive 'minor' tradition, with a study of Hume. It is a choice that, according to Jeffrey Bell in his *Deleuze's Hume: Philosophy, Culture and the Scottish Enlightenment*, has to be understood as directed against the post-Kantianism that was then dominant in the French academy and the first indication of Deleuze's life-long preference for English empiricism against French and German rationalism.[19] And Deleuze precisely wants to see in this an alternative to the Kantian impossibility of thinking the world outside a human subject. As he writes in his *Empiricism and Subjectivity: An Essay on Hume's Theory of Human Nature*: 'But let us suppose [against Kant] that the given is not initially subject to principles of the same kind as those that regulate the connection of representations in the case of an empirical subject' (*H*, 111). That is to say, for Deleuze reality does not exist only within the human mind because the human mind itself comes about only as an effect of reality. And this mind is not to be identified with Kantian subjectivity or consciousness because these phenomena arise only towards the end of a long genesis. Again, if reality is the effect of a certain 'brain', this 'brain' is only the reality it contracts or contemplates (*WP?*, 212–13). And this is also to say that it is 'empirical' reality itself that contains within it the power to think it. The conditions of real experience *are* the conditions of possible experience. Finally, indeed, more subtly than Meillassoux's and Speculative Realism's belief that it is possible to think reality outside consciousness – for which obvious self-contradiction it has been criticized – for Deleuze and Guattari it is not simply a question of thinking immanence or the plane of immanence, but of the always repeated *failure* to do so. As they write: 'The plane of immanence is, at the same time, that which must be thought and that which cannot be thought' (*WP?*, 59). That is, philosophy necessarily constitutes a certain transcendental origin for itself – in effect, a kind of subject within which reality is immanent – but its task is always to think the genesis or origin of this subject.

* * *

In fact, for all the early reviews of *What is Philosophy?* – which were only opinion, passed before we could properly know what the book was about – over the years there has been relatively little attention paid to it. Certainly, it is among the least discussed of Deleuze's many books. And, of Deleuze and Guattari's several collaborations, it is also amongst the least analyzed, receiving much less attention than *Anti-Oedipus* and *A Thousand Plateaus*. For all the obvious personal significance of the book – Deleuze speaks of it as a 'refrain' or 'ritournelle',[20] and it would prove to be the last that either would write – it has received virtually no sustained academic commentary. There are admittedly two relatively little-known and rarely acknowledged books that treat it: Eric Alliez's *Signature of the World: What is Deleuze and Guattari's Philosophy?*, and Iain MacKenzie's *The Idea of Pure Critique*. But neither of these takes up *What is Philosophy?* as a whole or offers a systematic exposition of its arguments. Alliez's book imitates the 'rhizomatic' style of *Anti-Oedipus* and *A Thousand Plateaus*.[21] MacKenzie's book uses *What is Philosophy?* to address the question of 'pure' or 'internal' critique that first emerges in Kant.[22] And neither book is regularly referred to in the literature on either Deleuze or Deleuze and Guattari. However, even in such surveys as Reidar Due's *Deleuze*[23] or Eleanor Kaufman's and Kevin Jon Heller's *Deleuze and Guattari: New Mappings in Politics, Philosophy and Culture*,[24] which seek to offer an overview of Deleuze's or Deleuze and Guattari's work, *What is Philosophy?* is rarely if ever chosen for sustained treatment. And, conversely, in those books that address selected 'themes' in Deleuze's and Deleuze and Guattari's work, such as Nathan Widder's *Political Theory after Deleuze*,[25] or Jay Lampert's *Deleuze and Guattari's Philosophy of History*,[26] *What is Philosophy?* is virtually never selected to be one of the books in which to see these themes or through which these themes are to be read. Even in the realm of specialist academic journals, *What is Philosophy?* is only infrequently addressed as the single or even principal subject of review. To our knowledge, there is only Isabelle Stengers' 'Deleuze and Guattari's Last Enigmatic Message',[27] which is an overview of the relationship between science and philosophy in *What is Philosophy?*, Arkady Plotnitsky's 'Chaosmologies: Quantum Field Theory, Chaos and Thought in Deleuze and Guattari's *What is Philosophy?*',[28] which is a discussion of how *What is Philosophy?* stands in relation to so-called quantum field theory, and Stephen Arnott, 'In the Shadow of Chaos: Deleuze and Guattari on Philosophy, Science and Art',[29] which looks more generally at the relationship of philosophy with science and art.

The obvious question must be asked: What explains this relative neglect of *What is Philosophy?* Why is the book so little read, for all the factors that would otherwise privilege it? Certainly – and this is again the predictive aspect of the book, the way it appears to take into account its own future reception – Deleuze and Guattari's own description of *What is Philosophy?* is essentially correct. The book appears to have been written in a hurry, 'in a moment of grace between life and death' (*WP?*, 1). There is a highly summarized aspect to the text, with its language abstract, condensed and abbreviated. Arguments and references from Deleuze's and Deleuze and Guattari's prior work – which we have attempted to elaborate here – are merely sketchily alluded to. The typical condensation and even encryptedness of Deleuze's writing, for all its surface clarity, is absolutely in evidence throughout. Take, for example, the discussion of 'conic sections' in the chapter on science (*WP?*, 129–30), which in fact raises the problem of perspectivism as treated in Leibnitz's 'Geometry and the Method of Universality' (1674). Or take the concept of the Other Person who makes 'any length a possible depth in space' (*WP?*, 18), which was first seen in the chapter 'Asymmetrical Synthesis of the Sensible' in *Difference and Repetition* and is actually an allusion to Merleau-Ponty. Material is taken from previous books, but now used in different circumstances or applied to different parts of Deleuze and Guattari's argument: calculus, for instance, which in *The Fold* is discussed in relation to the first dynamic synthesis and in *Difference and Repetition* in relation to the virtual Idea, is now seen in *What is Philosophy?* in relation to the second, static synthesis. And the 'plane of immanence', which refers to pure material movement in the cinema books, is now understood to speak of the abstract surface of philosophy, while that original plane of immanence in the cinema books is now called 'chaos' in *What is Philosophy?*

The effect of all of this is undoubtedly to make it seem as though *What is Philosophy?* has nothing new to say, that it is nothing more than a reiteration of everything that has come before. This has been more or less the explicit view of a number of commentators on the book. For example, Jean de Martelaere writes: 'In effect, to the question "what is philosophy?" is offered a response that is addressed only to those who, in the last instance, are already thoroughly familiar with the subject'.[30] Or, in a slightly more discreet way, Jay Conway suggests: '*What is Philosophy?* involves a slight remodelling of the distinction between the correct and incorrect ways of approaching philosophy'.[31] Or, in an interesting variant on this, Ian Buchanan speaks of the way that *What is Philosophy?* has 'all the hallmarks of an exercise in secondary revision'.[32] But this last comment, for all its overtones of Fredric Jameson, in fact opens up an intriguing new way of thinking about *What is Philosophy?* For it is to suggest that *What is Philosophy?* – and, indeed, all Deleuze's and Deleuze and Guattari's work – is 'allegorical'.[33] And what this means is that, beneath the ostensible subject of each book, something else is being played out. This is a view – which abstracts, dematerializes, decontenxtualizes, even counter-actualizes each book – that has gradually emerged in Deleuze and Deleuze and Guattari studies over the past twenty years; but we might suggest that it has achieved its highest form in the commentaries of Levi Bryant and Joe Hughes, which effectively suggest not only that each book by Deleuze and Deleuze and Guattari is allegorical, with each hiding its real content beneath some other subject matter, but that this hidden content is each time the same, that Deleuze and Deleuze and Guattari have been writing the same book throughout their careers.

And what is it exactly that each time is allegorized in Deleuze's and Deleuze and Guattari's books? It is suggested by Bryant and Hughes that it is a kind of *genesis*, moving from the unindividuated matter of a first, dynamic genesis, through the virtual immateriality of a metaphysical plane of thought and on to the individuated matter and conscious representations of a second, static genesis. Thus, as is argued by Hughes in his *Genesis of Representation*, we have in Deleuze's *Difference and Repetition* the passage from the three syntheses of time through the Idea and on to individuation and representation, in Deleuze and Guattari's *Anti-Oedipus* the passage from desiring production through intensity and on to social production and in Deleuze's *The Logic of Sense* the passage from an asignifying primary order through an incorporeal secondary organization and on to a signifying tertiary order. But the same trajectory is to be found in all Deleuze's and Deleuze and Guattari's books. In Hughes' later *Philosophy after Deleuze*, he takes up, for example, Deleuze's *Nietzsche and Philosophy*, in which there is a passage from a passive synthesis to an active synthesis through the will to power and the Eternal Return and Deleuze and Guattari's *A Thousand Plateaus* in which there is a passage from the forces of chaos through assemblages and on to the State and its apparatuses of capture.[34] However, it is undoubtedly true – this is also Hughes' contention – that each book emphasizes a particular moment in the overall genesis. Books on art and artists, such as *Proust and Signs*, *The Logic of Sensation* and the cinema books, concentrate on the first moment of genesis (although the second volume on cinema with its time-image takes us from the first moment of genesis to the second). Deleuze's doctoral thesis on Spinoza with its concepts of 'expressionism' and 'quasi-cause' obviously concentrates on how philosophy breaks with the materiality of the first moment of genesis and attains virtuality. Much of Deleuze's early work on Bergson and his later book on Leibniz are about the transition from the second to the third moment of genesis or how the virtual becomes actualized. And *A Thousand Plateaus*, as suggested by its organization by way of a series of historical dates or 'plateaus', is about that third moment of genesis or actualization, in an extension of that recoding and reterritorialization of capitalism addressed in *Anti-Oedipus*.

Each book by Deleuze and Deleuze and Guattari has its specific emphasis, and no book treats all three moments evenly. And, precisely insofar as it is taken up allegorically, this genesis is never explicitly spelled out. It is only ever through some other context (cinema, the work of a particular philosopher, historical social forms) that it can be seen. Even the names given to describe this 'genesis' in *The Logic of Sense* (dynamic genesis, sense and static genesis) are not the only ones. Here we might recall Deleuze's whole point regarding the necessary 'fictionality' or even 'science fictionality' (*DR*, xx) of his discourse, and *What is Philosophy?*

reminds us that in philosophy it is always a matter of having to communicate what cannot be communicated through propositions. But, we would argue, *What is Philosophy?* is the book more than any other in which this genesis is at stake. More than the short, disordered fragments of *The Logic of Sense*, each stage of genesis gets its own distinct chapter in *What is Philosophy?* The terms art, philosophy, science and logic of *What is Philosophy?* are at least as descriptive as the various moments of *The Logic of Sense* and as resonant with the rest of their work. And the question of the relationship between art, philosophy, science and logic, as we have seen, is directly raised at several points in the text, which is why we would say that one of the criteria in assessing any reading of *What is Philosophy?* is to what extent it understands them as inter-related and not separable (or even them being separated only as an effect of their inter-relationship).

To put all this otherwise, the question of genesis is the explicit subject of *What is Philosophy?* in a way it is not in others of Deleuze's and Deleuze and Guattari's books. For all the out-of-order presentation of the three stages of genesis, and passages in the book where Deleuze and Guattari appear to suggest that art, philosophy, science and logic are distinct, it is the relationship between them that is the fundamental issue that *What is Philosophy?* wants to explore. To put this even more strongly – and to repeat what we said a moment ago with regard to the brain – the answer to the question 'What is philosophy?' *is* this genesis, *is* this relationship between art, philosophy, science and logic. The 'philosophy' referred to by that name in the book is merely a component within a wider concept of philosophy, which also includes art, science and logic as its other components. And philosophy perhaps always includes itself as one of its components in this way (we might say that it always includes something that allegorically refers to it). It is again in this regard that Deleuze and Guattari can refer to their book as a work of 'old age'. It is a work of 'old age' in the same sense that they refer to Kant's *Critique of Judgement* as an 'unrestrained' work of 'old age' (*WP?*, 2). Alongside the First Critique of *Difference and Repetition*, in which the faculties enter into a relationship under a logical 'common sense', and the Second Critique of *Anti-Oedipus*, in which the faculties enter into a relationship under a moral 'common sense', in *What is Philosophy?* the faculties of art, philosophy, science and logic come together only in a 'dissension' (*WP?*, 51) that would also be their genesis. But – and here we return to that Nietzschean moment of the 'double' as opposed to 'single' affirmation – philosophy is not simply subject to genesis, but is also the thinking or affirmation of this genesis. What is most profoundly at stake in *What is Philosophy?* is the inseparability of genesis and the thinking of genesis, one because of the other.

All of this is why, to conclude here, Deleuze and Guattari in *What is Philosophy?* speak of philosophy in terms of a certain 'pedagogy' (*WP?*, 12) of the concept. It would be a pedagogy in that it is opposed both to the previous philosophical order of the 'encyclopaedia' and to the succeeding philosophical order of 'commercial professional training' (*WP?*, 12). Pedagogy, we would say, although it goes against that chronology Deleuze and Guattari lay out for it, corresponds to that moment of 'modern' philosophy, as inaugurated by Kant. For by pedagogy – Deleuze makes this clear in *Difference and Repetition* – Deleuze and Guattari mean that with philosophy it is a matter not of 'doing like' but rather of 'doing with' (*DR*, 23). And, more than 'doing with', they mean to refer to that famous Kantian paradox that what is being imitated – the philosophy one is 'doing with' – does not exist before it is imitated – the one doing with it. This is how we might think Deleuze and Guattari's concept of the 'Other' in *What is Philosophy?* The Other is not simply the Other to the Same, for the Same is also an effect of the Other. That is to say, the relationship with the Other, the one who follows or 'does with' a philosophy, is not merely outside or subsequent to this philosophy, but part of it and even what makes it possible. This relationship to the Other is exactly part of the genesis that philosophy both is and is about. But, again, this is also to say that philosophy is always about its own reception, the one who takes it up. If it necessarily awaits another to take it up, this Other is also taken into account by philosophy as part of its self-prophetic counter-effectuation. This once more is the relationship between philosophers that Deleuze and Guattari speak of in *What is Philosophy?* The history of philosophy is not a series of successive 'ruptures' or 'bifurcations' (*WP?*, 124) as in science, but of 'superimpositions' in a 'stratigraphic time' (*WP?*, 58), which is to speak of the way in which one philosophical system 'doubles' (*WP?*, 40) another, proposes a new plane of immanence that makes it possible, but in doing this only follows that first system of philosophy, which already is and is about this doubling, already its own genesis or self-transformation.

Indeed, Deleuze has written two great texts that, although having literature as their ostensible subject, address precisely this aspect of philosophy: the chapter 'Porcelain and Volcano' and the Appendix 'Zola and the Crack Up', both in *The Logic of Sense*. In 'Porcelain and Volcano', Deleuze analyzes the American novelist F. Scott Fitzgerald's famous confessional memoir *The Crack Up*, in which Fitzgerald tries to outline the chain of events that led to his going from handsome, wealthy and successful novelist in his late twenties to a seemingly washed up, broke and alcoholic hack by his early forties. Fitzgerald in his memoir seeks to locate when this crack up occurred and to attempt to explain it, as though to reverse it or even to lament the impossibility of ever going back to the way things were. (Of course, it is Fitzgerald who wrote the famous line 'there are no second acts in American lives'.) And, in a similar manner, Deleuze analyzes Zola's celebrated Rougon-Macquart series of novels, in which Zola follows the fate of a number of interconnected characters from a variety of social backgrounds in order to try to determine how their hereditary in combination with external circumstances produces a kind of destiny for them. (Of course, Zola is the great novelist of naturalism, who was deeply influenced by the theories of Darwin.) But Deleuze's point in both cases is that, despite the novelists' attempts to locate where the failure or breakdown occurs, and to explain it either by a flaw of character or inherited disposition, this 'crack-up' is finally unlocatable. It does not occur at a specific moment in time, but at once has already happened and is always yet to take place (and thus, in principle at least, is always reversible)[35]. It is endlessly explicable – in the mode either of self-confession or objective scientific discourse – and yet there is always something about it that defies explanation; and that, rather than being explained by either character or circumstance, appears (in that paradoxical reversal of quasi-causality we have previously spoken about) to explain or bring about this character and circumstance, or at least give them their explanatory power.

This is Deleuze's real point about the 'crack up', in both cases. It cannot be explained either by the authors' individual lives or by wider social conditions, but in fact precedes and explains them. And it is not simply to be diagnosed and corrected, but is creative and productive. Indeed, it is the very condition for something new to appear as what breaks with all biographical life and social determination. As against all historical analysis and efforts to give it a definitive meaning, this 'crack' is permanently open to the future and goes beyond any predetermined end. It is not so much death as the *death drive*, that which lives in humans but also lives on after them (*LS*, 178, 364). And we would say that this crack is not something transmitted – whether by those character flaws Fitzgerald cannot seem to escape or those hereditary traits of character that pass down the generations in Zola – but the very means of transmission. It is the crack itself that is passed on rather than any particular quality associated with the crack. As Deleuze writes of Zola, but it would apply equally to Fitzgerald: 'The crack transmits only the crack. Transmitting only itself, it does not reproduce that which it transmits. It does not transmit the "same". It reproduces nothing' (*LS*, 363). And Deleuze's ultimate point is that this crack is not something that is remarked on from the outside through a series of propositions, but – this is the impossibility of separating the author from what they write, in the case not only of Fitzgerald but also Zola – an effect of its narration, or it *is* this narration itself. It is its writing that is the crack or brings the crack about, in that doubling of things we have analyzed with regard to what Deleuze and Guattari call the 'mime' or 'counter-effectuation' (*WP?*, 159).

Indeed, the crack belongs to the order of what Deleuze and Guattari call the 'event', in *What is Philosophy?*, by which they mean philosophy. And by speaking of the way that the crack transmits only itself, Deleuze is suggesting that philosophy is given by its reception, its passage towards the other. That, before any actual content and allowing it, philosophy is defined by what it does, its becoming with the one who reads it. And it is this that forces us to reconsider the usual understanding of Deleuze and Guattari's criticism of certain forms of philosophy, by which they undoubtedly mean commentaries on philosophy: 'We will not say of many books of philosophy that they are false, for that is to say nothing, but rather that they lack importance or interest, precisely because they do not create any concept or contribute an image of thought' (*WP?*, 82–3). What they say here is true, and yet not the whole story, for if philosophy is subject to a certain loss through commentary, it is just this loss that *is* philosophy. A significant philosophical system, that is, is not merely subject to this loss but also attempts to formulate the rule of this loss. Indeed, insofar as philosophy is defined as a form of transmission, it must be understood first of all as its own loss, its own commentary. It is this quality that defines the greatest of philosophical systems: they are both transmission and the thinking of transmission, only the infinitely many different ways they are taken up and the thinking of this difference. And this constitutes a great test for philosophy, because this simultaneity can never be achieved: thought can never catch up with practice, just as practice can never be equal to thought. A philosophical system will always ultimately impose a limit on its readings, some subject or object to which it is immanent, something that all its interpretations must have in common.[36] And it is all of this that Deleuze and Guattari attempt to think in asking the question 'What is philosophy?' It is a question that marks philosophy from the beginning – indeed, from before the beginning, insofar as philosophy is a form of self-differentiation – and that can never be answered, insofar as it is part of its perpetual becoming. Philosophy is at once subject to this question and must always push it further in that transmission it both is and thinks. As Deleuze and Guattari write in almost the opening words of *What is Philosophy?*:

> [The question what is philosophy?] was asked before; it was always being asked, but too indirectly or obliquely; the question was too artificial, too abstract. Instead of being seized by it, those who asked the question set it out and controlled it in passing. They were not sober enough. There was too much desire *to do* philosophy to wonder what it was, except as a stylistic exercise. That point of nonstyle where one can finally say, 'What is it I have been doing all my life?' had not been reached. (*WP?*, 1)

NOTES

Chapter One

1. See Gilles Deleuze, 'On the New Philosophers (plus a More General Problem)', *Two Regimes of Madness: Texts and Interviews*, ed. David Lapoujade, Semiotext(e): New York, 2006, p. 144. This interview originally appeared in *Minuit* 24 (France), May 1977.
2. Félix Guattari (with Antonio Negri), 'Communist Propositions', *The Guattari Reader*, ed. Gary Genosko, Blackwell: Oxford, 1996, p. 253.
3. Saul Kripke, *Naming and Necessity*, Blackwell: Oxford, 1980, p. 106.
4. Gilles Deleuze and Claire Parnet, *Dialogues*, Continuum: London, 2002, pp. 16–17.
5. See François Dosse, *Gilles Deleuze and Félix Guattari: Intersecting Lives*, Columbia University Press: New York, 2010, pp. 423–7.
6. Gilles Deleuze, 'The Conditions of the Question: What is Philosophy?', *Critical Inquiry* 17 (3), Spring 1991, pp. 471–8. The essay includes at the bottom of its first page: 'This text, originally published in *Chimères* (May 1990), will appear as the introduction to Deleuze's forthcoming book *Qu-est-ce que la philosophie?*'.
7. Robert Maggiore, *La philosophie au jour le jour*, Flammarion: Paris, 1994, pp. 375–6. Cited Dosse, p. 9.
8. Félix Guattari, *The Anti-Oedipus Papers*, ed. Stéphane Nadaud, Semiotext(e): New York, 2006, p. 404.
9. Dosse will write: '*What is Philosophy?* was manifestly written by Deleuze alone, but he agreed to a co-author credit with Guattari as a tribute to their exceptionally intense friendship, suggesting too that the ideas developed in the book and its language were the fruit of their common endeavours since 1969' (p. 456).

Chapter Two

1. See Fredric Jameson, *The Political Unconscious: Narrative as a Socially Symbolic Act*, Cornell University Press: Ithaca, 1981, p. 22.
2. See Pierre Bourdieu, *Distinction: A Social Critique of the Judgement of Taste*, especially the chapter 'Towards a "Vulgar" Critique of "Pure" Critiques', Harvard University Press: Cambridge, MA, 1984.
3. Deleuze offers the following summary of his position: 'If the mistake of dogmatism is always to fill that which separates, that of empiricism is to leave external what is separated, and in this sense there is still too much empiricism in the [First] Critique (and too much dogmatism among the post-Kantians)' (*DR*, 170). We might compare Deleuze at this point to Derrida and his notion of the 'quasi-transcendental', which at once is 'more transcendental than the transcendental' and exists only in its 'folding back onto the empirical', Geoffrey Bennington, *Interrupting Derrida*, Routledge: London, 2000, p. 87.
4. We are referring here to Iain MacKenzie, *The Idea of Pure Critique*, Continuum: London, 2004.
5. Ronald Bogue, *Deleuze on Music, Painting and the Arts*, Routledge: New York, 2003, p. 176.
6. Elizabeth Grosz, *Chaos, Territory, Art: Deleuze and the Framing of the Earth*, Columbia University Press: New York, 2008, p. 28.
7. Joe Hughes, *Deleuze and the Genesis of Representation*, Continuum: London, 2008.
8. Levi R Bryant, *Difference and Givenness: Deleuze's Transcendental Empiricism and the Ontology of Immanence*, Northwestern University Press: Evanston, 2008.
9. *Deleuze and the Genesis of Representation*, p. 154.
10. Claire Colebrook, *Understanding Deleuze*, Allen & Unwin: Crows Nest, NSW, 2002, pp. xviii–xix.
11. See *Deleuze and the Genesis of Representation*, p. 20.

Chapter Three

1. Simon O'Sullivan, *Art Encounters: Deleuze and Guattari: Thought beyond Representation*, Palgrave Macmillan: Basingstoke, 2006, p. 1.

2 Isabelle Ginoux, 'De l'histoire de la philosophie considerée comme un des beaux-arts: le portrait conceptuel selon Deleuze', in *Discern(e)ments: Esthétiques deleuziennes*, ed. Joost de Bloois, Rodopi: Amsterdam, 2004, p. 23.

3 On the 'pre-human' status of art, it is notable that Deleuze and Guattari identify art with the 'animal'. As they write of Ahab in *What is Philosophy?*: 'Ahab really does have perceptions of the sea, but only because he has entered into a relationship with Moby Dick that makes him a becoming-whale and forms a compound of sensations that no longer needs anyone: ocean' (*WP?*, 169).

4 We see this in terms of the composers chosen to represent each 'movement' here, who are obviously not the usual ones. Beethoven and even Schumann can count as Baroque composers in Deleuze and Guattari's taxonomy because of their use of 'polyphony' (*TP*, 270). And again they will suggest that 'all of the baroque lies brewing beneath classicism' (*TP*, 380), as though it comes after it, when according to most histories of music the Baroque comes before Classicism.

5 In fact, this 'essence' is most properly found in art. As Deleuze writes, the substances of involuntary memory are much 'less spiritualized, less "dematerialized"' (*PS*, 62) than those of art. But this essence is 'Difference' – difference as what 'constitutes being, what makes us conceive being' (*PS*, 41).

6 For an excellent account of Deleuze's two volumes on cinema in these terms, see Joe Hughes, 'Schizoanalysis and the Phenomenology of Cinema', in *Deleuze and the Schizoanalysis of Cinema*, Ian Buchanan and Patricia McCormack (eds), Continuum: London, 2008, pp. 15–26.

7 Immanuel Kant, *Critique of Pure Reason*, A 102, Palgrave Macmillan: Basingstoke, 1985, p. 133.

8 For good accounts of Deleuze's conception of dynamic genesis and its relation to Kant, see Keith Faulkner, *Deleuze and the Three Syntheses of Time*, Peter Lang, Berne, 2005; and James Williams, *Gilles Deleuze's Philosophy of Time: A Critical Introduction and Guide*, Edinburgh University Press, Edinburgh, 2011. It should be noted that the version of the Transcendental Deduction that Deleuze works from and that we discuss here is the so-called A Deduction of the 1781 edition of the *Critique of Pure Reason*.

9 See Martin Heidegger, *Kant and the Problem of Metaphysics*, Indiana University Press: Bloomington, 1962, pp. 184–6.

10 This, however, is complicated. Although in each of our examples the third moment of synthesis is retrospectively seen as already there

– 'cosmic forces were always present from the beginning' (*TP*, 350), 'in the end, there are nothing but triptychs' (*FB*, 70), 'the signs of art give us an absolutely original time which includes all the others' (*PS*, 24), 'what the crystal reveals is the hidden ground of time' (*TI*, 99) – this is to be understood more in the sense of a 'third time in the series' (*DR*, 90) that is part of the permanent becoming of the Eternal Return than anything like Kantian apperception.

11 The difference here from Kant might be indicated by the fact that, as opposed to the final unity of the object within recognition in Kant, dynamic genesis concludes with an unknown object = x that is described throughout the chapter 'Repetition in Itself' as the 'in-itself of difference', 'self-different' and 'differently different' (*DR*, 119), that is, the work of art.

12 Edmund Husserl, *Ideas I*, Kluwer Academic Publishers: Dordrecht, 1998, p. 142. For a more detailed analysis of Husserl's critique of Kant in relation to Deleuze, see Joe Hughes, *Deleuze's Difference and Repetition: A Reader's Guide*, Continuum: London, 2009, pp. 88–96.

13 Edmund Husserl, *Formal and Transcendental Logic*, Martinus Nijhoff: The Hague, 1969, p. 250.

14 Deleuze's critique of Husserl is indebted to Jean-Paul Sartre's *The Transcendence of the Ego* (1957), which even more than Husserl's late subject placed in the world posits a subject that is possible only because of an Other that thinks it. This is that 'impersonal transcendental field' Deleuze and Guattari oppose to Husserl in 'restoring the rights of immanence' (*WP?*, 47) and that concept of the 'Other Person' (*WP?*, 17–19) they discuss towards the beginning of *What is Philosophy?*

Chapter Four

1 Here already we might begin to think the difference between philosophy and art: the sensations of art break with their object but do not determine it; the concepts of philosophy break with their object and also determine it. Deleuze in fact outlines three distinct moments in the determination of the concept (*DR*, 169): 'undetermined with regard to their object', in which the Idea comes 'first' without any object; 'determinable with regard to objects of experience', in which the Idea is differentiated in relation to an object; and 'infinitely determined with regard to concepts of the

understanding', in which the Idea is seen as exactly the same as its object. The resolution of the 'problem' is the passage from the first to the third of these, but the 'problem' is that all three moments co-exist and are inseparable from each other.

2 Gilles Deleuze, 'Qu'est-ce fonder?', Deleuze.com (online), p. 33. There is a good account of this text in Christian Kerslake, *Deleuze and the Vertigo of Immanence*, Edinburgh University Press: Edinburgh, 2009, especially in 'Introduction: The Problem of Immanence'.

3 As Miguel de Beistegui writes, 'the affirmation of immanence and the illusion of transcendence endlessly oppose each other', 'The Vertigo of Immanence: Deleuze's Spinozism', *Research into Phenomenology* 35, 2005, p. 89. It is an insight shared by James Williams in 'Immanence and Transcendence as Inseparable Processes', *Deleuze Studies*, 4 (4), 2010.

4 For a lucid explanation of the distinction between 'adequate' and 'inadequate' ideas in Spinoza, see Audrey Wasser, 'Deleuze's Expressionism', *Angelaki*, 12 (2), 2007, pp. 58–9.

5 Hence Deleuze's interest in differential calculus in which, even though the actual quantities of the derivative dy/dx might approach zero, the relationship between the two differentials themselves persists (*DR*, 172–3). See on this Simon Duffy, 'The Mathematics of Deleuze's Differential Logic and Metaphysics', in Simon Duffy (ed.), *Virtual Mathematics: The Logic of Difference*, Clinamen Press: Manchester, 2006, pp. 119–20. We will return to calculus in the next chapter, insofar as Deleuze and Guattari use mathematics as a way of explaining *static* genesis in *What is Philosophy?*

6 Daniel W. Smith, 'On the Nature of Concepts', *parallax*, 18 (1), 2012, p. 66–7. Deleuze once wrote an essay entitled 'How to Recognize Structuralism?'(*DI*, 170–92), which in effect aligned structuralism with what we are calling philosophy here. It has been remarked that in fact what Deleuze means by structuralism is more like *post-structuralism* (James Williams, *Understanding Poststructuralism*, Acumen Press: Durham, 2005, p. 53), and thus as well as thinking Deleuze's 'fold' as a concept or Idea, we might also consider Derrida's différance, Lyotard's differend and Baudrillard's simulation, among many others.

7 For the idea of the 'same' concept successively being 'differentiated' by each of its components, see Deleuze's references throughout *Difference and Repetition* on difference to the 'nth' power (*DR*, 8, 68, 141, 243). Deleuze also puts forward the notion, taken from Schelling, of 'finer, more varied and more terrifying flashes of

lightning' that take the form of always raised potentials, A, A², A³ (*DR*, 191) – and Schelling's idea of bringing 'difference out of the Identical' (*DR*, 191) tells us that it is always a matter of 'doubling' what is, providing a completely different explanation of it.

8   *Critique of Pure Reason*, p. 121.
9   See 'On the Nature of Concepts', p. 66. In fact, although Smith (and Deleuze in *The Logic of Sense*) speaks of both medical and scientific discoveries in terms of named concepts, in *What is Philosophy?* Deleuze and Guattari make a distinction between the name as it is used in science and the name as it is used in philosophy: 'It is clear that scientific propositions and their correlates are just as signed or created as philosophical concepts ... But however much the use of proper names clarifies and confirms the historical nature of their link to these enunciations, these proper names are the mask for other becomings' (*WP?*, 23–4). Indeed, that 'bifurcation' Smith speaks of with regard to the concept is more aligned to the scientific functive in *What is Philosophy?* (*WP?*, 123) and 'examples' would go more towards the 'differenciation' and not 'differentiation' of the concept (*DR*, 206–7).
10 If we could add something here to Deleuze's much-discussed remark that philosophy is a 'sort of buggery' ('Letter to a Harsh Critic', in Gilles Deleuze, Negotiations 1972–90, Columbia University Press, 1995 p. 6), it would be to say that what Deleuze is suggesting here is that there is only one hole or place for the commentator to insert themselves into the host system. Philosophy is a violent act, but it is also only undertaken with the 'permission' of its subject. This is why it is never a matter of philosophy beginning from nothing but only in terms of 'another' (*WP?*, 16). It is always a matter of entering or inhabiting what already exists, even if it exists only in retrospect.
11 Levi Bryant puts this 'reciprocality' between the various elements of Kant's system another way: 'In effect, Kant argues that the schemata, designed to function as intermediaries between concepts and intuitions, are made possible by the schematization of concepts', 'Deleuze's Transcendental Empiricism: Notes Towards a Transcendental Materialism', in Edward Willatt and Matt Lee (eds), *Thinking Between Deleuze and Kant*, Continuum: London, 2009, p. 35. There are two other essays in this volume that also put forward a reading of the *Critique of Pure Reason* through Deleuze: Matt Lee, 'Levelling the Levels'; and Edward Willatt, 'The Genesis of Cognition: Deleuze as a Reader of Kant'.
12 That is, beyond Kant, Deleuze sees Kant's rethinking of Descartes' Cogito as typical of the operation of philosophy itself. For Kant, the

'I think' is a determination that determines an undetermined 'I am' in time (*WP?*, 31). And similarly in Kant the '[undetermined] object of the Idea becomes indirectly determined by analogy with those objects of experience upon which it confers unity … Finally, the object of the Idea carries with it the ideal of a complete and infinite determination' (*DR*, 169).

13 Friedrich Nietzsche, Letter to Jakob Burckhardt, 6 January 1889, in Christopher Middleton, *Selected Letters of Friedrich Nietzsche*, University of Chicago Press: Chicago, 1969, p. 347.

14 Deleuze writes in *Nietzsche and Philosophy*: 'Affirmation is redoubled: as object of the second affirmation it is affirmation itself affirmed, redoubled affirmation, difference raised to its highest power. Becoming is being, multiplicity is unity, chance is necessity … Being ought to belong to becoming, unity to multiplicity, necessity to chance, but only insofar as becoming, multiplicity and chance are reflected in the second affirmation which takes them as its object' (*NP*, 189).

15 Immaneul Kant, *Critique of Judgment*, Clarendon Press: Oxford, 1952, p. 37.

16 Gilles Deleuze, 'The Exhausted', in *Essays Critical and Clinical*, University of Minnesota Press: Minneapolis, 1997, p. 158.

Chapter Five

1 Although it is translated as 'différentiation' (*WP?*, 126), it is in fact 'différenciation' that Deleuze and Guattari are speaking of here (*Qu'est-ce que la philosophie?*, Éditions de Minuit: Paris, 2005, p. 119). And throughout *What is Philosophy?*, the translator's mistake 'differenciation' for 'differentiation', this eliding an important distinction between 'differentiation' as the determination of the virtual content of the Idea and 'differenciation' as the actualization of this virtuality (*DR*, 207). We simply use 'differenciation' in our text when it is the equivalent in the original French.

2 To take just three of the more prominent examples of the attempt to rethink science on the basis of Deleuze's and Deleuze and Guattari's work: Manuel DeLanda, *Intensive Science and Virtual Philosophy*, Continuum: New York, 2002; Miguel de Beistegui, *Truth and Genesis: Philosophy as Differential Ontology*, Indiana University Press: Bloomington, 2004; and Peter Gaffney (ed.), *The Force of the Virtual: Deleuze, Science and Philosophy*, University of Minnesota

Press: Minneapolis, 2010. Our point here is that, before engaging in this 'rethinking', we must understand that science also occupies a structural position in Deleuze and Deleuze and Guattari, and is not simply science as such but one of the names, a number of which we detail here, for active genesis. Of course, these studies are not unaware of this, with DeLanda, for example, including an Appendix, 'Deleuze's Words', on *What is Philosophy?* in his book, which addresses in part this problem.

3 *Critique of Pure Reason*, B xxxviii, p. 34.

4 Daniel Smith writes in 'Genesis and Difference: Deleuze, Maïmon and the Post-Kantian Reading of Leibniz': 'The principle of sufficient reason says: for every thing, there is a concept that includes everything that will happen to the thing. The principle of indiscernibles says: for every concept, there is one and only one thing', in Sjoerd van Tuinen and Niamh McDonnell (eds), *Deleuze and the Fold: A Critical Reader*, Palgrave Macmillan: Basingstoke, 2009, p. 144.

5 This applies even to 'discontinuous' functions, in which the same function continues across a gap in ordinates or, put otherwise, in which two different values on the y-axis correspond to the same value on the x-axis. Here too, despite the apparent jump or gap, the function is continuous in terms of its solutions or abscissae.

6 Our argument that the passage from states of affairs to bodies corresponds only to the first stage of actualization or what Deleuze calls 'good sense' is evidenced by the fact that when Deleuze and Guattari speak of bodies 'renewing their individuation' (*WP?*, 123), in *What is Philosophy?*, this echoes Deleuze speaking of bodies being 'renewed locally for the sake of limited new actualizations and extensions' (*LS*, 125) in *The Logic of Sense* and things and bodies never 'stopping changing' (*F*, 65) in *The Fold*. We will see something of this in Deleuze's thinking about 'bodies' in biology in a moment.

7 In other words, the individuated 'body' in the sense we are describing it here is to be found not just in maths and science but also in biology. For Deleuze's argument that the individual is the carrier of transmissible difference in biological classification, see *DR*, 214–6. For an essay relating Deleuze to Darwin's theory of evolution, see Nathan Eckstrand, 'Deleuze, Darwin and the Categorization of Life', *Deleuze Studies* 8 (4), 2014, pp. 415–44.

8 Sean Bowden writes: 'Leibniz argues that each monad perceives the entire universe, but confusedly for the most part, in minute, unconscious perceptions. What the monad perceives or represents distinctly, on the other hand, are those monads "nearest" to it and

which compose its "body", 'Deleuze's Neo-Leibnizianism, Events and *The Logic of Sense*'s "Static Ontological Genesis", *Deleuze Studies* 4 (3), 2010, p. 305. See also Smith, 'Genesis and Difference', p. 143.

9 This is the meaning of Deleuze and Guattari speaking of the 'two poles' of the theory of functions, one in which, 'n variables being given, one can be considered as function of the $n - 1$ independent variables', the other in which '$n - 1$ magnitudes are functions of a single independent variable'. They explain this as the alternative in the 'problem of tangents' between summoning as many variables as there are curves, in which the 'derivative for each is any tangent whatever at any point whatever', which corresponds to differenciation, and dealing with only a single variable, which is 'the curve itself tangent to all curves of the same order, on condition of a change of co-ordinates', which corresponds to integration (*WP?*, 126). This latter description of integration with regard to the tangent should remind us of the 'body', and Deleuze and Guattari's point throughout is that, even though differenciation and integration are inseparable, it is always a 'prior' differenciation that allows the building up of 'integrated' bodies.

10 *Critique of Pure Reason*, A 51, p. 93.

11 Simon Duffy writes in 'The Mathematics of Deleuze's Differential Logic and Metaphysics': 'A power series expansion can be written as a polynomial, the coefficients of each of its terms being the successive derivatives evaluated at the distinctive point. The sum of such a series represents the expanded function provided that any remainder approaches zero as the number of terms becomes infinite; the polynomial then becomes an infinite series which converges with the function in the neighbourhood of the distinctive point', pp. 128–9. Duffy later discusses the nineteenth-century French mathematician Henri Poincaré's notion of 'singularities of the composite function' (p. 138) in similar terms.

12 Deleuze and Guattari furthermore go on to contrast the 'juxtaposition of reference' in science and the 'superimposition of layer' in philosophy (*WP?*, 128). It might be thought at first that it is science that is syntagmatic and philosophy that is paradigmatic, but precisely Deleuze and Guattari's point is that each new philosophical system does not *break with* the one that comes before, but as it were sits on top of it, and will be shown by another subsequent system, which doubles both, to merely sit *beside* it.

13 On this suggestion that scientists' names represent not just a good sense but also a common sense, Deleuze and Guattari write: 'Far

from distributing cardinal points that organize syntagms on a plane of immanence, the scientist's proper name draws up paradigms that are projected into necessarily oriented systems of reference' (*WP?*, 125).

14 *Critique of Pure Reason*, B 181, p. 183.

15 Admittedly, we are undertaking a number of interpretive risks in aligning the three moments of 'Dramatization' with the full span of ontological genesis, just as we are later in making the extension, intension and comprehension of the referent merely part of its 'denotation' in logical genesis. However, as Hughes argues in *Deleuze's Difference and Repetition*, the question of how Ideas function as rules for the production of objects is never entirely answered in Deleuze (p. 145). The great strength of Hughes' book is the underlying structure and the series of parallels between different parts he draws out in Deleuze's work, and it is this approach we follow here.

16 *Critique of Pure Reason*, A 109, p. 137.

17 See on this 'shifting and jamming' not only between ontological and logical genesis, but also between the various parts of ontological (denoted, manifested, signified) and logical (denotation, manifestation, signification) genesis, *LS*, 136–7. Deleuze will denounce Leibniz for his not overthrowing 'established sentiment' (*LS*, 133) after his discovery of incompossibility, but Deleuze himself does not simply do away with all logical categories through incompossibility, but rather traces its genetic role in their formation. In Deleuze too, this moment of incompossibility will ultimately be lost in the logical categories that come after it.

18 Jorges Luis Borges, *The Total Library: Non-Fiction 1922–86*, Penguin: New York, 1999, p. 363.

19 *The Total Library*, p. 365.

20 In truth, this denotation is of course the second of the prospects (*WP?*, 155), but we are trying to think it here as the first of the sequence denotation, manifestation and denotation that replays on the level of logical genesis the denoted, manifested and signified of ontological genesis.

21 Daniela Voss writes of Deleuze's conception of a 'sense' that would make Fregean 'truth' and 'referentiality' possible: 'To say that sense is an incorporeal or neutral "double" of the proposition should not be misunderstood: for Deleuze, the process of doubling up the proposition which expresses it does not imply "an evanescent or disembodied resemblance" to the state of things which are

denoted by the proposition. Instead, Deleuze insists both that sense is inseparable from its status as a neutral double and that it is "something unconditioned"', 'Deleuze's Rethinking of the Notion of Sense', *Deleuze Studies* 7 (1), 2013, p. 18. We will see something like this 'sense' in the 'mime', 'counter-effectuation' and 'doubling' (*WP?*, 159–60) that Deleuze and Guattari explore towards the end of 'Prospects and Concepts'.

22 For an example of these criticisms at the time, see Henri Lefebvre, *Les temps des méprises*, Stock Paris, 1975, pp. 160–1, 171.

23 To be clear here, with this 'terrified face' it is not an excess of the actual over the virtual but of the virtual over the actual. In fact, it is Slavoj Žižek who discusses Hitchcock's *Lifeboat* in similar terms in his *Looking Awry: An Introduction to Jacques Lacan through Popular Culture*, MIT Press: Cambridge, Mass., 1991, p. 144. The connection between Deleuze and Žižek has been made by Richard Rushton in 'What Can a Face Do? On Deleuze and Faces', *Cultural Critique* 51, Spring 2002, pp. 219–37.

24 Maurice Merleau-Ponty, *The Visible and the Invisible*, Northwestern University Press: Evanston, 1968.

25 Jacques Lacan, 'Of the Gaze as *Objet Petit a*', in *The Four Fundamentals of Psycho-Analysis*, Penguin: Harmondsworth, 1986.

26 Ibid, p. 96.

27 On the Other as depth and what allows the 'margins and transitions' of this world, see *LS*, 344–5. Deleuze and Guattari also speak of the Other in this sense in *WP?*, 16–17. And this necessity for an Other is seen in Deleuze's long-running admiration for Sartre's notion of an 'impersonal transcendental field' that precedes the self and restores an immanence against any assertion of a transcendent self (it is the Other that allows this self-possession or transcendence). See on this *WP?*, 47; *DR*, 64–5; *LS*, 112,118. See also on this Constantin Boundas, 'Foreclosure of the Other: From Sartre to Deleuze', *Journal of the British Society for Phenomenology* 24 (1), 1993, pp. 32–43.

28 It is this sense that genesis is complete and we can think only in opinions that is also to be seen in Deleuze's and Guattari's notion of artists having to struggle against cliché (*WP?*, 204). This argument is to be found also in Deleuze's book on Bacon, where in the chapter 'The Painting before Painting' he argues that the painter never begins with a blank canvas but only with a canvas already covered with models, preconceptions, 'things in his head' (*FB*, 71).

Chapter Six

1. Rodolphe Gasché, *Geophilosophy: On Gilles Deleuze and Félix Guattari's What is Philosophy?*, Northwestern University Press: Evanston, 2014, p. 112.

2. Mathias Schönher, 'The Creation of the Concept through the Interaction of Philosophy with Science and Art', *Deleuze Studies* 7 (1), 2013, pp. 26–52.

3. Deleuze writes in 'The Idea of Genesis in Kant's Aesthetics' that the sublime has the value of a 'model', insofar as the discovery of a 'dialectical' conception of the faculties, in which each comes about only in its 'discordant' relationship to the others, allows us to explain how the 'free accord' between faculties in 'The Analytic of the Beautiful', which can only be assumed there, actually comes about: '(1) The analytic of the beautiful discovers a free accord of the understanding and the imagination, but can only posit it as presumed; (2) the analytic of the sublime discovers a free accord of the imagination and reason, but under conditions that at the same time trace its genesis' (64).

4. In fact, it is at this point that Kant discovers not or not only the mind or 'Gemüt' but the 'soul' or 'Seele'. It is the 'soul' that is the 'point of convergence' or 'suprasensible unity' of the various faculties ('G', 68). In an excellent analysis, Joe Hughes traces the passage from the embodied 'mind' in 'The Analytic of the Beautiful' and the sections dealing with the mathematical sublime in 'The Analytic of the Sublime' to the immaterial 'soul' in the sections dealing with the dynamic sublime in 'The Analytic of the Sublime'. Hughes also raises the question of how Deleuze breaks with or goes beyond certain assumptions of Kant's analysis in putting forward his own account of the genesis of the 'soul', in *The Critique of Judgement*. For Deleuze, the soul is not any kind of noumenal or suprasensible 'origin' of the faculties, as it still is in Kant. Rather, the process of 'synthesis' is itself part of the sensible. This, indeed, is why not only is the soul aware of the faculties but we are aware of the soul. At the same time, however, the soul, or what Deleuze and Guattari will call the brain, is not simply in the world but adds a kind of allegorical, self-referential dimension to it. See Joe Hughes, *Philosophy after Deleuze*, Bloomsbury: London, 2012, pp. 102–8.

5. Žižek writes: 'The problem is how, from within the flat order of positive being, the very gap between thought and being,

the negativity of thought, emerges', *Parallax View*, MIT Press: Cambridge, MA, 2006, p. 6.

6   See on this Claire Colebrook, *Deleuze: A Guide for the Perplexed*, Continuum: London, 2006, p. 80.

7   See on this 'The Brain is the Screen: An Interview with Gilles Deleuze', in Gregory Flaxman (ed.), *The Brain is the Screen: Deleuze and the Philosophy of Cinema*, University of Minnesota Press: Minneapolis, 2000, p. 367. For good overviews of Deleuze and Guattari on the brain, see Andrew Murphie, 'Deleuze, Guattari and Neuroscience', in *Deleuze, Science and the Force of the Virtual*, pp. 330–67; and Sean Watson, 'The Neurobiology of Sorcery: Deleuze and Guattari's Brain', *Body & Society* 4 (4), 1998, pp. 23–45.

8   Thus when Deleuze in the second of his volumes on cinema writes of the new conception of the brain that 'the process of association increasingly came up against cuts in the continuous network of the brain, everywhere there were micro-fissures which were not simply voids to be crossed' (*TI*, 211), the only thing guaranteeing that this cut or gap remains and cannot be crossed is that it is not between the brain and somewhere outside it but between the brain and itself.

9   This goes towards Deleuze and Guattari's important distinction between an Idea that 'acts but is not' and a form that 'is but does not act' (*WP?*, 213) – and their preference for the second over the first. It is for this reason that they are able to say that 'withdrawal' is not the opposite but the correlate of the 'survey' (*WP?*, 211), which is to speak not just of the passage from art to philosophy but also of the way that some other principle arises out of or is at stake in the 'survey' of everything. The French philosopher of science Raymond Ruyer is very influential on Deleuze and Guattari's notion of the 'survey' and the way it breaks with while enabling both 'mechanical' and 'dynamic' conceptions of the brain (*WP?*, 233 n.11).

10 The 'fold' in this sense is at stake not only in the notion of the 'soul' developed in *The Fold* (*F*, 105–7), but also in that of 'habit' in Deleuze's book on Hume, *Empiricism and Subjectivity*: 'habit' there is a kind of folding or self-reference that produces something the 'same' out of something perpetually self-differing (*H*, 92–4). Indeed, Deleuze's argument here could be read alongside Samuel Weber's 'It' (*Glyph* 4, 1978, pp. 1–31), which conceptualizes habit in a similar way.

11 See Catherine Malabou, *What Should We Do With Our Brain?*, Fordham University Press: New York, 2008. p. 4.

12 *What Should We Do?*, p. 9
13 G. W. F. Hegel, *The Phenomenology of Spirit*, Oxford University Press: Oxford, 1977, p. 208.
14 *What Should We Do?*, p. 41.
15 For a detailed treatment of the connection between philosophy and Ancient Greece in *What is Philosophy?*, see Rodolphe Gasché, *Geophilosophy: On Gilles Deleuze and Félix Guattari's What is Philosophy?*, Northwestern University Press: Evanston, 2014, which unfortunately appeared after much of the drafting of this book was complete.
16 See *Philosophy after Deleuze*, pp. 57, 77; and Paul Patton 'Deleuze and Democracy', in *Deleuzian Concepts: Philosophy, Colonization, Politics*, Stanford University Press: Stanford, 2010. This is obviously a complex matter. It is perhaps the case that 'democracy' is the word for the recursive, reiterative 'failure' of thought we have identified throughout. In that case, 'democracy' would be a synonym for 'philosophy' in the way we have sought to define it here.
17 Immanuel Kant, *The Conflict of the Faculties*, Abaris Books: New York, 1979, pp. 151–3.
18 *The Conflict of the Faculties*, p. 153.
19 All of this is perhaps to say that immanence does not exist until it is folded or doubled or immanence itself is a certain folding or doubling. This might be one way of reading how Deleuze and Guattari explain the relationship between the 'relative deterritorialization' of the Greece State and the 'absolute deterritorialization' of philosophy: 'When relative deterritorialization is itself horizontal, or immanent, it combines with the absolute deterritorialization of the plane of immanence that carries the movements of relative deterritorialization to infinity, pushes them to the absolute, by transforming them (milieu, friend, opinion). Immanence is redoubled' (*WP?*, 90).

Chapter Seven

1 Robert Maggiore, 'Une bombe sous la philosophie', *Libération*, 12 September 1991, p. 19.
2 Xavier Delcourt, 'Les filles de Chaos', *La Quinzaine littéraire* 585, 16 September 1991, p. 21.
3 Raymond Bellour, 'Gais savoirs', *Magazine littéraire*, October 1991, p. 70.

4 Andreas Platthaus, 'Die Weisheit blieb bei den Griechen nur hängen', *Frankfurter Allgemeine*, 13 October 1996, p. 15.

5 Toni Negri, 'Qu'est-ce que la philosophie, selon Deleuze and Guattari', *Futur Antérieur* 8, Hiver 1991 (http://www.multitudes. net/Qu-est-ce-que-la-philosophie-selon/). Admittedly, this review appeared in France, but there are also reviews by Allessandro Delcò, 'G. Deleuze; F. Guattari: *Qu'est-ce la philosophie?*', *Filosofia* 43 (1), 1992, pp. 163–72; and Gianfranco Gabetta, 'Della sottrazione in filosofia', *Aut ... Aut* 247, 1992, pp. 13–23.

6 James Williams, 'An Affirmation of Independence: What is Philosophy? by Gilles Deleuze and Félix Guttari', *Journal of the British Society for Phenomenology* 26(3), 1995, p. 327. Other notable early reviews include Paul Patton, 'Here be Nomads', *Times Literary Supplement*, 23 June 1995, pp. 10–12; and Ian Buchanan, 'Review of What is Philosophy?', *Textual Practice* 10(1), 1996, pp. 217–22.

7 Erik Davis, 'The Witch's Flight', *Voice Literary Supplement*, Summer 1994, p. 41.

8 Roger Caldwell, '*What is Philosophy?*', *New Statesman and Society* 7 (318), September 2 1997, p. 37.

9 Robyn Ferrell, '*What is Philosophy?*', *Australian Journal of Philosophy* 74 (3), September 1996, p. 515.

10 Jean-Jacques Lecercle, 'The Pedagogy of Philosophy', *Radical Philosophy* 75, January–February 1996, p. 44.

11 See Slavoj Žižek, *Organs without Bodies: On Deleuze and Consequences*, Routledge: New York, pp. 183–4.

12 Anonymous, 'Das Leben nach dem Tod in Vancouver', *Süddeutsche Zeitung*, 10 June 1998, p. 15.

13 See Michael Hardt and Antonio Negri, *Empire*, Harvard University Press: Cambridge, MA, 2000, pp. 22–30.

14 See Peter Hallward, *Deleuze and the Philosophy of Creation: Out of this World*, Verso: London, 2006, p. 159, for the distinction between 'actual creatures' and 'virtual creatings' in Deleuze; and p. 162, for the way Deleuze 'offers few resources for thinking the consequences of what happens in the actually existing world'.

15 Alain Badiou, *Deleuze: The Clamour of Being*, University of Minnesota Press: Minneapolis, 2000, p. 45. See also Alain Badiou, 'Gilles Deleuze, *The Fold: Leibniz and the Baroque*', in Constantin V. Boundas and Dorothea Olkowski (eds), *Gilles Deleuze and the Theater of Philosophy*, Routledge: New York, 1994, p. 54.

16 See Quentin Meillassoux, *After Finitude: An Essay on the Necessity of Contingency*, Continuum: London, 2008, pp. 91–2.
17 See Ray Brassier, *Nihil Unbound: Enlightenment and Extinction*, Palgrave Macmillan: New York, 2007, p. 191. In this Brassier follows Meillassoux, who also sees Deleuze as a 'correlationist' in *After Finitude*, p. 37.
18 *Nihil Unbound*, p. 199.
19 Jeffrey Bell, *Deleuze's Hume: Philosophy, Culture and the Scottish Enlightenment*, Edinburgh University Press: Edinburgh, 2009.
20 See Gilles Deleuze, 'Nous avons inventé la ritournelle', in *Deux régimes de fous: textes et entretiens 1975–1995*, Éditions de Minuit: Paris, 2003, p. 356.
21 Eric Alliez, *The Signature of the World: What is Deleuze and Guattari's Philosophy?*, Continuum: London, 2004.
22 Iain MacKenzie, *The Idea of Pure Critique*, Continuum: London, 2004, pp. xv–xvi. Again, Gasché's *Geophilosophy* appeared too late in the drafting of this book to be included here. It would obviously merit a detailed response in any consideration of the reception of *What is Philosophy?*
23 Reidar Due, *Deleuze*, Polity Press: Cambridge, 2007.
24 Eleanor Kaufman and Kevin Jon Heller, *Deleuze and Guattari: New Mappings in Politics, Philosophy and Culture*, University of Minnesota Press: Minneapolis, 1998.
25 Nathan Widder, *Political Theory after Deleuze*, Continuum: London 2012.
26 Jay Lampert, *Deleuze and Guattari's Philosophy of History*, Continuum: London, 2006.
27 Isabelle Stengers, 'Deleuze and Guattari's Last Enigmatic Message', *Angelaki* 10, 2005, pp. 151–66.
28 Arkady Plotnitsky, 'Chaosmologies: Quantum Field Theory, Chaos and Thought in Deleuze and Guattari's *What is Philosophy?*', *Paragraph* 29 (2), 2006, pp. 40–56.
29 Stephen Arnott, 'In the Shadow of Chaos: Deleuze and Guattari on Philosophy, Science and Art', *Philosophy Today* 43(1), Spring 1999, pp. 49–56.
30 Jean de Martelaere, '*Qu'est-ce que la philosophie?*', *Homme et la société* 26 (1), 1992, p. 151.
31 Jay Conway, *Gilles Deleuze: Affirmation in Philosophy*, Palgrave Macmillan: New York, 2010, p. 140.

32 Ian Buchanan, *Deleuzism: A Metacommentary*, Duke University Press: Durham, 2000, p. 41.
33 Joe Hughes in *Philosophy after Deleuze*, Bloomsbury: London, 2012, speaks of Deleuze as a 'figural' writer in a similar way (pp. 19–21).
34 Hughes, *Philosophy after Deleuze*, pp. 34–77.
35 But this 'reversibility' must be understood very carefully. It is not any simple alternative to the way things happened, but rather an entirely other reason why things happened exactly as they did. Deleuze writes: 'Counter-actualization is nothing; it belongs to the buffoon when it operates alone and pretends to have the value of *what could have happened*. But to be the mime of *what effectively occurs*, to double that actualization with a counter-actualization, is to give to the truth of the event the only chance of not being confused with its inevitable actualization' (*LS*, 182)
36 All of this opens up complex issues, with two of them being the relationship of the philosophical friend to rival (*WP?*, 3–5) and the particular form of 'becoming' at stake in philosophy as opposed to art (*WP?*, 109, 173–4). There is also in the relationship between philosophy and the philosopher a coming together of the most singular and the most universal. It bears some relationship to how Deleuze sees the relationship between the individual life and the death drive in such texts as *The Logic of Sense* and *Pure Immanence: A Life* (Zone Books: New York, 2001). A great philosophy lives on exactly as the death drive does: through the substitution of one life for another, the life of the reader for that of the philosopher. It might almost be philosophy speaking in this passage from *The Logic of Sense*: 'And the impersonality of dying [but we might say philosophy] no longer indicates only the moment when I disappear outside of myself, but also the figure the most singular life takes on in order to substitute itself for me' (*LS*, 173–4).

INDEX OF NAMES

Alliez, Eric 179
Althusser, Louis 79
Artaud, Antonin 27

Bacon, Francis 10, 45–8, 49, 55, 57, 199 n.28
Badiou, Alain 142, 148, 176–7
Baudrillard, Jean 193 n.6
Beckett, Samuel 105
Beethoven, Ludwig van 41, 191 n.4
Bell, Jeffrey 178
Bellour, Raymond 171
Bergson, Henri 16, 54, 71, 158, 182
Bogue, Ronald 25
Borges, Jorge Luis 131, 133–5
Bourdieu, Pierre 18
Brassier, Ray 177–8
Bryant, Levi 26, 181, 194 n.11
Buchanan, Ian 181

Caldwell, Roger 172
Cantor, Georg 114
Carroll, Lewis 27, 47, 82
Chaplin, Charlie 55, 56
Chopin, Frédéric 41
Colebrook, Claire 27
Conway, Jay 181

Damasio, Antonio 159
Darwin, Charles 38, 185, 196 n.7
Davis, Erik 172

Dellcourt, Xavier 171
Derrida, Jacques 7, 190 n.3, 193 n.6
Desargues, Girard 124
Descartes, René 18, 74, 76, 81, 85–6, 88, 98, 101, 123, 194 n.12
De Sica, Vittorio 57
Due, Reidar 179

Einstein, Albert 122, 123
Eisenstein, Sergei 55
Epicurus 82

Faye, Jean-Pierre 163
Ferrell, Robyn 173
Fichte, I. H. von 21, 73
Fitzgerald, F. Scott 184–6
Frege, Gottlob 138

Gasché, Rodolphe 154
Giacometti, Alberto 44
Ginoux, Isabelle 33
Godard, Jean-Luc 55, 58
Griffith, D. W. 55, 56
Grosz, Elizabeth 25, 154

Hallward, Peter 174, 176, 203, n.14
Hardt, Michael 78, 174
Hardy, Thomas 35
Hegel, G. W. F. 4, 21, 24, 79, 162, 163, 166, 172, 202 n.13

INDEX OF NAMES

Heller, Kevin Jon 179
Herzog, Werner 55
Hitchcock, Alfred 45, 57, 58, 145–6, 199 n. 23
Hughes, Joe 26, 27, 29, 154, 181–2, 198 n. 15, 200 n.4
Hume, David 7, 93, 158, 177–8, 201 n.10
Husserl, Edmund 20, 21, 64–6, 71, 74, 131, 141–2, 148, 163, 166, 175, 192 n.14

Jameson, Fredric 17, 181

Kafka, Franz 133–5
Kant, Immanuel 18–23, 26, 38, 61–6, 71, 74, 80, 81, 84, 88–90, 94, 98–9, 100–5, 109–11, 111–12, 120–1, 123, 125–6, 129, 141, 151, 154, 155–8, 166, 167–8, 169, 177, 178, 179, 183, 184, 191 n.8, 192 n.10, 192 n.11, 194 n.11, 194 n.12, 200 n.4
Kaufman, Eleanor 179
Kierkegaard, Søren 92, 93
Klossowski, Pierre 95
Kripke, Saul 5, 150

Lacan, Jacques 148–9
Lampert, Jay 179
Lawrence, D.H. 5, 34
Lecercle, Jean-Jacques 173–4
Leibniz, G.W. 10, 16, 93, 101, 111–12, 116–19, 121–2, 124, 128, 133–6, 145–6, 182, 196 n.8, 198 n.17
Liszt, Franz 41
Lyotard, Jean-François 45, 193 n.6

MacKenzie, Iain 179

Maggiore, Robert 171
Mahler, Gustav 41
Maïmon, Salomon 21, 73, 90, 110
Malabou, Catherine 161–2
Maldiney, Pierre 43
Martelaere, Jean de 181
Marx, Karl 8, 12, 82, 143, 144, 164
Maxwell, James 125
Meillassoux, Quentin 177–8
Melville, Herman 35
Mendeleyev, Dmitri 122
Merleau-Ponty, Maurice 43, 148, 180
Mozart, Wolfgang Amadeus 41
Muyard, Jean-Pierre 7

Negri, Antonio 3, 79, 172, 174
Newton, Isaac 122, 123
Nicholas of Cusa 92
Nietzsche, Friedrich 19, 20, 80, 81, 92–7, 100, 101, 145–8, 169, 183

Ortega y Gasset, Jose 15
O'Sullivan, Simon 33

Pascal, Blaise 92, 93
Plato 4, 18, 74, 76, 81, 87–8, 92, 141–2, 166
Platthaus, Andreas 172
Plotnitsky, Arkady 179–80
Proust, Marcel 48–53, 59–60, 63, 69, 94, 182

Resnais, Alain 58
Rose, Steven 159
Rorty, Richard 4, 141, 165
Rossellini, Roberto 57
Russell, Bertrand 79

Saint-Hilaire, Geoffroy 82

Sartre, Jean-Paul 21, 192 n.14, 199 n.27
Schönher, Mathias 154
Schumann, Robert 191 n.4
Sherrington, Charles 159
Smith, Daniel W 82, 194 n.9
Soutine, Chaim 44
Spinoza, Baruch 19, 78–81, 83, 97, 100, 182, 193 n.4
Stengers, Isabelle 179
Strauss, Erwin 43

Tarkovsky, Andrei 58
Tinguely, Jean 88, 171
Tolman, Edward 159
Tournier, Michel 149

Uexküll, Jakob 38

Varela, Francisco 150
Vertov, Dziga 55

Wagner, Richard 41
Wenders, Wim 55
Whitehead, Alfred 159
Widder, Nathan 179
Williams, James 172
Wittgenstein, Ludwig 7
Woolf, Virginia 35

Žižek, Slavoj 154, 174, 176
Zola, Émile 184–6

INDEX OF CONCEPTS

affect/affection-image 27, 35–6, 42, 44–5, 55–6, 60, 64, 93, 109, 119–20, 140, 153–5
Aion/Chronos 29, 58, 60, 90–1
allegory 45, 55, 90, 104–5, 143, 150, 156, 181–3, 200 n.4
Ancient Greece 4, 31, 163–4, 175, 202 nn.15, 16
axiom 100, 143–4, 164–5, 166, 177

beautiful/sublime 22–3, 44, 53, 95, 102–5, 151, 155–6, 168, 170, 200 nn.3, 4
becoming 25, 30, 31, 41, 43, 44, 72, 110, 155, 158, 161, 164, 170, 186, 187, 191 n.10, 192 n.10, 194 n.9, 195 n.14, 202 n.16, 205 n.36
body 24, 107, 108, 109, 117–21, 122, 126, 128, 130, 131, 132, 138–9, 143, 176 n.7, 196 nn.6, 8, 197 n.9
brain 26, 30–1, 36, 37, 58, 71, 157–62, 178, 183, 200, 201 nn.7, 8, 9

capital/capitalism 8, 28, 143–4, 162, 164–9, 172, 173–5, 182
'cast a plane over chaos' 25, 29, 34, 70, 107, 154

chaos 5, 6–7, 24, 25, 26, 27, 28, 31, 36, 41, 42–4, 46, 52, 55, 59, 62, 69, 70, 72, 77, 84, 113, 117, 125, 131, 153, 180, 182
Cogito 18, 74–6, 81, 85–7, 98
common sense 17, 27, 102, 104, 112, 122, 126, 130, 131–4, 136, 143, 183, 196 n.6, 197 n.13
concept/components 5, 13, 16, 18, 20, 23–4, 26, 28, 29–30, 64, 67, 69–77, 79–80, 81–105, 108, 109, 110–11, 112, 116, 117, 119, 120, 140, 145, 151, 154, 155, 157, 158, 160, 161, 162, 167, 175, 176, 183, 184, 192 n.1, 193 nn.6, 7, 194 nn.9, 11, 196 n.4, 202 n.16
conic section 16, 180
coupling/vibration 109, 115, 116, 126–8, 129, 130, 143

dark precursor/obscure precursor 126–7, 129, 131, 139
Deleuze's/Deleuze and Guattari's books/essays (only when referred to at length)
Anti-Oedipus 143–4
Cinema I and *II* 53–9

Difference and Repetition
81–4, 95, 146–7
'Dramatization' 125–7,
129–30
Expressionism in Philosophy
78–80
Fold, The 117–9
Francis Bacon 45–8
'Idea of Genesis, The' 104,
156
Kant's Critical Philosophy
102–4
Logic of Sense, The 130, 133,
184–6
Nietzsche and Philosophy
96–7
Proust and Signs 48–53
depth 148–9, 150, 180, 199 n.27
deterritorialization/
reterritorialization 39–40,
42, 44, 47, 64, 70, 100,
143, 144, 164, 165, 166,
167–70, 202 n.20
differenciation 28, 85, 101, 108,
11, 194 n.9, 195 n.1, 197
n.9
differentiation 27, 82–3, 87, 95,
98, 101, 153, 187, 192 n.1,
194 n.9, 195 n.1
divergence/incompossible 16, 111,
127, 129, 130, 131, 133,
135, 138
doing with/doing like 31, 184
double/doubling 86, 100, 123,
135, 140, 150, 159, 167,
184, 186, 194 n.7, 197
n.12, 198 n.21, 200 n.20,
205 n.35
double genesis/quasi-causality 73,
77–8, 81, 99, 182, 185

effectuate/counter-effectuate 5,
6–7, 24, 78, 112, 145,
147–8, 167–8, 175, 181,
184, 199 n.21, 205 n.35
enthusiasm 167, 170
Eternal Return 20, 80–1, 95–6,
145, 146–8, 182, 192 n.10
explication 85, 120, 121, 134,
146–9

fatigue/exhaustion 105–6, 175
forced movement/inevitable
movement 45, 47, 48, 52,
59–60, 69, 109, 126–30,
136, 140
friend/rival 4, 87–8, 101, 163,
205 n.36
functive 107–8, 112–8, 121–5,
133, 136–7, 138, 139, 146,
153, 154, 155, 194 n.9

genesis passim, but especially
27–31, 35–37, 42–5, 54–5,
60–67, 71–3, 107–9, 125–6,
136–7, 140–1, 158–9, 169,
182–3, 191 n.8, 192 n.11,
193 n.5, 198 nn.15, 17, 20,
199 n.28, 202 n.16
good sense 17, 113, 126–7, 131,
132, 134, 143
ground/grounding 73, 76, 83, 86,
91, 103, 138, 144

'ideas men' 2–3, 143, 151, 175
implication 79, 81, 146–9
individuation 24, 28, 70, 109,
111–2, 115, 116, 117, 123,
126–7, 128, 130–2, 133,
136, 137, 138–9, 140, 143,
153, 158, 181, 196 nn.6, 7
intensity 27, 28, 42, 44, 52, 59,
61, 69, 70, 80–1, 95, 98,
102, 109, 112–3, 115, 116,
118, 120–2, 126, 128, 143,
146, 149, 181

Kantian faculties 22–3, 50, 61,
    62–3, 65–6, 84, 101–4, 110,
    155–7, 183, 200 nn.3, 4
Kant on Cogito 81, 88–90, 123,
    194 n.12

mime 20, 169, 186, 205 n.35
monad 111–12, 116–17, 118,
    119, 122, 124, 126, 127–8,
    131, 136

'No' 23, 155, 156

old age 6–7, 12, 22, 151, 183
opinion 3, 4–7, 17–18, 24, 26,
    46, 49, 66, 87, 99, 107–9,
    112, 119–20, 138–45, 150,
    151, 153, 159–60, 163,
    166–7, 170, 171–2, 175–6,
    179, 199 n.28, 202 n.16
Other/Other Person 21, 74,
    149–50, 180–4, 192 n.14

partial observer 124, 126, 127,
    131, 132, 136, 148, 153,
    155
pedagogy 12, 31, 48, 59, 172, 184
percept/perception-image 35–7,
    42, 44–5, 55–6, 58, 60, 93,
    109, 119–20, 140, 153–5
persona 6, 67, 70, 72, 92–9,
    100–1, 102, 104, 105, 153,
    155
phenomenology 21, 65–6, 142
plane of composition 26, 37, 44,
    52, 63–4, 67, 69, 72, 75,
    93, 153
plane of immanence 18, 19, 26,
    28, 59, 60, 67, 69, 72,
    75–81, 83, 86, 92, 93,
    94–8, 100–2, 105, 115,
    144, 170, 178, 180, 184,
    197 n.13, 202 n.20

problem 15, 25, 34, 71–2, 78, 83,
    95, 97, 100, 112, 124, 139,
    150, 180, 193 nn.1, 9
prospect 99, 107, 112, 133,
    136–40, 198 n.20

reserve 18, 76, 81, 145
resonance 44, 45, 48, 51, 52,
    59–60, 109, 126–30,
    139–40
revolution/French Revolution
    167–8, 170

schema/schematism 34, 61, 89,
    98, 110, 120, 125–6, 194
    n.11
self-positing/autopoetic/
    self-creation 24, 67, 73, 81,
    150, 167
sense 24, 27–9, 139–40, 149,
    182, 198 n.21
soul 22–3, 53, 102, 125, 158, 200
    n.4, 201 n.10
spider's web 24
state of affairs 20, 24, 93, 107,
    115–9, 121, 130, 136, 137,
    138, 139, 145, 146, 168,
    196 n.6
survey 16, 29, 30, 37, 67, 70, 85,
    99, 153, 160–1, 201 n.9
synthesis/syntheses 27, 40, 47–8,
    57, 58, 60, 61–5, 69, 71,
    74, 81, 84, 94, 95, 96, 97,
    101–2, 109–10, 112, 120,
    125, 126, 128, 130, 143,
    146, 148, 180, 181–2, 191
    n.10, 200 n.4

taste 23, 87, 100–1, 103, 107,
    139, 155, 175
thermodynamics 81, 146–7
thing 24, 115–7, 119, 121, 128,
    138–9, 196 n.6, 198 n.21

thought/thinking 5, 6, 15, 16, 17, 18, 19, 20, 33, 53, 58, 60, 63, 74–7, 80, 84, 86, 89, 93–4, 97, 105, 109–10, 120, 141, 144, 148, 156, 158, 159–62, 163, 166, 168–70, 176, 177, 178, 181, 186, 187, 200 n.5

transcendental empiricism 19, 20, 84

variable 114, 115, 117, 118, 119, 121, 132, 136–7, 140, 142, 153, 197 n.9
variation 16, 75, 85, 87, 153
variety 34, 37, 72, 85, 153

www.ingramcontent.com/pod-product-compliance
Lightning Source LLC
Chambersburg PA
CBHW070337240426
43665CB00045B/2158